JOHN COWPER POWYS IN SEARCH OF A LANDSCAPE

John Cowper Powys
in Search of a Landscape

C.A. Coates

First published 1982 by
THE MACMILLAN PRESS LTD
London and Basingstoke
Companies and representatives
throughout the world

ISBN 0 333 32476 5

Typeset and printed in Hong Kong

For John, Peggy and John

Contents

Acknowledgements

The author would like to thank Laurence Pollinger Ltd., and the Estate of John Cowper Powys for permission to use the quotations from Powys's work which appear in this book. Thanks are also due to Powys's publishers, Macdonald & Jane's Publishing Group Ltd., Pan Books Ltd., and the Village Press.

The author would also like to thank the following: Glen Cavaliero, Angus Wilson, George Steiner, Jeremy Hooker, Belinda Humfrey, G. Wilson Knight, Derek Langridge, Kenneth Hopkins, Walter Allen, John A. Brebner, Philip O'Connor, H. P. Collins, Ninian Smart, Frederick Davies, J. B. Priestley, George Dangerfield, Peter Green, Colin Wilson, Philippe Jullian, the *Sunday Times* for permission to quote from Cyril Connolly's review; the *New Statesman* for permission to quote from V. S. Pritchett's review; The Society of Authors and the Estate of Llewelyn Powys; Macdonald Futura Ltd., and the Estate of Louis Wilkinson; the Estate of Richard Heron Ward; the Estate of Lloyd Emerson Siberell; the Estate of Arthur Machen; the Estate of G. K. Chesterton.

While every effort has been made to contact the copyright holders of works quoted, the author regrets that in a few cases this has not been possible. The author apologises for this and will, in any subsequent edition, amend the situation should any unacknowledged copyright holder get in touch with the publishers.

Preface

Both the size and the uneven quality of John Cowper Powys's work make selection vital. This book is not intended as a survey guide to the whole, but a discussion of one aspect of it. Without referring to his non-fictional writing, there are still too many novels to discuss adequately. Selection, however, is relatively easy. There are a handful of novels that make Powys one of the great novelists of the twentieth century. The rest are interesting to the interested. In this book, I have concentrated on *Wood and Stone* (1915), *Ducdame* (1925), *Wolf Solent* (1929), *A Glastonbury Romance* (1932), *Weymouth Sands* (1934), and *Porius* (1951). *After My Fashion*, written just after the First World War and published recently for the first time, is also mentioned. *Wolf Solent, A Glastonbury Romance* and *Porius* need no defence. But it may be asked why *Rodmoor* (1916), Powys's second novel is omitted, while *Wood and Stone*, his first admittedly very weak novel, is discussed. Or why *Maiden Castle* (1936) is hardly mentioned, or why *Owen Glendower* (1940) receives such scant treatment.

The reasons are both ignoble and rational. This is a partial study, and I have chosen those novels I prefer. The study is of one aspect of Powys's work, and the omitted novels either do not fit in with my theme, or repeat it without developing it. But, perhaps more importantly, the omitted novels are, if not aberrations, at least eccentrics, untypical of the rest of the work, and not of Powys's essence.

Rodmoor is a pessimistic tale of self-destruction. The setting is the coast of East Anglia, and the sea is rendered as alien and menacing. The novel is perhaps worth reading for the vividness of the land and seascapes, but the characters are unconvincing and the plot is static. Moreover, it has a quality of unfocused neurosis that is off-putting. Powys's first two novels are unrewarding for the general reader, and I feel that in discussing *Wood and Stone* I spend enough time on his early work.

Maiden Castle deserves far more attention. But here, the rich complexity and physical density of the earlier novels is missing. The probable reason for this was Powys's desire to avoid the sort of libel threat that followed the publication of the minutely particularised *A Glastonbury Romance*. Dorchester in *Maiden Castle* is a vague unspecified locality. The novel is valuable, especially in its presentation of the nervous tensions, attractions and repulsions of particular relationships. Powys is always sensitive to the ebb and flow of irrational moody involvements, but *Maiden Castle* contains the greatest number of these, and they are very closely observed.

Owen Glendower is a novel of great power and shows very clearly that Powys could triumphantly present an objective public world. It is a detached, accessible novel, containing Powysian themes, but subsuming them into the historical material. It is the easiest of Powys's novels to read. Because of this, my discussion of it is limited. The novel deserves more, but it is the most un-Powysian of the work, and in pursuing my theme, I have not spent time on it.

The later writings after *Porius* seem to me to be playthings, toys for a writer no longer intent on real creation. They are interesting, amusing, sometimes silly, but they are not serious. They are reworkings, relaxations, fantasies, and are better left until the major novels are read.

My theme is Powys's obsession with landscape and nature, and his long struggle to embody his response to them. This may sound narrow, but it was his central preoccupation, and I have tried to isolate it in his best novels with the intention of evoking his real achievement.

I have tried to avoid generalisation without, I hope, falling into the trap of too rigidly applying myself to the words on the page. I have endeavoured also to avoid unsupported assumptions about Powys's personality, although the temptations are great. It is more than necessary to impose limits on the discussion when John Cowper Powys is the subject. He is too vast and Protean and the clumsy Menelaus clutchings of literary criticism seem to catch only a little bit at a time. The bit that I have attempted to grasp is his attitude to landscape. His deliberate cultivation of a way of seeing and experiencing his environment is intimately connected with the developing subtlety of his style. I feel that this leads towards the essence of Powys.

Obviously, with this limited theme, much is left out. I would like to make much clearer the humour of the novels, the diverse and interesting secondary characters, the acute psychological portraits. In fact, Powys is very much more interesting than I have shown. I would advise any new reader, regardless of his or her opinion of my discussion, to read *A Glastonbury Romance* and *Wolf Solent*.

Abbreviations

Introduction

It is necessary for those interested in Powys's novels to admit that there is some substance in the case against him. But it is also necessary to show that some of Powys's characteristics are not faults, merely unfashionable qualities. One complaint against Powys's novels is that they are 'long', not too long, but long, as if length in itself were a fault. The length of the novels may indeed have put off some readers, but it is the nature of the length itself which presents problems to the hasty. Powys's novels are not long in the sense that *War and Peace* is long, encompassing huge public events, several private lives and a considerable span of time. Powys uses length to evoke the intense duration of a day, or a week, of an individual discovering and developing the ways, the subterfuges he can use to try to live his life in the face of almost intolerable difficulties. In this quest, he may encounter heroic events, or not. It is not the events but how he deals with them that is Powys's concern in the novel. His novels are long in the sense that a day spent by oneself is long, not in the way a war is long. They require patient, careful reading, and in some cases the reader must persevere, as with the first chapter of *Porius*.

Despite the gentleness of Powys's attitudes, the worlds he creates are intense and overwhelming. There is nothing apologetic about them, no concessions to the reader any more than in the Rabelais or Balzac he admired. The combination of strength and length may be offensive to those readers who seem to appreciate a certain diffidence in an author, not too much of a creative gusto, a defensive irony or caginess about the vision he offers. Powys is never defensive.

The preference for modest length and lack of pretension in the British novel has spared us the American mammoths, prefabricated white elephants full of symbols for the professional researchers. Possibly Powys's reputation has been tainted by this not entirely misplaced caution. Surely, it may be thought, a book as long as that must be self-indulgent or prefabricated. This is a

1

query only referred to twentieth-century writers. It may be understandable caution, but the result is that there are not enough critics providing the scholarly apparatus necessary to establish Powys's reputation and promote the study of his books.

Glen Cavaliero has remarked that there is no commonly held view of what is important in Powys.[1] In Lawrence or Forster criticism the same passages reappear and are accorded a similar degree of emphasis by different writers. The reader of Powys must decide for himself what is important. In his excellent summary 'The Difficulties of Reading John Cowper Powys',[2] George Steiner gives considerable attention to this absence of a critical Baedeker in Powys's case. The lack of a general biography tends, he also suggests, to promote gossip, an 'in group' atmosphere, which may repel those outside it, and hinder the placing of vital elements in Powys's work. The lack of a generally accepted critical introduction makes it easy for emphatic and sweeping dismissals of Powys's work.

In a sense these points in the case against Powys are merely incidental and will no doubt be remedied in time, as another mentioned by Steiner has already partially been; the lack of readily available texts. If these were all that prevented his work from establishing itself as its importance deserved, there would hardly be a Powys problem. There are, however, more vexed issues. It would be hard to pretend that Powys's subject matter was very familiar in the English novel, or that it was calculated to attract all readers. We are used to a novel of moral debate, examining a particular problem, depicting the personality in some social or sexual setting. The key words are 'choice', 'maturity', 'awareness'. The frame of reference is the public realm; the difficult path to individual happiness or ripe judgement through the hazards of a series of choices. It is a frame of reference radically inapplicable to Powys's work. He is not concerned with a moral obstacle race. Powys's characters are not 'mature'. (Perhaps we have heard too much of this word. 'Maturity' so often seems a stick with which the boring beat the interesting. The more modern hero's 'maturity', a kind of cynical alienation, is equally uninspiring.) Powys's wisdom is reached through a world of private fantasy, myths, taboos, day dreams and secret ritual. Often moral choice is seen as factitious and irrelevant.

There is perhaps an inhibition against admitting the important role this world of private fantasy has in most people's lives, a notion that it is merely childish and should be denied. But it plays a larger part than conscious moral choice, probably fairly rare in most experience. The novel cannot afford to neglect so vital an area. If, as Cavaliero has said, Powys is the novelist of

> the yearning child within the man, the aspect of people that never grows up, the child that is not left behind but becomes the core of the personality[3]

then this is an asset rather than a liability. The 'childish' aspects of the inner world need a novelist who realises their significance. If one compares Powys with a writer much more commonly associated with the 'stream of consciousness', Virginia Woolf, one is struck by the more central importance of Powys's subject, and the far greater realism of its treatment. Virginia Woolf's work is thin in texture compared to Powys's, but it is also much more structured and artificial. The inner world of her characters may be just a little disordered but it remains thoroughly dignified and adult in tone. It is far easier to accommodate to the expectations of readers and to the 'moral and mature' English novel than the sprawling, undignified Powysian attitude, but it is less realistic. It is worth mentioning here that Powys, as well as being acutely aware of the elements of the child in the man, is also very sensitive to the inner world of the child. The portraits of children in *A Glastonbury Romance*, *Maiden Castle* and *Wolf Solent* are most perceptive.

Powys's sexual views often prove difficult to accept, and not only for the inhibited or overearnest reader. Steiner candidly admits Powys's 'giggly' quality, although he declares, surely correctly, that it is held in place

> by very strong clamps of commonsense, of sudden gusts of almost luminous simplicity and self-correction.[4]

Despite a remarkable and even brutal frankness in many areas of sexual experience, giggling 'ocular' sadism, and masturbation have not quite established themselves in literature. Writers are content to deal with wickedness and depravity, with amoral sex, even with sex seen in political terms, but not with the silly and merely undignified. It must be admitted that this element of

Powys's world is offensive and distasteful to some readers. It is difficult to argue with this reaction, although one might observe that Powys's sexual attitudes are free from the least trace of cruelty or exploitation. It is difficult to see how anyone who accepts the off-centre sexuality of *Women in Love* and *Lady Chatterley's Lover* could object to Powys's unpretentious explications. For the rest, it seems a pity to make heavy weather of what could incur no great moral blame in any sane or sensible code.

It is, however, worth repeating what Belinda Humfrey has emphasised, that Powys

> probably provides the fullest and most emotionally entrancing descriptions of 'normal' hetero-sexual relationships in twentieth-century literature.[5]

The memorable celebration of the 'normal' love of Nell and Sam is far more important than the 'abnormal' relationship of Mary and John in *A Glastonbury Romance*.

There is perhaps one criticism that is more relevant. It was once said to me that Powys was not interested in relationships, that his characters were selfish. This can be superficially refuted. Nearly all the Powysian characters desperately attempt to form significant relationships. But this is not shown to be ultimately important. The real relationship in the Powys novel is the one between the inner self and the whole outside world. The real struggle is to live one's life, and while this includes personal relationships, it is far more than this. Perhaps the criticism is based on an invalid premise. Personal relationships are not the whole of life, or even of those parts of life which people agree to call important. This prescriptive criticism is based on a humanist bias not universally shared.

Criticism is often directed at Powys's prose. There are two points to be made here. Firstly, as in any distinctive stylist, there is always a tendency for manner to harden into mannerism, for the quirks of Powys's prose to become self-parody. In works of such size, some excesses are to be expected. For the same reason, there is also a certain carelessness; hyperbole; repetition; exhausting parenthesis; enormously long sentences, eccentric or silly names of characters. Unevenness of style is a hazard to which all readers of long novels are accustomed. But Powys's circumlocution cannot be regarded as an incidental fault. It is integral to Powys's whole approach to life. It was not just that he simply found it difficult to come to the point. His sceptical, relativist approach to experience resulted in his prose in endless conditional clauses, while his expansive, inclusive attitude entailed adjectives in abundance. Those readers who confine their attention to tight, economical prose will find Powys very difficult.

1 Beginnings and Echoes

Because John Cowper Powys died recently (1963), and because his novels have qualities generally regarded as 'modern', it is necessary to realise that he was born and brought up in a world that has entirely and utterly vanished. Also, despite the fact that many people who knew Powys are still living; despite the candour of his autobiographical writings; despite the many memoirs that feature him; his personality remains enigmatic. Powys needs a George D. Painter or a Gittings to produce a full-scale life. Anecdotes cannot serve as biography, but they can perhaps help to suggest an atmosphere.

Born in 1872, he was the eldest of the eleven children of Charles Francis Powys and Mary Cowper Johnson. His father was a clergyman in the Church of England, and both parents were the children and grandchildren of clergymen. C. F. Powys had inherited a solid fortune, which while ensuring his very respectable position in the upper middle classes, also enabled him to cultivate a detachment from and contempt for it rather difficult to manage today. The huge family had its own intense self-sufficiency. It is tempting to compare it with Ivy Compton-Burnett's convoluted family communities, but perhaps hardly fair. Certainly Compton-Burnett suggests the isolation and intensity of the large family in the country rectory, but all reports of C. F. Powys's household emphasise the happiness and friendship of the siblings. They remained friends, with developing rather than static relationships with each other. The friendship between John Cowper Powys and his brother Llewelyn, for example, is one of the themes of both writers.

Powys's childhood and boyhood were spent in Derbyshire, Dorchester, Weymouth and Montacute. His father was appointed vicar of Montacute, Somerset, in 1886. Llewelyn Powys, in his essay on 'Montacute House' in *Somerset and Dorset Essays*[1] remarks that in his childhood he had lived two lives, one in the eighteenth century and one in the twentieth. This was prompted by a memory of a noticeboard with 'Beware of Man Traps' still legible. He relates the story of how the Squire's father impoverished his estate. One wet afternoon in Weymouth, he staked a bet on one of two flies crawling up the window. When his insect lost the race, he was heard to remark 'There go Sock and Beerly', the names of two of his farms near Ilchester. This anecdote sounds as if it came from some Jeffrey Farnol costume romance, but it adds point to Llewelyn's observation that his father's job as clergyman was to stand between the landed gentry and the people of the village.

This seemingly archaic role was perhaps literally true in 1886. Gladstone's reforms of 1884 and 1885 had extended the vote to the agricultural worker. Llewelyn Powys describes the Montacute Squire as a kindly despot, constantly resenting the democratic assertiveness of the working classes. Ham Hill, where many Montacute workers were employed, was a favourite place for political demonstrations. Montacute-born George Mitchell held rallies there to support Joseph Arch in his work to unionise and enfranchise the agricultural worker. Anyone visiting the quiet, prosperous village now, surrounded by mechanised, subsidised agricultural land, Montacute House a beautiful shell neatly kept by the National Trust – will be mistaken if he feels that this is the authentic atmosphere of Powys's boyhood home. The political disturbances of *Wood and Stone* (set in Montacute) and *A Glastonbury Romance* were probably based on memories and gossip, and were not so very unlikely, however unrealistic and unimportant they seem now.

Powys's host of Shakespearean beggars and rustics are not purely literary either. Llewelyn Powys describes Nancy and Betsy Cooper (who figure in his brother's novels), as beggars that no-one would dare invent, strange creatures from an old ballad, yet they came to gather sticks in Montacute Park.

John Cowper Powys describes how, as a boy, hidden in a hedge near this park, he heard Mr Phelips, the Squire, say to some guest, 'Yes, that's the Vicarage; Powys is the name; a very good family'.[2] It is obvious from *Autobiography* that he found this irksome, that in England he felt limited by 'the perpetual psychic question, "*Is* he a gentleman? *Has* he been to a decent school?"' His reaction was to move away from the position and place where such questions could be asked, rather than to react aggressively to any questioner.

Powys's account of his 'decent school', Sherborne, is vividly uncomfortable in *Autobiography*. It is perhaps unnecessary to relate the details of the difficulties experienced by a sensitive introspective boy in a public school. They have become literary clichés. What is interesting is Powys's method of dealing with the jeering bullies. He talked at them. He describes how he stood up after supper before the whole of his house, and instead of denouncing them, he denounced himself, exposing every idiosyncracy for which he had been mocked in a great flood of inspired words. The wild self-mockery of his 'apologia' had its effect and was met with applause. Powys was to deal with many situations by flooding them with tumultuous self-denunciations and self-revelations. It is difficult to decide whether this sort of reaction stems from masochism or contemptuous pride. It is because of a 'malice-dance' of this nature that Wolf Solent loses his job as a lecturer and has to find a living in Dorset. Perhaps Powys danced his own 'malice-dance' before his First World War audience when he was asked why he was not at the Front. Despite his age and ill-health, he had repeatedly tried to join up, but his reply was that he was afraid of German bayonets. Frederick Davies has pointed out[3] that Powys's imaginative awareness turned his pride into humility, that he learned to play the Fool to his own Lear, but he also warns against too explicit belief in the malicious exaggeration of his self-revelations.

John Cowper Powys went up to Corpus Christi, Cambridge, in 1891. He made some friends, read widely although not in his subject of English History, but the most important event of his stay there had nothing to do with people or books. It was an inexplicable ecstasy he experienced in a quiet leafy footpath behind the Fitzwilliam Museum. This sensation was evoked by a glimpse of moss, grass and stone-crop growing on a forgotten wall. Powys says he cannot describe it, but that sensation was 'beyond sensation' and as he was writing of it in *Autobiography (A*, p. 199) over forty years later in upstate New York, he experienced again that ecstasy. The scene was like a sunken treasure ship in his memory upon which he could always draw.

What Powys learnt from Cambridge was an intensification of what he had had to learn at Sherborne: the ability to escape into what he really valued, to hide his real identity from the social world and give it to his encounters with the inanimate world. This is how he put it in *Autobiography*. How much of this was present in the consciousness of the graduate of twenty-two is debatable. But the young Powys had enough self-knowledge to declare his unwillingness to become a clergyman, the profession expected of him. Instead he became a lecturer to girls' schools in West Brighton. This suited him in many ways. Firstly, because he thought that these hordes of young females – '*Schools* of girls! I saw them like gleaming porpoises; (*A*, p. 204) – would minister to his developing need to stare at the slim limbs of anonymous young women. In fact, Brighton beach, rather than Brighton schools, provided for this need. It was the solitary nature of his work that was particularly congenial. Belonging nowhere, visiting briefly to talk about books, without director or colleagues, Powys could live his own particular life with very little hindrance. He wrote derivative poetry. He pursued his long walks, his voyeuristic tendencies, a self-punishing asceticism, and a bewildering array of fetishes and obsessions. In *Autobiography*, the 'Southwick' chapter which describes these days shows intense neurosis, the appalling tyranny of supersensitive fastidiousness, recoiling in particular from women – 'A gulf of femininity opened beneath my feet. It made me shudder with a singular revulsion' (*A*, p. 222).

Powys married Margaret Alice Lyon in 1896. Her brother Harry Lyon figures in *Autobiography* and appears to have lived with them at some time. There is evidence of disagreements between Powys and Lyon, but Powys says nothing of his wife in *Autobiography*, which out of gentlemanly or cowardly reticence makes no mention of individual women. In 1902, Margaret Powys bore a son, Littleton Alfred. The couple drifted apart during Powys's American years.

Powys began lecturing for a wider adult public through the University Extension movement in 1902. His first lecture was, appropriately enough, on Arthurian myth. He travelled widely throughout England, visited the Continent, enjoyed a half-hearted attraction to the Roman Catholic Church, and was invited to lecture in the USA in 1905. His unconventional, enthusiastic, 'Dithyrambic Analysis', as he called his lecturing method, enjoyed a great popular success. He seems to have been a cultural Evangelist, a literary Billy Graham, whose message was not Christ, but Dostoievsky. In the USA, where he was to spend more and more time, he made enough money to support his family in Sussex, educate his son at Sherborne, and distribute to needy friends and acquaintances. His own private life remained rigorously simple. He spent it in cheap hotel rooms, in trains, in long solitary walks, in obsessive hunts for the anonymous slim limbs of his feminine ideal. His asceticism had provided him with agonising duodenal ulcers, for which he had several operations. He often lectured brilliantly in such pain that he could hardly stand upright.

The disturbing candour and odd reticences of *Autobiography* give only a partial picture of Powys's adult life. He remarks that the real reason for becoming an author was simply that Arnold, his business manager, had become a publisher. He adds that the war was a contributory cause. Certainly, his first work published by Arnold Shaw in 1914 was a pamphlet, 'The War and Culture: A Reply to Professor Munsterberg'. The war fired Powys with heroic zeal, and he spent some time attempting to enlist, not because he had any illusions about the justice of the war, but merely, it seemed, because it was there – 'Persons of spirit hurried to get *as close to the flames* as they could' (*A*, p. 583). He was rejected as unfit, and for a while lectured about 'War Aims', afterwards realising from the Versailles Treaty that his war aims and those of Lloyd George differed in many respects.

It was at this time that he began his fiction-writing career. In 1915 Powys was forty-three. He had spent twenty years reading, lecturing, travelling and writing. Only poetry – 'those two little booklets of copy-cat verse' as Powys described them in *Autobiography* – and one story survive from this period, but a book on Keats had certainly been written. *Wood and Stone*, his first novel, was published in November 1915. A book of literary essays, *Visions and Revisions*, was published in the same year.

Wood and Stone is a rather uninteresting novel. Possibly I may seem to discuss it at greater length than its merits suggest, but I would like to use it as a focus for the ideas and attitudes with which Powys was concerned at the time. It contains the seeds of Powys's major themes and hints at his later methods.

Powys's locality in the novel is the minutely described region of Montacute and Ham Hill. Some names are changed, but the landscape, village and great house are vividly present. They are far more vividly presented than the rather improbable action of the novel. Romer, the rich businessman and new owner of the great Elizabethan 'Nevilton' house, is a powerful and subtle tyrant. Too many overanalysed and unconnected characters engage in personal clashes and religious and political debate, but the main theme is the thwarting of the tyrant and his equally sadistic daughter, Gladys. Romer's victims eventually escape, after much lengthy discussion on the nature of power and the nature of sacrifice.

The novel is dedicated to Hardy. After the publication of *Odes and Other Poems* in 1896, the older novelist had thanked Powys for a poem addressed to him. From this an acquaintance progressed, and in *Autobiography* Powys describes the awe, excitement and reverence he felt when waiting for Hardy and his first wife to arrive at Montacute. The poem itself is very bad, but from it one senses rapturous enthusiasm particularised by a special relationship,

> O Master, thine a special meed of praise
> From me whose heart is all thy sweet West's own.

Wood and Stone has some obvious and superficial echoes from Hardy. James Andersen, the 'educated' stone-mason, has the same sort of ambivalent social position as Jude in *Jude the Obscure*, but it is not this that drives him to his death. His madness is brought about by a supersensitive pity for the victims of the world. His love for Lacrima, Romer's particular victim, is merely unreturned, not thwarted by strange events. Clavering, the naively self-ignorant vicar of Nevilton, is very like Angel Clare, and even, in fatalistic mood, stretches himself on the parish bier in the church, under the indifferent stars. The country girls have more than a touch of Tess or Marty South. Powys's narrative comments, as Hardy's did, on the effect of board school education or states that the nervous systems of some are too sensitive to secure their survival. There are many such incidental echoes.

A more important connection is the emphasis both writers place on the importance of the interaction of the individual and the landscape. Powys says many years later in a letter to Louis Wilkinson,

> And from T. Hardy I learnt long, long ago, to see all human feelings, gestures, actions and everything else! – my own and everybody's – against the inanimate background of Nature.[4]

Hardy's most sophisticated use of figures in a landscape is in *Tess of the d'Urbervilles*. Landscape and Tess relate and interact in various ways. When Tess wanders the night woods in the months following her seduction, she intensifies 'natural processes round her till they seemed part of her own story'.[5] She sees Nature as reproachful; rain and wind were 'formulae of bitter reproach'. Hardy points out that 'the world is only a psychological phenomenon'. Therefore, Nature was reproachful. But he does not allow Tess to create her own landscape without comment. He qualifies it by remarking that it was entirely mistaken, based on Tess's conventional morality. She is not out of harmony with the natural world at all; she merely thinks she is. Hardy describes her fantasy, says it is valid, then dismisses it as mistaken. He sees Nature as neutral. Tess may extend her emotional landscape into the natural one, but it is not valid objectively.

The most important use of landscape in *Tess of the d'Urbervilles* has already been discussed by Dorothy Van Ghent.[6] It is contained in the scene where Tess creeps through the uncultivated garden to listen to Angel Clare playing his harp.[7] The evocation of a rank, damp, blighted garden, overgrown and wild, is given in particular detail immediate to the senses – 'offensive smells', 'sent up mists of pollen at a touch'. The 'profusion of growth' is almost menacing: the cuckoo-spit, thistle-milk, slug-slime and sticky blights that Tess encounters; the last leaving blood-red stains. The garden is explicitly connected with Tess's attitude.

Hardy uses the garden imagery in a subtle twofold way. Tess, rapt and adoring, feels that the garden is a manifestation of her love and their union. His music, her sensibility, colour and sound blend together intently. But what of smell and touch? Unhealthy juices exude, slime and blight cover her; underfoot are the cracked oozy remains of snails; red stains are on her arms; cuckoo-spittle fouls her dress. Amid the dense, damp and rank undergrowth, she is already metaphorically, as she is soon to be in reality, reviled and betrayed. This highly sophisticated two-fold handling of nature imagery ensures that the Tess characterisation has a particular quality of depth. Hardy uses various devices and transitions: the association of conscious character and environment, where Tess sees the woods as grieving at her sin; the association for the reader between character and nature, for example, the maiden Tess and the secluded and engirdled Blackmoor Vale, or Tess in love and Talbothays in Spring. There is also Hardy's own attitude to Nature in his authorial comments. He sees it as purely neutral.

In *Wood and Stone*, the description of Nevilton Mount, the wooded conical hill behind the village, owes much to Hardy's description of Tess's garden. Clavering, the vicar, clambers up the hill, torn by his conflicting thoughts and feelings about Gladys, Romer's attractive daughter. The description of the undergrowth, overpoweringly pungent, rank, tangled and unhealthy, is Clavering's own state at the time, 'the bindweed, which entwined itself round many of the slenderer tree stems, became a symbol of the power that assailed him'.[8] As Hardy does, Powys has transferred to the landscape certain aspects of the human situation so that the result is an objective presentation of a landscape of the mind. Clavering fights his way through the tangled undergrowth of nettles, grasses, burdock, red-campion and newly planted firs; the rank smells of ivy and elder fill his nostrils, branches strike his face while his feet stumble over fern fronds. He feels pursued and hunted. The clergyman, suspicious of all natural pleasures, attracted against his will to Gladys, is caught up by conflicting desires and impulses. Again, as Hardy does, Powys shows that the character associates external phenomena with his own moods. Clavering connects the bindweed with the power that Gladys draws from the erotic.

But there is another aspect of association in this scene.

> He vaguely associated with his thoughts, as he struggled on, certain queer purple markings which he noticed on the stalks of the thickly grown hemlocks.

These marks are not made into symbol, as the bindweed is; they merely remain as external phenomena, unselected, associated 'vaguely' with his thoughts at the time his eye fell upon them. It is a random association, certainly far less artificial and literary than any 'symbolic' natural object, and far more psychologically accurate. Lacking any artistic qualities, or symbolic importations, the queer purple markings of weeds become important because the eye falls on them at a moment of stress. This almost random associative process is not derived from Hardy.

Powys's particular use of thematic imagery also seems entirely his own. The novel is based round a dualism centred in the natural scenery of Nevilton and Leo's Hill (Ham Hill) which is explained in the Preface. Here Powys makes clear that his aim is to

> get to the bottom of the world-old struggle between the 'well-constituted' and the 'ill-constituted', which the writings of Nietzsche have recently called so startlingly to our attention.

The first two chapters, 'Leo's Hill' and 'Nevilton Mount', suggest that the two hills are the foci for two opposed mythologies, the 'Mythology of Power' and the 'Mythology of Sacrifice'. Leo's Hill, once a Roman military encampment, now a sandstone quarry, shaped like a crouching lion, is tyrannical, dominating, pagan and powerful. Nevilton Mount, the site of the Holy Rood of Waltham, wooded and tower-topped, is meek, Christian and submissive:

> the two opposed Mythologies – the one drawing its strength from the impulse to Power and the other from the impulse to Sacrifice. (*W&S*, p. 2)

It is not just the characters, but the author who uses landscape for symbolic purposes – as 'formulae' as Hardy says in *Tess of the d'Urbervilles*. In fact, Powys builds his plot round it, using his symbolic landscape as the vehicle for philosophic and moral debate. These symbols, Leo's Hill and Nevilton Mount, appear to exert influence on the characters. Powys superimposes a philosophic pattern on the landscape of his parents' home, intensifying it into a psychic dualism. Landscape expressionism works better in art than literature, and the novel is far too explicit, but this is the raw material of the great influences of Glastonbury and Maiden Castle, inanimate objects of terrifying potency in his later novels.

Powys had a strong belief in dualism at this time, not only, as he states, through reading Nietzsche. *Confessions of Two Brothers* was published three months after *Wood and Stone*, in February 1916, containing two essays by John Cowper Powys and Llewelyn Powys. It records that this feeling was deeper than a belief; it was innate. Powys states that emotions 'find their place and their justification in some underlying duality beyond the confines of rational logic'.[9] Certainly, dualism explains evil and cruelty. At the same time he rejects William James's pluralism, saying 'to call it a "multiverse" is to use language which makes language impossible' (*CTB*, p. 48). By 1930, his opinions had altered. In the most popular of his books of 'philosophy' for the layman, *In Defence of Sensuality*, he rejects dualism in favour of pluralism. Perhaps by 1930, language for him was becoming more malleable. (I use these terms, 'dualism' and 'pluralism' as Powys uses them in his 'philosophical' books, taking them, I imagine, originally from William James's *Varieties of Religious Experience*.)

It is interesting to discover that awareness of the limitations of dualism was present in Powys's thought as early as 1902. *The Hamadryad and The Demon*, a slight fantasy by Powys circulated in a family magazine at this date,[10] contains traces of ideas which were later to be developed fully.

The story describes the love that two isolated young people bestow, one on a pagan and one on a demonic presence. Lovel's feelings for Nature take their ultimate form in love for a hamadryad. Her tragic slender pathos has a beauty far beyond the human.

> It is something primitive – unspeakable – something so far down into the root of things that it has passed beyond Good and Evil.

Lovel is a Roman Catholic and strains to comprehend something outside and beyond this moral dualism. When the Roman Catholic priest has exorcised both the hamadryad and Rachel's demon, the two realise the uniqueness of what they have lost. What they had found for a short while was something that reduced their city, families and religions to nothing and pointed beyond the moral categories evolved from them. Powys never lost interest in dualism. In a late work, *All or Nothing*, 1960, he plays with the theme in a context of fantasy science-fiction.

The dualism of *Wood and Stone* takes the particular form of Power and Sacrifice. Power resides not only in Leo's Hill, but in its capitalist owner, his daughter Gladys, and her seducer, Luke Andersen, a young stone-cutter. He is obviously based on Llewelyn Powys, and Luke has all the heathen charm and good looks ascribed to Llewelyn Powys before his tubercular illness of 1909. Luke's life-hungry attitudes are like those of one who has narrowly escaped death, and are similar to expressions in the writings of Llewelyn Powys. Both brothers faced serious illness in this year; John Cowper Powys had a severe stomach disorder which almost made him abandon his lecturing career. Kenneth Hopkins has suggested that *Wood and Stone* was begun at about this time.[11] There is a long meditation on death, when Luke watches over his brother's body, which seems unnecessary in the novel, and may reflect external concerns dating from this period.

Sacrifice is implicit in Nevilton Mount and a host of misfits, pariahs and depressives that no self-respecting Somerset village could possibly support. These are the weakest figures in the novel. The main character here is Lacrima who is to be married off to a brutish farmer to satisfy Romer's sadistic feelings towards her. Luke's brother, James (based on Powys himself) is, in his madness, the only one really aware of the cosmic struggle focused in the landscape and working itself out with Romer and Lacrima. Although, in his Preface, Powys mentions Nietzsche, he owes more to Dostoeivsky, as his writings on him show. But Lacrima has none of the transfiguring power of love that Sonia shows in *Crime and Punishment*. Indeed, what emerges is a personal obsession, the sado-masochistic relationship, rather than what Powys on Dostoeivsky calls 'the mad struggle always going on between the strong and the weak'.[12]

But certainly the Russian model is there: the collection of heterogeneous ideologues; the uprooted intelligentsia fond of philosophical and political debate; the absorbed obsession with different religious experiences. The scene of a stormy clash between the reactionary Romer and the rioting mob led by Christian socialists and nihilists seems to be composed of a mixture of Joseph Arch and Dostoeivsky.

The ultimate spokesman of Sacrifice is the nun-like Vennie Seldom, last of the old family of Nevilton House, who, in the new-found power of her Catholic conversion, removes the victims from the tyrant's grasp. She takes them to the sea, beyond Wood or Stone. Perhaps the enclosed stifling atmosphere of inevitable fatalities, which has an unpleasantly morbid effect in the novel, reflects Powys's own attitude to the pulls of Montacute. Weymouth and the sea are described in terms of freshness, rebirth and the rebuttal of 'Wood' and 'Stone'. In his childhood, Weymouth, his grandmother's home, was a longed-for haven. *Confessions of Two Brothers* is explicit about his need for an '*escape*' (*CTB*, p. 87), which he found in desert or sea, but not in lush vegetation. Weymouth offers escape to Vennie and the victims. The powers of Nevilton and Leo's Hill, so great that they kill James Andersen and can still animate the conversation of his dead parents, are negated by the sea.

Powys presents these forces as if they were effective in fact as well as psychologically powerful, apprehended by the sensitive. Clavering connects the lush abundance of the Nevilton landscape with Gladys. So does Lacrima, the poor relation who is tormented by her. She escapes from the great house and wanders in a lane full of the smell of fungus and honeysuckle: 'The Nevilton scenery offered her no escape from the insidious sensuality she fled' (*W&S*, p. 294). Powys takes the situation further. He does not discriminate, as Hardy does, between what the characters imagine about the landscape and what the novel uses as images for it. The lush foliage not only seems symbolic to Lacrima; it is symbolic in the novel. The connection between man and landscape or woman and landscape is more powerful and personal than Hardy shows. The porcine Goring is not only symbolic of the mud and clay of his farm. He is strengthened in his boar-like earthy attitudes by contact with it. Tess of the d'Urbervilles may have been 'akin to the landscape' but she was not its occult representative. Similarly Romer's autocratic powers are strengthened by contact with sandstone, which is also their symbol. In Chapter 3, Powys describes the noon sunlight falling on the sandstone pavement of Nevilton House. At the same time, Romer conceives the idea of the sexual torment of Lacrima. The midday sun was more than an agent of heat and light. Heathen, powerful and worldly, it is pro-Romer, if such a thing could be said, and it can influence him. Sandstone was the planetary matter which sustained him most. Therefore, noon on his sandstone terrace was Romer's most auspicious time. This slight hint was expanded in *A Glastonbury Romance* when the heathen sun was hostile to Matt Dekker, the clergyman, and determined to torment him. In *Wood and Stone*, Powys is trying to show connections between man and landscape, an interaction that verges on the occult or magical, but his tentative efforts are marred by the overriding dualism of his theme. It is in *A Glastonbury Romance* and *Maiden Castle* that this relationship is fully explored.

There are moments in *Wood and Stone* when Powys approaches a different sort of attitude to landscape. It is far more realistic than the occult thematic attitude, although both were developed in the later novels. Clavering 'vaguely' connects the hemlock markings with his thoughts at the time. Again, a clump of dandelions casually glimpsed by Dangelis 'mixed oddly' with the 'obscure workings of his brain' (*W&S*, p. 119) or a gesture is linked for the rest of his life with 'the indefinable smell of cut flowers' (*W&S*, p. 126). Here, the imagery relates to an experience, a consciousness received, not through the rationalising mind, but through the senses.

In *Visions and Revisions*, Powys shows boredom with the modern tendency to 'describe scenery'. He even objected to Hardy's eloquence. His admiration for Dostoievsky was partly based on the Russian's ability to convey landscape and weather without set pieces of descriptive prose, giving a 'general effect' by means of 'innumerable little side-touches' (*VR*, p. 24). Landscapes 'associated in detail after detail with the passions and sorrows of the persons involved' are the most effective. Dostoievsky's presentation of the movements of the individual consciousness in relation to its physical surroundings had some influence on Powys's attempt in this, which was to be the area of his greatest originality and achievement. It is probably true also that both Powys and Dostoievsky owe something to Dickens in this matter. It is possible that Clennam's return to London in *Little Dorrit* (1857) may have influenced Dostoievsky's portrayal of Raskolnikov's urban wanderings in *Crime and Punishment* (1866). In view of Powys's own distrust of literary influences (though his wide reading shows clearly throughout his novels), and his extreme individuality, it would be unwise to offer this as more than a suggestion.

In *Little Dorrit*, the outcast observer Clennam, with a heavy load of personal unhappiness, wanders through a nightmarish London.[13] Dickens describes a landscape of the mind; a use of landscape as symbol fundamentally similar to that which Powys later comes to reject, but the grotesque nature of the imagery has all the oddity of a private fantasy. The imagery which expresses Clennam's concerns is consistently quirky, although the causes of his misery have objective existence and are capable of rational description. This kind of Dickensian grotesqueness can be seen in many of Powys's interior settings; for example, Mr Smith's house in *Wolf Solent*.

The link between Powys and Dostoievsky is more substantial

and may be best observed in certain specific features of Raskol-nikov's personality and mental processes. These features may have suggested certain characteristic Powysian procedures and preoccupations. Raskolnikov's mental state is extremely private and idiosyncratic. He is an outcast, oversensitive, unbalanced figure, wandering in a monomaniac trance through the city. He has inexplicable impulses to malice and hilarity. His wanderings are remarkable for the minute description of every mental process which Dostoievsky gives,

> He began almost unconsciously, by some kind of inner com-pulsion, to examine carefully everything he happened to come across on his way.[14]

This absorption in his surroundings is marked by capriciousness and quirkiness, and a stress on unexplained coincidence and feelings of significance.

Despite his heightened, indeed border-line mental condition, Raskolnikov is reacting in a detached yet cogent fashion to the very lay-out of streets and houses. His mind follows its own course, ebbing and flowing in a non-linear, non-rational fashion. Joy and despair alternate. These movements of the mind, though they relate strongly to the urban environment, relate to it in an extremely personal, idiosyncratic way. Odd and quirky as Dickens's images had been, they had ultimately been rational and explicable. There is an occasional sense in Dostoievsky of a personal mythology which seems to anticipate Powys. There is even a sense here of the role memory and habit play in Wolf Solent's sensations.

> This magnificent view always struck a strange chill into his heart; this gorgeous sight filled him with blank despair. He had always wondered at this gloomy and enigmatic impression of his, but having no confidence in his ability to find a solution of this mystery, put it off to some future day.[15]

This sensation, which he almost planned, is entirely irrational. There certainly appears to be a parallel in Dostoievsky for the sense Powys frequently gives of the mind revelling with excited preoccupation, in scraps of thought and sensation.

It is unnecessary to dwell at length on Raskolnikov's fascination with pain and cruelty, and his absorption with his own response to it. Powys's own purely cerebral attraction to sadism is frankly described in *Autobiography*. The most complete picture of a sadist in his work is Evans in *A Glastonbury Romance*. His recurring, eagerly sought imaginative vision of a blow on the back of a head with a stick is similar to Raskolnikov's obsession with the hatchet.

Such hints and suggestions as these do not go far to proving anything in the nature of an 'influence', but they do offer a possibility of an original for some elements in the Powysian scene. There are other, very minor echoes. The melodramatic chapter 'Auber Lake' in *Wood and Stone* reveals Powys borrowing from Edgar Allen Poe. It was Hardy himself who suggested that Powys should read Poe. It was not a useful recommendation. The intense sensitivity to natural things that Powys shows was not helped by Poe's oversensitivity to his own Gothic imaginings.

Powys remarks in *Autobiography* that up to forty he tried desperately to 'arrange my feelings' according to the books he admired, but since that age,

> I struggled to find out what my real feelings were and to refine upon them and to balance them and to harmonize them, according to no-one's method but my own. (*A*, p. 403)

It is worth remembering this when looking at literary influences on Powys. Here is stressed not only the influences that are apparent, but also the deliberate turning away from them at the time he began writing novels to 'explore' and 'refine' his own 'real feelings'. This is the quest of his novels.

2 The Outline

Although Powys published widely and variously after *Wood and Stone*, nine years separate the publication of the two novels, *Rodmoor*, 1916, and *Ducdame*, 1925. This gap has now been explained by the recent publication of *After My Fashion* which Powys put aside after rejection in 1919.

Although chronologically *After My Fashion* belongs nearer *Wood and Stone* and *Rodmoor*, it is a far less diffuse and congested work. It is self-critical rather than self-indulgent. Although the themes are familiar, there is much interesting and original material in the novel.

The Powys-hero, literary critic Richard Storm, returns to England after the Great War. He goes to Sussex where his family roots are. This was Powys's married home, and Francis Powys, in his Foreword to the novel, has identified Selshurst and Littlegate as Lewes and Burpham. Descriptions of the landscape, however, are far fewer than in the two earlier novels.

In the familiar return journey which begins so many Powys novels, Storm has a definite artistic purpose. Dissatisfied with French culture and his own work he needs to find expression for a particular 'vision' he finds only in England. To do this, he feels he must escape from the erotic pull of his mistress, Elise. In Littlegate, where his grandparents are buried, he meets Nellie, an unsophisticated young girl whom he associates with his 'vision of things'.[1] They are attracted to each other and marry, despite Nell's previous engagement to the artist, Canyot. The relationship begins to wither. Nell's jealousy and Storm's half-loyalty to Elise are contributory causes. They accompany Canyot to New York, and the deterioration continues rapidly when Storm meets Elise again. After realising that Storm and Elise have taken up their adulterous affair, Nell, now pregnant, returns to England. Storm follows her; tries and fails to effect a reconciliation, and dies of a heart attack.

There is much that is familiar in this: most obviously there is the Powys-hero caught between two women of different types and answering to different and contradictory needs. However, what emerges most clearly and most self-critically is the central Powys preoccupation: the nature of his 'vision'. And, with greater clarity than in any other novel, there is shown the need to express it fully and particularly. *After My Fashion* repeatedly connects this 'vision' with 'England' and the 'English temperament'. This is very much a novel of homesickness, unless, as seems likely from the book, Powys was trying to rebut American criticism of his work. The emphasis on the 'Englishness' of his vision and art was not developed in later novels. Individuality and privacy are the English qualities necessary for Storm's art,

> the obstinate right of every Englishman to meditate upon his own sensations in reserved isolation....(*AMF*, p. 27)

He rejects his previous concern with technique and analysis, realising that his 'vision' would evoke 'its own expression in accordance with the intensity of its accumulative purpose' (*AMF*, pp. 22-3). The dualism of sex and the meddling of possessive women are the main enemies of his 'vision'. This 'vision' is described and, despite Storm's rejection of analysis, analysed in different ways in *After My Fashion*. It is more than an aesthetic ambition: it can 'save' one from 'fear and remorse and from the fret and the fever of this perpetual choice and rejection' (*AMF*, p. 17). It is described in explicitly religious terms (*AMF*, p. 110), and yet it is solely an English 'vision' (*AMF*, p. 219). There are Platonic references (*AMF*, p. 75). Like Storm, Powys is groping towards definition by description, but the evocation of 'the balance, the rhythm, the lovely poise of things' (*AMF*, p. 24), eludes Powys as it does Storm, perhaps by the very variety of the descriptions.

Storm gropes towards 'entrance into some larger consciousness' (*AMF*, p. 89) which he sometimes connects with the past generations of the human race, or a 'half-conscious soul of the earth' which is 'nearer the Goat-Foot Pass than any vague dream of the old Gnostics' (*AMF*, p. 90). The apprehension of this 'vision', more Pan-like than Gnostic, yet more mystical than earthy, depends ironically enough on physical well-being and a personal detachment. Powys is better at describing Storm's responses to alien elements than he is at evoking the 'vision' they threaten. His analysis brings to mind the lecture theatre rather than 'the lovely poise of things'. But he does make clear that Storm is striving to convey a particular individual quality, not 'mere mystical sensation, inchoate and indistinct' but to link the poignant and transitory 'little things' of experience

> with some dimly conceived immortal consciousness that gave them all an enduring value and dropped none of them by the way. (*AMF*, p. 89)

Art is the real subject of the novel, as the title suggests. 'After My Fashion' surely refers to the struggle to convey his own theme in his own way. This is far more a genuine autobiographical concern than is found in either *Wood and Stone* or *Rodmoor*. Criticism of both his 'vision' and his art is also found in *After My Fashion* and it is easy to believe here that Powys was probably voicing contemporary criticisms of his novels and poetry.

In Chapter 17, Elise the successful dancer derived, according to Francis Powys, from Isadora Duncan, criticises both Storm's poetry and his personality. Firstly she accuses him of being afraid to lose his 'precious personality' (*AMF*, p. 216) in a love affair with her. She connects his wooden insistence on his own nature with British imperialism. He is 'made like that' (*AMF*, p. 218) and other breeds must alter. (Powys is particularly aware in this novel of the selfishness inherent in the particular temperament he describes. Here it seems to be linked with British imperialism!) Elise criticises his poetry, so 'overloaded with sensations' (*AMF*, p. 219), it conveys no emotion. Storm, whose sensations and emotions have become disastrously muddled over Nell, cannot understand this. He replies that his purpose has been to capture the 'essence of the English country', surely a 'sensation'. Elise replies that it may be – 'to an Englishman'. She attacks Storm's theory of description by 'accumulation' by saying that his 'indiscriminate piling up' of natural detail is 'heavy and dull':

> It seems to get in the way of something.

He replies that:

> Any English person reading what I've written would be reminded of the happiest moments of his life.

These are moments 'associated with old country memories' (*AMF*, p. 220), though 'dull' to her. Elise is questioning all that is most important to Storm. She pokes 'with a hayfork into the most sacred recesses of his soul'.

Elise states that such writing is not 'art' because it does not 'make such impressions universal, so that everybody feels them'. He may be content to 'write about ponds and ditches for the benefit of English people' but 'It's the merest personal sensation of one individual'. There is here a criticism that was levelled at Powys for most of his career, a complaint about the inaccessibility of his material. This is the criticism Storm feels most keenly, and about which he can do little. The aesthetic theories of 'Bohemians' in New York are of little help. Elise and Storm indulge in a pointless exchange about 'art'. He has tried, in the tradition of the English poets, to capture 'the magic of the earth soul' without becoming too vague. But while Storm still uses such phrases as 'the magic of the earth soul' he will not avoid the vague, mystical or portentous. Elise laughs at this, saying that Shelley and Keats were no doubt beautiful and right, but 'You've got to say something new'.

Storm's rage and humiliation are intense. His personal male vanity is upset, but more deeply his artistic purposes are questioned. He has to write about what is important to him. He cannot change his subject. Without 'those old delicious sensations' (*AMF*, p. 221) he can contact nothing deep. But he wonders if Elise is right in her attacks upon his 'mystical sensationism'. She says his poetry is self-indulgent, self-satisfied, vague personal feelings not conveyed to anyone else. 'It's as if you had never really wrestled with life.' Storm has no answer to this but a mood of brutal, cynical resentment. Her criticism of his personality and art can only be answered by more and better writing. If one can undertake the sometimes very delusive activity of equating author and fictitious character, the novel shows Powys as lonely and self-critical. Storm's art and subject matter, and therefore because of the personal nature of his 'vision', his personality, are called into question in the most fundamental way. Because of his theme, he is accused of not tackling 'life'. But his theme is the most important part of his life, and it is imperative that he evoke it.

Perhaps *After My Fashion* gives its own answer to this. It has frequently been regretted that Powys never wrote an 'American' novel. The second half of this novel is set in New York, but description of it is flat and unoriginal, using the familiar image of the machine, dehumanising and impersonal, with mechanical movement and noise. Storm is very depressed: 'All about him were iron girders and iron cog wheels and iron spikes' (*AMF*, p. 177). Their 'Bohemian' circle of acquaintances are equally shadowy. Far too many insubstantial personalities are introduced in the second half of the novel and are barely characterised. Although Storm's moods dominate the whole novel, and no character save his own is given much individuality, the English characters seem more placed, especially Nell's father and her cynical old friend Mrs Shotover, than the Americans.

The Americans do, however, have some embryonic symbolic function, as does New York, in the novel. They embody different ways of living and feeling. Storm's feelings of revulsion and hatred about New York are tempered by a stray feeling of exultation. America like 'some great wedge of iron' (*AMF*, p. 172) bored its way 'through the thick sensuousness of his nature and laid his deeper instincts bare'. 'It was a process of spiritual surgery, painful but liberating.' He was compelled to 'fall back upon his own soul for vision and illumination'. Later, when entangled with Elise, resentful of the responsibility of his unborn child, conscious of his lack of 'human warmth', irritated and depressed by Nell's possessiveness, he sees New York as a 'huge shout of defiance' (*AMF*, p. 233); a place which took to itself the 'right to deny the whole traditional order'. The chaotic impersonality of the New World (which he hated) had evoked some 'completely new attitude to life'; where camaraderie replaced love, honesty to self took the place of loyalty to others, cynical courage submissive piety, 'reckless indifference to death' 'the old sad resignation'. This attitude suited the particular exigencies of Storm's character with its independence and hatred of the personal. It is liberating, and he feels that he can incorporate some of this attitude into his poetry. He also feels that Elise's criticisms are plausible. New York has a strengthening as well as depressing effect on Storm, and it is extremely interesting for the Powys enthusiast to read these early descriptions of America. But they fail as descriptions in the novel. This was not Powys's real subject.

But Elise's criticism of Storm's work needs answering. His 'vision' of the 'lovely poise of things' has to be made more accessible to the reader, and less abstract and expository. There is in the novel in the description of the death of Nell's father, the Rev. Moreton, a clue towards Powys's eventual solution to this problem. Moreton is a more realised character than most in *After My*

Fashion. Having lost faith in God, that 'Eidolon Vulgaris' (*AMF*, p. 55), he changes the Anglican service so that it is a worship of Christ Only. The figure of the heretical priest is one that remained a preoccupation with Powys. Moreton is a milder, more human heretic than Hastings in *Ducdame*, but he has the same 'fierce, fanatical pride' (*AMF*, p. 56) in his own opinions, and he is a dualist, seeing the world as a perpetual conflict between 'God' and 'Christ', one renounced, the other worshipped in the Mass (*AMF*, p. 76).

Moreton, like Powys's father, is a keen naturalist and he shows some of the Rev. C. F. Powys's tastes in food and botanising walks. He dies after overexerting himself by walking, and the description of his death at the end of Chapter 10 is one of the most interesting parts of the novel. Powys describes how Moreton's dying mind integrates random scraps of thought, memory, fantasy and sense perception into a 'stream of consciousness' which becomes the individual life-flow of that particular man.

Individuality, irrationality and myth-making are the characteristics of Powys's presentation of the dying man's thoughts and sensations, and in his death Moreton becomes vividly alive for the first time in the novel. Here is a glimpse of Powys's mature style.

In his reverie, the dying man forgets dualism and theological abstractions. The concept of God seems to perch on his bookcase like a 'whimsical but not unfriendly goblin' (*AMF*, p. 145). The crucified Christ hovers in the air, the arms waving 'like the wings of a butterfly'. 'What butterfly was it?' Everything becomes smaller under the waving of the butterfly wings. His happiness grows. He floats in blue space, conscious of the word 'annihilation', aware of the musical quality of the sentence 'the immortality of the soul' (*AMF*, p. 146) but unable to remember whether it has any meaning. 'He was going to sleep now; going to sleep upon velvet-black butterfly wings (*AMF*, p. 147). He hears weeping and his last sensation is 'an ecstasy of indescribable peace' as he shouts 'Mother'. But, the nature of such sensation being incommunicable, to the watchers by the bed the great last word of his life sounded like 'the meaningless syllables "Blub-blub"'.

Here is the beginning of Powys's mature use of scraps of sensation, floating phrases, nebulous irrelevant memories flowing together until the moment of consciousness is evoked. Powys had only to connect this style with his 'vision', the way he apprehended certain aspects of landscape, to answer the criticism that his novel makes about itself. Both *After My Fashion* and *Ducdame* are trying to work out the artistry of *Wolf Solent*. *After My Fashion* tries to understand the intellectual nature of Powys's ambition, presenting the criticism that must have been levelled at him, and in a sense admitting its plausibility. *Ducdame*, a much more finished and highly wrought novel, tries to answer the criticism artistically.

Richard Storm is the only Powys-hero who has Powys's own artistic ambition in this overt form. Wolf Solent and Dud Noman may write, but they are not greatly concerned with aesthetic theories. The particular Powys-hero temperament is embodied, criticised and discussed in much of Powys's fiction, but it is made far more clear here that it is the temperament of a creative artist. The detachment necessary for the apprehension of the 'lovely poise of things' is also the detachment necessary for the writer to embody his 'vision' in words. Too much personal emotion is destructive of both. *After My Fashion* confirms that Powys was a *conscious* artist, intellectually intent on his ambition and aware of valid criticism. The novel shows perhaps too much self-awareness for comfort; there is a moral and intellectual scrutiny of Storm's motives and behaviour which is rather like the spiritual self-examination of the religious. There is a relentless analysis of Storm's responses, especially in his relations with women. Scenes where the personalities of Storm and Nell irritate, attract, mislead and elude each other are well described. There is present a sad awareness of the isolation of the individual personality and the difficulty of communicating emotions and sensations accurately. This is essentially a book of debate and discussion with a highly self-critical, self-conscious element.

After My Fashion does not, however, succeed as a novel. It is too short and sketchy to convey adequately the personalities of the main characters, and secondary characters appear and disappear with little obvious function. The pace of the novel is badly judged with emphasis placed on events which have little further relevance; for example, the death of Canyot's mother, which is given disproportionate space in the first half of the novel. Canyot's strange quixotic attitude to Nell is never explained. Roger Lamb and Olive Shelter have no function in the novel. In writing such a short novel, Powys may have been following contemporary advice, but he has deprived his art of one of the things most necessary for it – length.

Powys's other publications at this time included reviews, essays, poems and pamphlets of popular 'philosophy'. He was greatly in demand as a lecturer. The massive audiences he commanded all over the United States remind one of those accorded to the great nineteenth-century lions, Dickens, Thackeray or Oscar Wilde, rather than a twentieth-century literature lecturer. Financially, those long and lonely tours were very rewarding. His father's death in 1923 strengthened his economic position while lessening his ties with England, his son being now adult. Powys's base in the USA was in Greenwich Village, New York, where Llewelyn Powys was working and getting published as an essayist, and his sister Marion ran her lace shop. Here were friends, contacts, visits from other Powys brothers and sisters; cultural support and encouragement, especially from Llewelyn Powys, until his return to England in 1925, after the recurrence of his TB. The success of their brother, T. F. Powys, and his growing celebrity in the 1920s must also have been an encouragement to his fiction-writing. This was the time, as John Cowper Powys remarks, when the name 'Powys' meant, in literary circles, Theodore Francis only.

Ducdame, written during this time of financial security and popular acclaim, gives an impression of intense sadness. The mood of *Rodmoor* is neurotic, that of *After My Fashion* depressed, that of *Ducdame* tragic. Although the action is tragic, ending in the murder of the main character, this is not where the sadness lies. It lies in the intolerable strains Rook, the Powys figure, has to undergo, because of the inadequacies or special qualities of his particular temperament. Powys has presented a complex character, soon to be familiar in his fiction: a man capable of intense visionary awareness who walks into trap after sordid trap of his own making; whose blind selfishness contrasts with quixotic conscience-stricken pity; whose detached erotic attraction towards women is frequently submerged by his deep revulsion from them and whose ecstatic delight in the natural world combines with a book-long drift towards death. Rook Ashover is the first version of Wolf Solent, but he is also a considerable achievement in his own right. The action is seen mainly through his eyes, yet he is objectively presented. The unbearable tensions of his life are rendered accessible to the reader – not an easy task given their nature – without the self-pity which makes *Rodmoor* rather distasteful.

After *Rodmoor's* desolate East Coast setting and the rich glimpses of Sussex scenery in *After My Fashion*, Powys returns to the Wessex manor-house and village; not to Montacute, with so many recognisable details, but to an unspecified Dorset village on the river Frome, 'Ashover'. Rook is 'the impoverished Squire of Ashover, doing nothing but walk and eat and sleep',[2] as he is described by an outsider taxing him with idleness. Rook is not ambitious; he is not socially concerned; his 'account', as he calls it, is with the universe. His tragedy is precipitated by his action of bringing his barren and socially unacceptable mistress, Netta, into Ashover House, where his mother still lived, a woman obsessed with the need to have an heir to the family. In retaliation, she invites Lady Ann, Rook's cousin, beautiful and brilliant and in marked contrast to the bedraggled, pathetic and preferred Netta.

Observers of this battle are Lexie, Rook's consumptive brother (based on Llewelyn Powys); Hastings, the nihilistic vicar; his wife Nell who is in love with Rook; and some minor characters; Corporal Dick an illegitimate hanger-on of the House, an idiot boy, a fortune-telling wandering woman and several servants. Rook makes Ann pregnant and Netta is persuaded for Rook's sake to leave secretly. Rook and Ann marry. Rook, sickened with remorse at Netta's loss and revulsion against Lady Ann, faced with the prospect of Lexie's death, with sympathy only from Nell, tries to come to terms with his life. His marriage particularly oppresses him. Hastings, who spends most of his time writing a philosophy extolling 'Nothingness', hates Rook and on the night of his child's birth, kills him.

The plot is very simple, and there are few digressions. The number of characters, also, is small. What action there is takes place in Ashover House and its immediate surroundings with only a couple of excursions to the nearby town. *Ducdame* is a far shorter and more concentrated work than most of Powys's novels. This was due to Llewelyn Powys's influence. Powys remarked in a letter many years later, that he changed the end of the book completely, having read it 'chapter by chapter'[3] to his brother. Llewelyn Powys's 'compressing and revising hand' has resulted in an excessively pruned novel. The chapter in *Ducdame* is far more of an obvious artefact than in Powys's other novels. The use of the chapter as a kind of essay on a theme is more of a feature of Llewelyn Powys's own style, especially in *Skin for Skin* published in 1926.

If *Wood and Stone* was a cartoon or sketch for the later works, *Ducdame* is perhaps the film version of the novel, a manageable and workable plot-summary, script, stage-directions and set. The stage-directions and set are perhaps what suffered most in the compression. The flow of the novel is interrupted by set-piece chapters which, like scenes in a rather early symbolic film, have a definite character of scenery, weather and atmosphere to match the moods and actions of the characters.

Although this sounds like the symbolic staginess of Powys's first novel, the landscape in *Ducdame* is far less abstract. Powys presents a far more immediate landscape through the minute-by-minute reactions of the characters, especially Rook. His intention in the novel is to show that atmospheric conditions affect the imagination and the nerves; not only to show it, but to show it happening. The excessive pruning of the book probably throws too much emphasis upon the natural scenery and its effect upon, or reciprocity with, the characters. Each chapter becomes stylised, and one can speak of the snow-scene, or the rain-storm or the March or June set. This formal pared-down emphasis is reminiscent of an early Bergman film in the way the scene follows the event or the event the scene.

Powys's style is still too expository and conscious. He does not give himself time to create each character as a full focus for the sensations he describes them as having. The intensity of their experiences only enhances the vacancy of their characters. Powys does not succeed in conveying the deep psychological inter-relations between the mind and what it observes. He complains in *The Pleasures of Literature*, 1938, that twentieth-century novelists allow the universal to swallow up the particular. In D. H. Lawrence the grotesque, pathetic, unique, 'never-to-appear-again'[4] human creature is lost in 'symbolic sex reactions'. In *Ducdame*, it could almost be said that symbolic nature-reactions have 'levelled out and drained away the mysterious uniqueness of all separate living persons'. Almost, but not quite. Rook, the main focus of the book, is an individual. For the rest, Powys has left little room in so brief a book for anything but the simple narrator perspective which merely tells the reader. For example, a West Country December afternoon of 'a warm trance-like stillness', 'had an especial appeal to the nerves of women' because of its 'self-amorous quiescence' (*D*, p. 74).

These generalisations frequently take the place of individual experiences. The result, in this case, of Lady Ann and Mrs Ashover being encouraged in their plot to entrap Rook into marriage and propagation, seems to be the action of puppets rather than people. One is more convinced of Rook's experience and reaction.

> He loathed the sodden, relaxed clay with its incense-reek of insidious mortality. He longed to escape from it all, into some clean, purged, bitter air. He felt homesick for the tang of the salt, unharvested, unfecund sea. (*D*, p. 80)

It is not just that Ann is relaxed and mellow with the warm damp December afternoon, and that Rook is happier with a hard, black frost. There is an attempt at creating the experience of the character's particular response to atmosphere and landscape and weather; to get between the personality and his surroundings and capture the flavour of the interchange between both, to see what it consists of and to present it. To do this for several characters requires the length which Powys has denied himself in this novel. 'Impressions' abound – whose they are is not so obvious. Lacking real personalities to which to cohere, they return back to the author and become part of the conventional omniscient author technique, so that the narrative is overburdened.

These problems were solved in *Wolf Solent*, 1929. The novel depends entirely on the focus of Wolf and every impression is strained through his consciousness so that nothing exists without him. Rook is less central. His impressions are fully given, but although he is the main, and most credible character, he does not encompass the others as Wolf does. Mrs Ashover, Ann, Netta, Nell, Lexie and Hastings exist partially and unsuccessfully in their own right. The technique of the long, multicentred narrative was not mastered until 1932 with *A Glastonbury Romance*.

The successfully presented character, Rook Ashover, is shown as the victim of a crazy battle between dualist extremes. Dualism is not an abstraction here, or a thesis. It takes the form of the wild theories and obsessions of cranks and madmen. The dualism is distanced by this, but it is still important. Mrs Ashover, insanely inhuman through brooding over the Ashover family, sees her son merely as an agent for propagation. It is she who, perhaps too explicitly, voices one of the extremes of the book: creation. Her dead husband's bastard brother, Dick, Lady Ann and the tombs of the Ashover family are part of this dualist drive. The tombs are a powerful symbol in the book. Here is present the pressure of the past, its atmospheric intensity, its power to disturb the nerves, that Powys uses to such great effect in his later novels. Rook twice hears an uncanny sound suggesting 'the united exultation of a host of people buried underground' (*D*, p. 125). Ann is supported by emanations from the Tombs, while Hastings is obsessed with the living power and influence of the dead.

The other dualist drive is voiced by the vicar of Ashover, Hastings, whose nihilistic theories are shown to be a destructive force by the effect of his obsession on his wife Nell's nerves. Nell believes Hasting's book is evil, but the novel does not show dualism as simply good and evil. Powys tries to avoid dualism as merely moral or religious antithesis. He takes it further than this. Good and evil exist in both drives of a complex dualism.

The dualism is located in actual people, rather than in the lugubrious landscape of *Wood and Stone*. It is given some, although not full, psychological credibility. Rook's choice of the barren Netta, Lexie's imminent death: these are causes sufficient for Mrs Ashover's concern, if not obsession. Hasting's nihilism is a result of his morbid oversensitivity, outraged pity and loneliness. Dualism in *Ducdame* is not simplistic, although it seems like cowardice to make three of the spokesmen of the dualist drives partially mad, two of them homicidally so.

Rook and Netta are outside these drives. Rook is a pluralist. He is shown as a detached 'sensationist', enjoying most his walks and the experiences and thoughts he has upon his walks. Would he have these experiences, would he be receptive to these influences, these sensuous and sensual sensations, if he and they were part of a grinding necessity? For this sort of sensitivity, he has to have a philosophy of Pyrrhonian scepticism, and a situation which does not tax it too severely. From the beginning, three things are stressed about him: his detachment from ordinary relationships (*D*. p. 2); his feeling of 'reciprocity' with natural scenery; and his awareness that it had 'something' behind it, some Platonic essence, some astral dimension.

Rook is the centre of a tentative exploration of nature and the 'strange correspondency' (*D*, p. 7) of nature and mind is put forward by him. There is a sense in *Ducdame* that Rook and Powys are looking at all natural objects with a gaze that takes in new aspects of the reciprocal situation and ponders them. Rock's detachment from the dualist battle is due to his 'dehumanized ponderings upon life' (*D*, p. 236). The remark that 'these pine-trees had been the background of his imagination as long as he could remember' (*D*. p. 6) is expressive of a move away from nature as symbol and a step towards the building-up of an atmosphere in the mind, produced from the action of certain aspects of natural scenery on the imagination and nerves.

Rook's ponderings are part of his 'life-illusion' and in *Ducdame* we have the first attempt at conveying the whole psychic bubble of a man's 'life-illusion'. This phrase from Ibsen, so rightly and brilliantly interpreted by Powys, is of great significance.

> A human being's life was not a thing of outward possessions, of outward circumstances. It was a thing of a certain, secret abiding life-illusion, that *must* be in some measure satisfied or all was lost. (*D*, p. 384)

Rook marries the wrong woman and his 'life-illusion' becomes annexed as a battle-ground for the forces of Creation and Destruction, as Ann's pregnancy and Hastings's destructive secret (Netta's address) claim his entire attention. His independent life was being reduced to a 'meaningless cipher' (*D*, p. 347) by them. Powys here realises that dualism implies loss of personality and individuality.

In the first chapter, Rook's appreciation of the watery, moonlit Somerset fields is firstly sensuous experience; he could 'feel' (*D*, p. 13) their essential chilly dampness. He then takes in the whole sensation of the 'thereness' of the landscape; he apprehends the 'indrawn breath of multitudes upon multitudes of grass blades' (*D*, p. 14) responding to the pull of the moon. This goes further than description, and becomes an involvement, a relish of the senses and the mind. This relish is tightened up by the thought of his brother's imminent death, the sadness becomes part of the landscape, screwing up Rook's participation until it becomes exaltation. And the exaltation shades off into the infinite, invades that part of the mind whose ramifications are eternal, beyond

> the border line between death and life... to some unearthly ghost garden, far from all human troubling, where nothing but

solemn milk-white cattle moved up and down through a pearl-
gray mist, (*D*, pp. 14–15)

The texture of Rook's 'life-illusion' is made up of these exalted
moments. For them to occur, he had to be free from responsibilities, free from domestic cosiness, free from the demanding
love of a woman who was his equal. He could be a good son and
brother, he felt, and he could in a detached way feel pity and love
for the undemanding Netta. But Powys emphasises that she is
barren. In the later novels, he emphasises that the nature of the
love between his protagonists is sterile. Even in *Ducdame*, Powys
is turning away from the presentation of normal love. Rook's
misogyny is not disguised, as Ann points out – 'They're awfully
fastidious, men are. You'd think sometimes that they'd never seen
anything born or anything die' (*D*, p. 100). Rook's 'life-illusion'
involves getting away from the natural. This is rather obscure in
Ducdame and is much more fully described in *Wolf Solent*, where
Wolf turns away from the superb natural beauty of Gerda to the
strange asexual Christie. In *Ducdame* the essence of the
relationship between Rook and Netta is only hinted by the
reading of *The Phoenix and the Turtle* in Chapter XI. There is a
similar strange unworldly compatability of the 'twain' who 'had
the essence but in one' and yet

> Leaving no posterity
> Twas not their infirmity
> It was married chastity. (*D*, p. 150)

Netta is necessary for Rock's 'life-illusion'. But the detachment
which is also necessary to preserve what Mrs Ashover calls 'the
crazy unreality of your own fancy' (*D*, p. 130) leads him to behave
cruelly towards Netta and falsely towards Ann and Nell. People
are only half-real to him, or real as phenomena of the present
with no development into the future. The results of this are
disastrous. Powys faces the fact, here and later, of the selfishness
of the sensationist who, living most completely in his own world,
meddles with others without real commitment. Rook's disasters,
like Wolf Solent's, are his own fault. And what is the 'life-illusion'
after all? Towards the end of the book. Powys ironically suggests
that it is a monstrous piece of egotism. Netta refuses

to have pity upon his life illusion, pity upon his soul's inmost self, pity upon that ultimate reflection of himself before himself which lay in the abysmal mirror of his self-deception as the sky lies in a mirage of water above arid sands. (*D*, p. 395)

Rook can offer Netta nothing but a place inside his secret landscape where her image could function for his benefit.

But the sensations that go to make up his 'life-illusion' are of extraordinary significance. It is not just their entrancing beauty – often it is not conventionally 'beautiful' scenes that produce the sensations – it is their significance that affects Rook. There are many passages in *Ducdame* where Powys tries to analyse this significance (*D*, pp. 313–15). It is obvious that the struggle to convey the meaning of the landscape to him is behind all his attempts to show landscape as symbol or influence. In Chapter XIX he notes the feeling of a 'world' lying all the while behind the 'face of crude reality'. This suspicion of an imminent and immanent higher plane is echoed in his poems of the time ('Omens by the Way', 'Duality', 'Wayfarers', 'The Willow Seeds', 'Saturn', 'Exiles'). This secret, inner life of Rook's responds to certain scenes which answer to his 'deepest aesthetic exigencies' (*D*, p. 314) and produces a 'magic' quality.

Wilson Knight has spoken of *Ducdame*'s 'earth nature etherealised' into a 'sense of an etheric dimension,'[5] and there is always the feeling that events, like the swan Rook and Lexie saw (*D*, p. 330), sent ripples out into eternity, or that the view through the trees was of some Fourth Dimension.

The significance of Rook's encounters with landscape may be 'Platonic' but the other dimension they imply is often described as a dream landscape of insensibility and death. It is a land of lotus-eaters, a Pre-Raphaelite rather than a mystical vision. Other images of the 'other world' also seem to come from an imagination that has not fully come to terms with the real significance of what it is trying to convey. One such is the 'Cimmery Stone' (*D*, pp. 262–5), a crystal which reflects the dream landscape of Rook's 'life-illusion'. The most important symbol of the 'etheric dimension', and the one most in accord with the action of the novel, is the meeting of Rook with the rider on horseback. This is both the culmination and the response to a process of growing despair in Rook, which Powys renders with extraordinary vividness.

The boring, deadening nature of dualism is responsible for Rook's despair, although the creative urge seems more destructive to him. One is reminded of Gerard Manley Hopkins's tragic imperative, to sacrifice the 'dapple' of existence for the stark dichotomy of right and wrong in 'Spelt from Sibyl's Leaves'. His predicament, caught between sensuous delight in the variety and expression of natural things and a rigid moral duality, was one that could be appreciated by Powys. He shows Rook caught in the 'two flocks, two folds', and the nervous depression which follows the loss of freedom and vision, 'For earth, her being has unbound, her dapple is at an end'.

The procreative urge takes on an especial image in the mind of Rook. In Chapter VI, on the day Powys describes as being particularly attuned to women's nerves, Rook irritably striding away from the matchmaking of his mother and cousin, has to stop his march across the fens, unable to cross two ditches that bar his way. They are black, choked with dead vegetation, 'the very final exhalation of the dead flesh of the world!' (*D*, p. 80). This menacing obscenity seems to be the reverse of the fallow implacable earth waiting for the 'hour of the sowing of the seed' (*D*, p. 78), but it is shown to be not so much its reverse as its underlying element. The impression is reinforced only four pages later. Rook, revolted by the ditches, recoils and sees Nell by the church. As they embrace, the image that comes to her mind is of 'black pools, stained with pale blood' (*D*, p. 84) once seen on the Dorset coast. It was these 'livid pools' that 'offered an escape to her soul'. This is an obvious echo of the ditch image and its association with sexuality is emphasised as Nell connects the pools with the 'dark flood' of Rook's desire for her. His sensation among the fen ditches fuses with his own nervous resentment of women (what Powys would call 'the feminine principle'), and becomes a working symbol.

That it is a fertility symbol becomes obvious in Chapter XII in a description of Spring. The word 'Spring' refers to the 'very greenness of hyacinth stalks, the very blueness of hedge-sparrows' eggs' but it also carries the mind back into 'the dark rain-soaked background which gave all these things birth,' a place of 'heart-hurting memories' (*D*, p. 162). Powys stresses that life continues at a cost, and that creation implies death and loss. Immediately after this, Ann tells Rook that she is pregnant. That same day

Netta leaves Ashover. Rook is repelled by the real death-in-life behind the 'suppliance' of Spring and creation, the cruelty implicit in the whole evolutionary urge. The whole love instinct, whether maternal or sexual, with its urge to possess another, and to force out of this possession a smothering loving disregard of the other's psychic entity, as Mrs Ashover, Ann and even Nell seem to do, is questioned here. The novel is weighted, probably unintentionally, towards the nothingness of Hastings. Rook's psychological drift is away from life altogether, while Netta after his death complains that 'Life must be rushing, jerking, trailing, dancing, howling forward, just the same' (*D*, p. 449) like the strident whirligig at the fair.

The life urge is more fully treated, perhaps because of Rook's revulsion from it, and the image he half-creates, half-receives for it – the ditch. The ditch image persists throughout the book. The next important example of it is Chapter XIX, when Rook is utterly weary of his life, gazing into 'the green slime of a cattle-trodden ditch' (*D*, p. 303). Seeing this, he realises the extent and cause of his misery; his marriage has profoundly outraged his 'life-illusion' and blurred the very essence of his identity.

> He felt as though this female creature...fungus-like and carnivorous,...devoured his flesh and drank his blood. (*D*. p. 306)

As Ann becomes the embodiment of the ditch, Rook is shown that it can have another reconciling character. The colours of the landscape change to grey – the colour of his dream landscape – and a rider on a tall grey horse canters up. It is his 'son'. Rock tries to explain the 'indescribable horror' of his lost 'life-illusion', and in the effort reaches some sort of resolution; self-acceptance or suicide (*D*, p. 308). His son points out a heron to him, and again Rock reaches a conclusions; that no-one is worthy to live

> who doesn't know that all life asks of us is to be recognized and loved! (*D*, p. 310)

This is important but equivocal in several ways. The theme of the necessity of self-acceptance becomes stronger in Powys as the novels mature, but here it is the words 'kill himself and end it' that hover in the air. The conclusion that life should not be questioned, but enjoyed, loved and recognised is triumphantly reiterated in *A Glastonbury Romance* but surely an unborn messenger from an etheric dimension must undermine the premise that it is *all* life asks of us? It takes a careful reading to realise that this is meant to be a conclusion. It seems merely a sentence as Rook does not act upon it until a few hours before his death.

Both the ditch and the rider are seen on Rook's last night, just before he is killed and when Ann is in labour. The emphasis is changed. Stars, reflected in the ditch, shine like 'drowned but not quite extinguished' glow-worms while twigs float between them

> as if they floated above a crevice in the terrestrial orb itself which sank down into antipodal gulfs. (*D*, p. 431)

Here the ditch itself becomes an annexe to the etheric regions, no longer a swampy pit of decaying fecundity. Rook is happy, at peace, reconciled. After this, he again catches a glimpse of the rider and knows that his son is born. This is an aspect of the pro-creative urge he had not until then experienced. At the time of his death, he is reconciled to living happily with Ann.

Powys may not originally have meant to end with his murder. Llewelyn Powys made him 'change the end of the book completely'. But Rook's death is in accord with the mood of the novel if not with his conclusions. In Powys's first four novels the protagonist ('hero' is inappropriate) is dead by the end. The first four novels end with water, rain, sea or river. The last chapter of *Wood and Stone* describes a month-long downpour which makes Nevilton almost a village under water. In *Rodmoor*, Adrian Sorio and Philippa are swept out to sea, 'out of reach of humanity'. In *After My Fashion*, Richard Storm dies of a heart attack in the rain after rescuing a sheep from a dew-pond. Rook dies in the river Frome and the novel ends with penetrating, isolating rain. In *A Glastonbury Romance*, the flood is far more obviously and successfully cleansing and all-resolving. In the earlier novels, it seems to emphasise the depression always present.

Ducdame is only partially successful. It is, however, worth reading despite its minor status because of Powys's robust intellectual desire to do two things: to slough off his weakening interest in a boring dualism and present a pluralism; and to understand the effect of landscape on the mind, even the very process of the effect. The two things are brought together in the character of Rook. One could call *Ducdame* an outline for his next novel. Having called his 'fools into a circle' Powys could go on to write *Wolf Solent*.

3 Wolf Solent

Novels in which 'Nature' is an important element have not been accorded major status since Hardy's death; unless, as in the works of Lawrence or Forster, natural scenery is symbolic, there to prove a point, either about society or an individual. Even Forster's Howards End is very convenient for the London train and it is only the suburban comic-tragic figure of Leonard Bast who does any real walking and seeing.

Until Ted Hughes, twentieth-century 'nature' poetry was regarded as a minor mode, and 'Georgian' was a particularly demeaning adjective to use about it. Often in reading accounts of the Georgian 'nature' poets, one is forced to conclude that their reputation for insipid mediocrity is partly due to their ignorance of the coming of the First World War. George Dangerfield's very readable account of these years, 1910–14, *The Strange Death of Liberal England*, describes the 'England' of the Georgian poets – 'where sorrow dies with sunset and even despair is crowned with new-mown hay'[1] – and dismisses the impulse behind this sort of landscape imagery as childish. Certainly many of the Georgian poets (they include W. H. Davies, Robert Bridges, James Stephens, John Masefield, Ralph Hodgson, Walter de la Mare, Edward Thomas) wrote deliberately simple straightforward poetry as a reaction against the tortured emotionality of the poets of their youth. As G. K. Chesterton wrote, referring to the 1890s, 'The World was very old indeed when you and I were young'. This response to the 'Decadents' implied a return to childish things, simple country pleasures enjoyed spontaneously, Rupert Brooke eating honey at Grantchester, or Ratty and Mole eating rather more on another river bank in *The Wind in the Willows*.

Peter Green in his biography of Kenneth Grahame also discusses what he considers to be the motivating force behind the literature of the time; its 'stock themes', 'food and drink, tobacco, sleep, travel, walking, nature mysticism' are 'drugs', 'escape routes' from reality.[2] Powys, perhaps because of his long exile or

slow maturing or merely his long life, belongs to several
traditions. His work contains the sexual and emotional
ambiguities of the Decadent poets. He uses the 'stock themes' of
the Georgians – food and drink, sleep, walking, nature-mysticism, and one of his key words is 'escape'. Escapism was the basis of
his philosophy. He never felt that escapism was of a low moral
tone.

But in *Wolf Solent*, 1929, the prevailing impression is of the
seriousness of engaged moral concern, the freshness of imagery,
the individuality of thought. It is not a rehash of stock themes. It
does not depend, for any power it may possess, on recollection of
earlier literary models. One cannot say, as Dangerfield says of the
Georgians, that their subject was,

> the rural England of Shakespeare and Milton and Words-
> worth... gone very soft at the heart.[3]

There is very little softness at the heart of Wolf Solent's Dorset,
and although it could be said that there was indeed 'nature-
mysticism' it should be placed against the background of literary
'nature-mysticism'.

Richard Jefferies' is the classic voice of this emotion at the turn
of the century (*The Story of My Heart*, 1886). Jefferies does not
express himself in theological language. He does not try to force
his feeling of transcendent reality into a proof of anything. Nevertheless, he says, he has an authentic sense of the existence of a
whole world beyond the life of the senses: 'A great life – an entire
civilization lies just outside the pale of common thought'.[4]

It is this feeling, expressed by a writer of far less sophistication
and education than Powys; a feeling which should more accurately be called 'numinous' rather than 'mystical', that Jefferies
exemplifies. Nature points beyond herself:

> holding out my hand for the sunbeams to touch it, prone on
> the sward in token of deep reverence, thus I prayed that I
> might touch to the unutterable existence higher than deity.[5]

Place this quotation by the side of a characteristic passage from
Wolf Solent. The Powys passage is just that sort of intense description of the inner life, that attempt to capture the flavour of a
state of mind most people have probably felt but few described,

to which the word 'mysticism' has been loosely attached.

Wolf, is walking with Gerda, near a river bank,

> There came rushing headlong out of that ditch...a whole
> herd of ancient memories! Indescribable! Indescribable! They
> had to do with wild drenched escapes beneath banks of sombre
> clouds, of escapes along old back-waters and by forsaken sea-
> estuaries, . . . [6]

These memories are the 'very essence' of Wolf's life. They are his 'secret religion'. At no point, however, is there any suggestion of their being a hint of the supernatural. They are part, to use an ugly phrase, of the data bank of experience. There is a sense in Jefferies' rather artful, consciously 'beautiful' style with its absence of humour, of a contrived effect, of an aetherealising of experience. He remains God-haunted.

Powys, by contrast, humorously refuses the temptation to exaltation in describing Wolf Solent's collection of memories and the energies they release for him. Although he collects these 'filmy growths' like a 'mad botanist' for 'no purpose', they are connected with 'that mythopoeic fatality' which drives him. Powys did not arrive at this all-embracing and irreverent style at once. It is interesting to note, for example, the evolution of the sense of nature melancholy in his work. Pater provides an example of nature-melancholy in literature at a time when Powys's imagination was beginning to germinate. In Chapter XXV of *Marius the Epicurean* (1886), appropriately entitled *Sunt Lacrimae Rerum*, Pater remarks on a sense of deep sorrow in the essence of things: a grief 'in things as they are',[7] beyond the often removable 'griefs of circumstance', an 'inexplicable shortcoming...on the part of nature', a constant sense of time passing and death. This is the Victorian dilution and secularisation of the doctrine of original sin.

In *Ducdame* the traces of this feeling remain though it is drained of explicit theological meaning. The passage of description conjured up by the word 'Spring' has already been quoted. It is full of revulsion and even fear. By the time of *Wolf Solent*, this importation of the doom-laden into nature has ceased. Wolf feels

> his soul invaded by that peculiar kind of melancholy which
> emanates at the end of a spring day from all the elements of

earth and water.... It is a sadness accentuated by grey skies, grey waters and grey horizons. (*WS*, p. 94)

This passage is worth noting because of the way in which it shows Powys playing down wider metaphysical and cosmic statements. The fatality in nature is simply the recognition of death. There is in grey skies and grey waters a perfectly satisfactory explanation of its special force at certain times.

(It is interesting to remember that the mature Powys saw in Walter Pater none of those elements of Weltschmerz which are so evident in his writings, but which Powys had obviously lost interest in. In his essay on Pater (*VR*, p. 171) Powys shows him as another Nietzsche, emphasising his irreverent, pyrrhonist and hedonist elements, and including an unlikely vignette from Edmund Gosse, of Pater dancing on his lawn in the moonlight.)

It is perhaps necessary to return to the earlier, first-generation Romantics in considering the nature of Powys's attitudes. At the end of *Wolf Solent*, Wolf explicitly compares himself with 'another blundering mystic', (*WS*, p. 611) the Wordsworth of *Ode on Intimations of Immortality*. Even without the explicit reference, the presence of Wordsworth is inescapable, although, as in the case of Jefferies and Pater, there are crucial differences.

What strikes most readers about *Wolf Solent* is its originality. Powys can be distinguished from those writers whose names have here been associated with 'nature'. There are varied reasons for this. Freedom from literary reminiscence set him apart from the Georgian poets; absence of theistic assumption from Jefferies; and lack of a prevailing mood of deep melancholy from Pater. The combination of psychological accuracy and serious philosophical intention add to the stature of his work.

The language of *Wolf Solent* is fully equal to the originality and subtlety of the theme. Critics have complained of the longueurs inherent in narrative strained entirely through the consciousness of one man who spent much of his time staring over hedges. Powys himself says that he was for some time in thrall to Henry James's style. But *Wolf Solent* shows what Powys was striving for, when in 1915 he stated his desire to create a language that would present actual physical sensation.

It is through an examination of style and manner that Powys's matter is reached, and here plot summaries and 'themes' are unhelpful. Cyril Connolly's admission, in a *Sunday Times* review of G. Wilson Knight's *Neglected Powers*,[8] that he could not even get through a plot summary of *A Glastonbury Romance* is beside the point. A resumé of the 'action' of *Wolf Solent* would leave many readers surprised and bewildered that it was printed at a time when *Lady Chatterley's Lover* was banned. A mother-dominated, middle-aged man arrives in Dorset to write a porno-graphic history for a wealthy old homosexual necrophiliac. He seduces a young girl, Gerda, and marries her, having also fallen in love with her friend, Christie, the daughter of the bookseller who supplies Wolf's employer with his questionable literature. Malakite, the bookseller, has another young daughter, born of an incestuous union with his eldest daughter, now dead. Wolf also meets the Otter brothers, the older a homosexual depressive poet, the younger a depressive school teacher who marries the illegiti-mate daughter of Wolf's father. The alcoholic Tractarian vicar of the village, also given to 'unholy love', is persecuted by Urquhart, Wolf's employer, who feels that the priest is responsible for the mysterious death of Wolf's predecessor, Redfern. Wolf becomes more and more puzzled over Redfern's death, especially when his grave shows signs of disturbance. Later he watches while Urqu-hart, his sullen servant, and Round, the half-mad inn-keeper and uncle of the lesbian bar-maid, disinter the body. Weevil, the grocer, has been encouraged to cuckold Wolf, while Wolf himself refrains from seducing Christie. Christie leaves Blacksod, after probably killing her father, and Gerda captures the attention of Wolf's rich and womanising relative, Lord Carfax. It is interest-ing to compare this melodramatic farrago with the actual im-pression of reading *Wolf Solent*.

Perhaps the most useful way of examining Powys's nature imagery and his psychological understanding at the beginning of his mature period is by a close examination of one chapter of *Wolf Solent*. Since the style gains its effects by consecutive ac-cumulation and modification, one does not do Powys justice by picking threads and incidents here and there from the great fabric of the novel. This kind of darting selectivity tends to exaggerate the eccentricity of Powys's fiction, as well as falsify it. To study Powys's subject and themes exclusively, would be to lose the essence of the novels. (How far would a study of the Grail myth help in an understanding of *A Glastonbury Romance* for example?) This type of criticism interrupts the trains of thought, of description, conversation or incident from which the leading images appear. Not only does this make Powys seem neurotic when he is above all, sane, but it robs him of what is his special quality, a fidelity to the moment-by-moment working of certain mental/physiological processes (not always thoughts in the strict sense) which have never been caught so exactly. The plot summary above gives no impression of *Wolf Solent* and it destroys the tactful and beautifully placed hints and allusions, the gentle and humanising quality of the style.

I propose to discuss Chapter 16, 'A Game of Bowls', very closely, pointing out allusions and references to other parts of the novel to try and show how Powys's style works. The chapter traces Wolf's currents of mind over some five hours. It begins with Wolf working on Urquhart's collection of scandals in the library of the manor-house at King's Barton. Compelled to work up the 'spiteful commentaries and floating fragments of wicked gossip' into a book, he has begun to be interested in the style, his contribution to the work.

> and although it had been evoked under external pressure, and in a sense, had been a tour de force, it was in its essence the expression of Wolf's own soul – the only purely aesthetic expression that Destiny had ever permitted to his deeper nature. (*WS*, p. 316)

His work – 'the only aesthetic expression' allowed to him – 'lent itself to the breathless peacefulness of that gray afternoon'. The afternoon was one of 'autumnal atmosphere' – the dew on the fallen leaves 'giving them that peculiar look, for which he had been craving'.

The work, the afternoon, the view from his 'escutcheoned window', so reminiscent of the Gainsborough view in the diningroom – all blended and combined to give Wolf a sense of wellbeing. His writing, the style he had evolved, is Pateresque, 1890s' aestheticism, as is the original picture of Wolf sitting in the window-seat of the old manor-house, elegantly transcribing obscenities.

He rewrites one of Urquhart's pieces of wicked gossip about a girl corrupted by the 'troubling symbol' (*WS*, p. 317) of the Cerne Giant. The first transcript is heavy and ponderous, full of coy abstract nouns, and loaded with prurient meaning – 'procured him his famous infamy'. The revision moves towards a detached and intelligent view of the subject, a more immediate style whose whimsical euphemisms recall those of Pater. The studied, rather precious prose is amoral in effect. It changes the phrase that judges its subject, 'corrupt rogue' and replaces it by a morally neutral one; 'baffled idolator of innocence'.

His style has come to be of great importance to Wolf. It is a part of himself and he refines and winnows it with great care. But what in fact is he doing? He is putting an aesthetic gloss upon some rather dubious material. He is aware of this, and becomes far more so when he realises that Urquhart, instead of merely noting down interesting and scurrilous tales, is presenting the material in such a way as to suggest an explanation of his own life-style, the fastidious gentleman, recoiling in disgust from lewd countrywomen, interests himself in strange rare books, and dreams of the ideal friendship (perhaps with young Redfern?) which 'is misunderstood by a lewd parson'.

It is also worth nothing that the relationship between the Cerne Giant and the unknown female is an ambiguous parallel of the situation Wolf has just witnessed on Poll's Camp with his wife Gerda. Wolf grows obscurely jealous of the 'strange non-human eroticism existing between the heathen soil and that sleeping figure' (*WS*, p. 313). The heathen hill seems hostile to Wolf and his desire, his 'platonic' desire for Christie which is associated with the 'chastened' and 'mediaeval' Somerset Vale. The heathen malice of Poll's Camp reminds him of Urquhart.

This passage he transcribes, while being what he feels consciously to be propaganda for Urquhart, is also more remotely a hint of what is happening to Wolf. His ideal 'platonic' friendship with Christie is in direct contrast with Gerda's straightforward eroticism.

It is the reminder of Urquhart's 'special pleading' reinforced by his own phrase, 'natural enough, therefore, for this baffled idolator of innocence to become a mysogynist and to turn –' which brings Wolf up sharply. He begins to think, without knowing why, of Redfern. The preceding passage has made quite clear why the thought of Redfern should intrude at this moment. The 'shadowy Redfern', previous secretary to Urquhart, had died prematurely, and to Wolf his personality is a focus for ill-defined suspicions, suppositions, and sympathies. Certainly he feels that Urquhart's attitude, behaviour, and feelings for Redfern were questionable.

Thinking of Redfern, and Urquhart's ambiguous relationship with him, produces a revulsion in Wolf's attitude to the book. Staring at the flower beds, which earlier had seemed in perfect accord with his work, he now becomes conscious of 'a clear revelation of something in nature purer than anything in man's mind' (*WS*, p. 317). He realises that despite his 'stylistic inventions' the book's drift is apparent. He must come to terms with the sordid intentions of the book and its possibly evil influence. Although he hated 'traditional terminology', Wolf's 'life-illusion' was obsessed 'by the notion of himself as some kind of protagonist in a cosmic struggle'. He mentally opposed

'his own secret mythology' to some equally secret evil in the world around him.

'Cosmic struggle', 'primordial dualism': these are terms from *Wood and Stone*, and *Ducdame*, evoking as they do the relentless dualism of Powys's early work. But the struggle, however 'primordial' and 'cosmic' is only taking place in Wolf's mind. It is a part of his psychological make-up (*WS*, p. 8).

He cannot do otherwise than see the world as a place where 'good and evil' oppose one another. His 'life-illusion', the way he manages to feel comfortable in this sort of world, consists of pretending, feeling, dramatising his role so that he becomes, in the shadowy theatre of his imagination, a heroic figure on the side of 'Good'. His secret weapon, his trick to outwit 'evil' is the 'mythology' of his sensations. His 'life-illusion' and his 'mythology' are described in Chapter I, where Wolf, travelling down to Dorset, reviews his life. His 'mythology', at its baldest described as 'certain sensations' (*WS*, p. 7) or 'sinking into his soul', is what in *Ducdame* Rook called his 'dehumanized ponderings'. These were produced by certain natural objects (originally the sea at Weymouth) and the 'sensations', a mixture of imaginative and sensuous excitement, were pervasive and powerful enough to affect Wolf's dramatic inner struggle. His 'magnetic impulses' resemble 'the expanding of great vegetable leaves on a still pool' the spontaneous movement of which makes a difference to 'the great hidden struggle' between good and evil. Into the 'still pool', however, the drop of 'ice-cold rain', the doubt, had fallen. This raises the question, almost the challenge that Wolf threw out at Dorset, when he arrived. Would there be something or someone able to do what no outward events had yet done – break up this mirror of half-reality and drop great stones of real reality – drop them and lodge them – hard, brutal, material stones – down there among those dark waters and that mental foliage.

Wolf's attitude to 'reality' is ambiguous. In the last quotation he seems aware that the 'charmed circle of the individual's private consciousness' is only 'half-reality' and that 'real' and 'material' reality could disrupt it fatally. His life in London, his 'material' life held no such threat to his 'half-real' life. But he also feels that 'true reality' is only present in the mind.

Outward things, such as that terrible face on the Waterloo steps, or that tethered cow he had seen at Basingstoke, were to him like faintly-limned images in a mirror, the true reality of which lay all the while in his mind – in these hushed, expanding leaves – in this secret vegetation – the roots of whose being hid themselves beneath the dark waters of his consciousness.

The face and the cow had some existence until he saw them, but when he had seen them, they took on a significance as of remote and archaic figures, and this significance reverberated and echoed in his mind. The strength of Wolf's subjective 'true reality' gave him a complete armour against the world, his 'life-illusion', but it could also result in gross selfishness and terrible mistakes, as Christie points out (*WS*, p. 450).

His literary style was 'the expression of Wolf's own soul' – the only purely aesthetic expression that Destiny had ever permitted to his 'deeper nature'. This sentence links it up with his 'sensations'. Both are aesthetic and amoral, but both are radically involved with the moral issues Wolf cannot but see as pervading the universe.

There is no author's voice with its knowledge of objective truth. There is no final authority. There are no facts. Everything stated appears by way of reflection in Wolf's consciousness, the 'mirror of half-reality'. Urquhart may be 'evil'. What is certain for the reader is that as far as Wolf's 'true reality' goes, Urquhart is very evil. But Wolf is also assailed by doubts. He begins to doubt his own suppositions. This begins when he, Urquhart and Jason Otter watch Weevil and Lob, two Blacksod youths, bathing in Lenty Pond. In the atmosphere of sentimentality and well-being

(*WS*, p. 285) Wolf finds himself wondering if his whole subjective vision of the struggle between good and evil is not a 'fancy of the brain'. This doubt of his most firmly held conviction shakes his whole sense of identity and purpose. He has a sense of 'moral atrophy'. Is Urquhart evil or not?

> And the placid sun-burnt sympathy he felt for the man's amiable passivity seemed seeping in upon him like a warm salt tide – a tide that was outside any 'dualism' – a tide that was threatening the banked-up discriminations of his whole life.

Although this doubt is described in entirely untheological language, it is shown as something as serious as the undermining of a religious conviction. It is not a half-serious rethinking of sexual moeurs. The whole atmosphere of the 'Giorgione-like fête-champêtre' made Wolf feel 'awkward, ill-at-ease, and even a fool', not, as has been made clear, because Urquhart and Otter are enjoying the spectacle of boys bathing. It would, he considers, make no difference if they were girls. It is because the atmosphere is so harmless, so enjoyable. Wolf cannot condemn Urquhart and perhaps his moral categories are meaningless.

Again, the 'moral atrophy', the 'placid sunburn sympathy' can be seen in Wolf's literary style in Chapter 16. His revisions are away from moral judgements. And yet this style, this 'warm salt tide' of acceptance is 'the expression of Wolf's own soul'.

Here there is the conflict already seen in *Ducdame*, the opposition of two philosophies, dualism and pluralism. Although in *Wolf Solent* both these systems exist within one mind, the conflict survives. It is not explicit, however, as in the earlier novel. *Wolf Solent* is so rich and subtle that to analyse 'philosophies' is to pull out two fish to describe the multiple personality of a river.

Wolf's thoughts return to Redfern (*WS*, p. 318), and his habit of wandering round Lenty Pond in the autumn evenings. To this thought is added the image of himself wandering the world far from Christie, and then he picks up the alabaster paperweight which reminds him of soap. These three reveries are transitions which reinforce the concluding image, the memory of Urquhart remarking that the decision to commit suicide would transform all the little things one's eyes happened to fall upon, as for example, a bar of soap. Wolf's half-formed notion that Redfern was driven to his death or suicide by Urquhart's unnamed evil

which centred round his book, almost leads him to decide to give
up his job. But the result of this would be to lose his mother,
Gerda and Christie, an impossible eventuality, and absent-
mindedly picking up the paperweight, he is again clearly
conscious of suicide.

Powys, by his use of these easily overlooked, seemingly
haphazard associations, conveys significance through the dense
texture of his writing. Dialogue is the only way in which other
people can claim objective attention in the novel. There can be
no objective third-person narration which can tell the reader
anything. Wolf's conscious reveries are reinforcements, discoveries, decisions, definite mind-happenings. But the low-key,
half-aware, background noises, almost unacknowledged, are
released to the reader only by chance objects, quick associations,
asides of feeling liberated by some unimportant object. The
object sometimes becomes the feeling. Certainly in Wolf's mind
the object becomes the shorthand for the feeling, like Christie's
'grey feather', (*WS*, p. 169) or the bowl of violets in her room
(*WS*, p. 235).

Monk, Urquhart's rather menacing servant, invites Wolf to
come to the 'Farmer's Rest', the pub in the village of King's
Barton where a bowling match is to take place. In 1929, Powys
still included the Squire, country-house and village as part of his
setting, although Wolf lived in Blacksod (Yeovil) and spent much
time travelling, both actually and imaginatively, between Somerset and Dorset.

There are two rather eerie episodes before the match. Wolf is
first disturbed by the strange cries 'Jesus, Jesus, Jesus' of the
obsessed landlord, Round. He is then joined by Malakite,
Christie's father, for tea in the little parlour.

Malakite's strange obsessive gaze of a 'fixed monomaniacal
intensity' (*WS*, p. 323) further disturbs Wolf. It has no human
meaning.

> It seemed directed towards some aspect of universal matter
> that absorbed and fascinated it.

What information already given of Malakite fits in with this livid
gaze of monomania. He has had incestuous relations with his
daughter, who bore his child. He was friendly with Wolf's shameless father. He provides pornographic books for Squire Urquhart.

But it is through Wolf that the full significance of this stare is realised.

As Wolf leaves the School Treat at King's Barton in Chapter 18, he catches sight of Bess Round and a younger girl. He recognises that he 'is in the presence of a passionate perversity' (*WS*, p. 385). It causes an extraordinary excitement in him which in itself startles him. He senses that if he let it, this pulse-throbbing excitement could become an obsessive quest. He could feel 'the sort of scoriac desolation – all delicate intimations become cinders and ashes in the mouth – that would possess him'. He could even feel 'the actual expression' his face would come to wear as he went on his 'maniacal pursuit'.

Malakite's obsessive mania is described and explained through Wolf's sudden realisation that he could become like this through sexual obsession. Powys's own obsession for sylph-like anonymous limbs and his occasional orgies of reading pornography are described in *Autobiography*. He shows Malakite as so totally obsessed as to lose any connection with ordinary humanity. His livid gaze seemed 'to eat the air'. He is a very well presented 'dirty old man', seen through Wolf's eyes as disturbing and disturbed. Wolf's own 'deadly sweet' insight throws a beam on Malakite rather like his own desolate stare. It is only a glimpse but it shows Powys's awareness of sexual disturbance. In *A Glastonbury Romance* the whole poisoned ashy world of the sadist Evans is developed at length.

Wolf is curious about the landlord and asks Malakite about him. He rebuffs him rudely. Wolf finds himself beginning to entertain 'wildest imaginings' (*WS*, p. 325) about Mr Round, and this is another strain of thought to add to the whole King's Barton mystery, that he persists in weaving. When closely questioned by Wolf, Torp, his father-in-law, gives him some reluctant information, that Round feels responsible for Redfern's death. He cannot be persuaded, however, to tell Wolf what Round did say to Redfern, and this mystery further complicates the muddle of Wolf's thoughts about King's Barton.

Lenty Pond itself has become a more and more ambiguous image in Wolf's mind. His irritation with Torp comes out in an exasperated request not to let Lobbie bathe in 'that damned pond' (*WS*, p. 327)

'Tis a pond that would drown the likes of you and me, maybe. But they boys! Why they'd bathe in Satan's spittle and come out sweet. Lenty Pond's nothing to Lob Torp, sir. You can rest peaceful on that.

Torp's reply is ambivalent. It half-reinforces, half-denies, the feeling of the strangeness of Lenty Pond. Powys allows the reader to be totally sceptical about King's Barton and its mysteries, and about Wolf and his 'mythology'.

The image of Lenty Pond as a 'good Darset duck-pond' seems incongruous after Wolf's fascinated ruminations, and shows the relativity of experience. What to Wolf is a still pool of ambiguous evil, to Torp is a good pond to slide on. But Torp's allusion to drowning is taken up much later when Wolf feels that finishing Urquhart's book has killed his 'life-illusion': the loss of his 'mythology' has rendered his present life intolerable and 'the alternative to London was the bottom of Lenty Pond (*WS*, p. 525). Torp's speech is the reverse of comforting to Wolf. While Torp speaks, Wolf begins to be aware of a growing conviction. A fancy concerning Lenty Pond presses upon him, that everybody knows something about it, 'something that was absurdly simple, that fitted together with mathematical precision, but to which he was himself completely blind' (*WS*, p. 327)

It transpires, later on, as Bess Round tells him (*WS*, p. 487) that there is a superstition concerning Lenty Pond, the Urquharts and various young men down the generations, which gets attached by Monk, Round, and the village elders, to Wolf himself. But this actual, communicated fact seems almost incidental to the real phenomenal place the pond occupies in Wolf's mind. Perhaps the haunting quality of the image of Lenty Pond in Wolf's imagination is partly due to the fact that his 'mythology' is expressed through the imagined experience of great quiet vegetation expanding in still green water (*WS*, pp. 4, 8) or the movement of fish.

> Wolf felt the familiar mystic sensation surging up... Up, up, it rose, like some great moonlight-coloured fish from fathomless watery depths. (*WS*, p. 27)

This early reference to the 'moonlight-coloured fish' of his 'sensations' is referred to again in Chapter 21 after Wolf has finished and accepted payment for Urquhart's book, and quarrelled with Gerda, and suspects that Christie may, after being

disappointed when Wolf refused to sleep with her, have excited
her father's old incestuous feelings. Wolf fears that his mythology
is 'dead as Jimmy Redfern'. Lob Torp has just caught an
enormous perch in Lenty Pond. The dead fish reminds Wolf of a
childhood incident at Weymouth when his father made him
return a small fish to an inland pool. The young Wolf had a
sympathetic ecstasy as the fish swam away and Powys presents an
intensely realised description of 'that lovely translucent underworld' into which the fish escapes (*WS*, p. 485).

Wolf connects the fish with Weymouth 'where his mythology
had first been revealed to him'. As he picks up the fish 'and
entered into the overpowering emanation of its dead identity – its
pale blood drops, its sticky irridescent scales, its mud-pungent
smell' he is seized with a craving for Weymouth, for the old
native-land of his mythology. '"Which of us five men", he
thought, "is most like a fish? It's the best symbol of the Unutterable there is!"'

Powys, through Wolf, deliberately asks the reader which of the
men is most like a fish: the answer to this, after Wolf's 'mythology'
and all its pond-pool-lake imagery, is of course Wolf himself. He
is the 'great moonlight-coloured fish from fathomless watery
depths'. He is the small fish that swam away safely in the
Weymouth backwater when his 'mythology' began.

But Dorset had dropped 'great stones of real reality...down
there among those dark waters and that mental foliage' (*WS*, p.
9) and the great 'out of season' and rare perch caught roughly at
dawn by his young relative out of 'that lovely translucent underworld' is Wolf himself. His mental landscape of 'aqueous dimness'
has dropped away. Other quotations support this reading (*WS*,
pp. 426, 542).

The 'fish' recurs in the name Powys gives to the self – 'ichthyo-
saurus ego' in *In Defence of Sensuality*. Perhaps the most important 'fish' in Powys's novels is Sam Dekker's vision of the Grail
and its shadowy fish in *A Glastonbury Romance*. The fish seems
to be a symbol for the human personality at its highest level.

This is the shadowy meaning weighing on Lenty Pond; that it is
the environment of Wolf's mind. And the young lesbian lady's
gnomic ramblings of a face on the water waiting for Wolf to join
it (*WS*, p. 498) are peripheral; they sound, and are meant to
sound, like vulgar village gossip. Here Powys has achieved a
sliding scale of importance. In *Ducdame*, 'Cimmery land', the

Gorm signpost, the cry of the ancestral tombs, Rook's 'sensations', Netta's vision, the ghost of Rook's son: all these things, psychic supernatural, superstitious and imaginative, were jumbled up in no sort of scale of importance. They had to be sorted out.

The scale of importance in *Wolf Solent* is so finely managed that the reader is hardly aware of it. Because Wolf's mind sorts through experience with the reader, only those experiences remain which really work upon his consciousness and imagination. Thus when Bess Round 'warns' him of the danger to him in King's Barton, his response is to notice a poetical expression she uses, and to wonder at his own rather perverse attraction to her. Her 'warning' is hardly bothered about. It is only important as an external fact about the sort of people with whom he had to deal. The mythic personalities of Urquhart, Monk and Round in his mythopoeic world are what are important.

After the game of bowls (Chapter 16) Wolf is overcome by a 'disconcerting feeling as though the whole of his life at the present moment were unreal' (*WS*, p. 328).

> It hung upon him like a wavering dizziness, as full of meaningless blotches and sparkles as the glass coffin lid of King Aethelwolf in the Abbey.

This is a reference to his visit to the Abbey with Miss Gault one evening to see the newly found coffin of King Aethelwolf. Striking a match, he throws a weird light on Miss Gault's even more weird face, and produces a vision he can only call 'bestial' (*WS*, p. 305).

Taking the match as close to the glass-covered aperture as he can, he can distinguish nothing but the reflections of the match on the glass. He peers desperately at 'sparkles, black wavering spots, fluctuating blotches of reddish-yellow, little orbs of blackness rimmed with lunar rings; and then again darkness! Nothing!' He cannot make out the bones of the ancient king for the reflection of his own match, just as he cannot make out the material reality of King's Barton for the reflection of his imaginative, creative 'true reality'.

Wolf recalls this occasion at the bowling-match because he is again 'vexed and perturbed' – 'something was teasing him. What was it?' (*WS*, p. 328).

The same situation recurs: he is trying to make something out;

it is as disproportionately worrying to him that he cannot grasp what is on his mind, as it was that he could not distinguish the royal dust. The clue to what is 'fretting him' is already there in his mind; in the 'random association' of Aethelwolf's tomb. It is the memory, unrevealed to him in the 'Farmer's Rest', of Miss Gault's hideous face lit suddenly by his match (*WS*, p. 305). The 'glimpse' of something 'ghastly' echoes or prefigures Malakite's gaze of 'ghastly livid illumination' (*WS*, p. 325) and it is this which teases Wolf's nerves as he stands gazing at the bowl on the grass, talking of the bowling-match, and feeling as unreal and dizzy as the sparkles on the glass coffin.

Powys uses echoes and associations of incidents and ideas, much as they actually occur in life. A man trying hard to think of what is actually worrying him, recalls a random image from a scene that took place some weeks before. It recurs, quite unconsciously, because the striving to concentrate and see something is paralleled in both situations so strongly that the man actually feels himself at that moment take on the characteristics of the visual image he retains from the first incident. But what was accessory to the first scene, the ghastly face, and less important at the time than the effort to see, is a parallel to what is the cause of the effort to see in the second scene.

It is this subtle presentation of the actual movements of the consciousness (not just the workings of the mind) which is Powys's original and exciting achievement.

His effortless use of psychological reality is never strained, and the achievement of what is surely 'stream of consciousness' is not gained by loss of other levels in the book, the story for example. Virginia Woolf achieves 'stream of consciousness' by minimising plot and use of tense. Powys shows this to be unnecessary. He also progresses further than Virginia Woolf. While she uses random objects (the sad furniture in Mrs Ramsey's summer house for example, sets off a memory train about the Swiss maid)[9] to release memories and reminiscence, the random objects become the imaginative symbols of the thoughts and emotions they release in J. C. Powys. Mr Bankes is watching workmen building a house while he ponders over the beauty of Mrs Ramsey.[10] Their activity is set in parenthesis in the middle of his ruminations. Wolf's concentrated striving becomes the visual image of this remembered mental activity. It is worth noting the differences between Powys and Virginia Woolf. Although her novels made a far greater stir in the 1920s and 30s, Powys is the more technically innovative 'stream of consciousness' writer.

Another example of this is Wolf's attitude to the 'delicately polished bowl, of a dark chestnut colour, that lay on the grass close to Darnley's feet' (*WS*, p. 328). A small flower-seed had balanced itself on the bowl. As Wolf gazed at it the niggling worry became the flower-seed. He could feel it 'tickling the skin of his mind', which had become the bowl.

A better example of how Powys's style, through Wolf's imagination, makes thoughts into entities is Wolf's reverie before sleep on his first night in Dorset (Chapter 3). All his thoughts and experiences of the day, his trip from London, what he saw from the train, his meeting and dinner with Urquhart, became material, as his personality became the polished bowl. The moments of drifting into sleep where random associations and images float among evaporating consciousness are described. Some clear hints are also given as to Wolf's future in Dorset.

Wolf remembers the waiter at the Lovelace Hotel and the tragic face of a tramp he had seen on the steps of Waterloo Station, and his mind becomes suddenly full of the 'unknown personality' of Valley, the vicar of King's Barton. The strength of this image is due presumably to Squire Urquhart's contempt for the man he nicknames 'Tilly-Valley'. This is reinforced by Wolf's impression of Urquhart's ritualistic delight in the altar, despite his lack of Christian faith. The extraordinary picture had come into Wolf's mind of Urquhart, stark naked and pot-bellied, kneeling alone in a dark church. This strange spectacle clearly evokes the sort of 'actual evil' Wolf comes to believe embodied in the Squire. It is an atmosphere of incense-smelling Satanic obscenity that leads straight to his suspected necrophiliac activities. It is Urquhart's contempt for and persecution of Valley that first excites Wolf's sense of moral drama, before he has heard of Redfern. His imaginative sympathy for Valley comes into his mind with such force, because he was thinking of the face he saw on the Waterloo steps. The face of a tramp, casually seen, becomes for Wolf the actual experience of suffering.

While the syllables 'Tilly-Valley' repeat themselves senselessly in his mind, they cease to refer to any one personality but become a 'queer-shaped floating object' which must be 'straightened out' (*WS*, p. 39). What prevents Wolf from helping this to be done is the 'thick and heavy' port-wine-tasting influence of Urquhart. (When, at the end of the novel, his 'mythology' dead, and left only with his awareness of sensations, he experiences the horror of the slaughterhouse (*WS*, p. 595), it is in the same image as this experience of Urquhart's evil. By this time a vital change has taken place in Wolf's perception of the world, especially the nature of evil. Pain and cruelty in a universe of chance have taken the place of Evil in a moral dualist universe. It is as if Hamlet, instead of being killed, is brought to realise at the end that his father died naturally, hoping Gertrude would marry Claudius, that no-one spies on him or plots his death, that he is assured of the Danish throne; and that his real pain is caused by the point-less suicide of poor Ophelia. A Hamlet, realising that there is no great evil to revenge, but only pain and loss to experience, is what Wolf is at the end of the novel. He casts no long tragic shadows.)

In his early reverie, Wolf invokes the memory of his 'mythology' which will make straight the 'bent twig' which Tilly-Valley, and the oppression he represented, has become. When the calm swelling of his will to good rose to the surface 'all would be well' (*WS*, p. 39). With a multiplication of images, this means that the cow at Basingstoke seen from the train, would 'stop eating and lie down'. That this is not such an unrelated transition can be seen by looking at the passage about the cow, which

> gathered to itself such an inviolable placidity that its feet seemed planted in a green pool of quietness that was older than time itself. (*WS*, p. 5)

It is therefore a natural transition from the constant pool imagery of his 'mythology' to the memory of what that day had seemed to be an animal in the natural environment of his mythology. This is much more natural than the introduction in *Ducdame* of the similar image of the swan on the lake (*D*, p. 330), cited above.

In *Ducdame*, Powys is trying to explain the significance of the image to himself – why did the swan on the lake mean so much more than it actually was? Why did his impression of it have so many more implications and intimations than the real swan and the real lake could possibly contain? Which was more real – the swan or his image of the swan? Which really existed? In *Wolf Solent* Powys has answered many of these questions. The cow did exist 'for the space of a quarter of a minute' (*WS*, p. 5), but as 'faintly-limned images in a mirror, the true reality of which lay all the while in the mind' (*WS*, p. 8).

If the cow would 'lie down' it 'would be a beautiful green mound covered with plantains' (*WS*, p. 39). It would be, in fact, his father's grave, visited by him that day for the first time. Miss Gault, however, had pulled all the plantains from the grass-covered mound. If they were allowed to grow, they would become the mental peace of his 'mythology'.

> but the cow couldn't quite lie down. Something thick and heavy and sticky, like port wine, impeded its movements (*WS*, p. 40)

The repose of both Wolf and his father is prevented by Urquhart.

Further into sleep, images rise like the starry spangles on the inside of eyelids, everything becomes an object. His mind becomes a 'little bluish-coloured thing' and his slow-welling mythology 'rising out of the dead leaves' is blue also. But this 'material' blue thing recalls the 'Millions of miles of blue sky' that he gazed at in Ramsgard that day. And what the immense blue and the 'pure unalloyed emptiness' had conveyed to him was a conviction: 'that the whole affair was a matter of thought' (*WS*, p. 10).

There are, from the beginning, faint traces of disparity between his pluralist pyrrhonism, his insistence that 'nothing is real except thoughts in conscious minds' (*WS*, p. 474), and his conviction 'that he was taking part in some occult cosmic struggle' (*WS*, p. 8). They are inextricably bound together in Wolf, but philosophically they are opposed. This is the point where Wolf's view of things is vulnerable. There is always a slight tension, for example, this matter of the blue sky. If it 'almost proved' that the universe only consisted of what one imagines about it, then how can it also be the colour of the up-swelling and powerful will to good against evil that is Wolf's 'life-illusion'? The answer is that Wolf creates this also. It is a way of viewing life rather reminiscent of George Eliot's when she remarked that God was inconceivable, immortality unbelievable, duty peremptory and absolute.[11] She could not imagine it otherwise, although her basis for belief had been rejected by her intellect.

Although Wolf creates his own world ('I am god of my own

mind') (*WS*, p. 423) he intends to be Jesus also, and redeem it
(*WS*, p. 5). The heroic necessity in the moralist universe, Christ,
Hamlet, King Arthur: they must go out and do battle in a world
of moral absolutes that exist for them alone. Wolf intends to
preserve his 'life-illusion' by not sleeping with Christie. Sam
Dekker in *A Glastonbury Romance*, less selfishly, renounces Nell
Zoyland in his battle, and after months of fasting and hard work,
has a vision of the Grail. Both these men discover by themselves
the ends they pursue. It is not surprising that Wolf likens himself
when he has lost his 'life-illusion' to those Christian people who
know they are damned (*WS*, p. 553).

Powys's theories of the way the mind functions help to explain
this tension. He explains them in *In Defence of Sensuality* (1930).
The mind is compelled to ascribe the whole multiverse to an
ultimate First Cause.[12] He later modifies this to say that *his* nature
required an Ultimate Cause, taking the form of duality. But the
first consideration was that the human personality should
recognise itself as

> a bare lonely 'monad' or 'soul' contemplating this limitless
> floating mass of mental impressions.[13]

Wolf is aware of the contradiction between his distaste for
'metaphysical unity' and his polytheistic religious feeling on the
one hand and his moral dualism, his intense sense of the
dichotomy of good and evil on the other,

> one is compelled to accept hopeless contradictions in the very
> depths of one's being. (*WS*, p. 293)

It is this tension in Powys's mind between his pyrrhonism and
his dualism that produces the richness of his style and the depth
of his thought. His pyrrhonism, the flux of mental impressions,
aided by the extraordinary vividness with which these natural
objects define and clarify his inmost mind movements, determines this style. The profound significance that his mythologising
and dualistic mind ascribes to these images, determines the depth
of moral drama in *Wolf Solent*. There is a delightful sense of
recognition for the reader in the passage describing Wolf's reverie
before sleep. Powys has caught the exact tone of an idiosyncratic
private world. It is an ordinary state, not an extreme one. Many

of Powys's contemporaries, for example D. H. Lawrence, could render abnormal states of tension or despair with great power, but Powys presents an ordinary situation with refreshing and minute fidelity.

When Wolf becomes aware of what is troubling him, and even more when he is told that Malakite has 'just traipsed off' (*WS*, p. 329), he relaxes and his mind recovers from the unreality which had previously dominated it. The 'relaxed jocularity' of the men, 'the gathered volume of masculine personalities', among them Darnley and Jason Otter, conspire to build up about him 'a sort of battlemented watch-tower, from the isolation and protection of which his days began to fall into a measured, reasonable order, such as he had not known for many a long week'.

(This sense of serenity induced by a sort of bodyguard of men, the feminity of Bess Round counting for no more than 'petticoats on a line', is given a more questionable meaning from wider reference. Wolf has begun to look on Darnley as a source of strength and when he plans to marry Mattie, Wolf asks himself if his 'mood of miserable apathy' (*WS*, p. 539) is caused by Darnley's marriage as much as by 'the loss of his great secret'. He is prompted to ask himself this question, however, only after Miss Gault, his mother, and Valley have told him that, like Jason or Urquhart, he was a man who hated women (*WS*, p. 506).

Miss Gault names the two people who, it seems, have had the most power to torment Wolf and have not spared themselves. They were also his companions when the boys bathed in Lenty Pond. His mother glancingly alludes to this (*WS*, p. 524), while Valley is more explicit (*WS*, p. 539).

These hints as to Wolf's sexual nature are not meant to be taken for anything more than casual hints. They are another shade of meaning added to the palimpsest of Wolf's personality, and his particular environment. It is the sum total of all these shades of meaning that is important. Powys is not disposed to exaggerate the role of sex in the personality.)

Wolf's disturbance sank away and his peace of mind returned with the upwelling of his 'life-illusion' and a memory of Weymouth (*WS*, p. 330). Weymouth as in *Wood and Stone* becomes the answer to some unasked question. Feeling strong in his 'mythology', he wishes he could pour great handfuls of such memories on the 'face of the Waterloo steps' until he suddenly wonders whether one day 'by the turning of the terrible engines' he should look like that face.

Walking back that evening, Jason Otter begins to attack his 'life-illusion', ending with a malicious blow hinting that he might become a cuckold if he wasn't careful.

Wolf walks on towards Blacksod by himself, wondering if he was 'the conceited fool' Jason thought him, with his walks and his stick. Jason is an enemy of his 'life-illusion', reducing it to its least dignified level: 'When you look over gates on your walks and think that nature is something' (*WS*, p. 419).

Wolf sees Jason as a man who has 'stripped himself of every consolatory skin'. Does this necessarily produce a glimpse of real reality? Wolf emphatically denies this, refusing to believe 'that there's such a thing as "reality", apart from the mind that looks at it' (*WS*, p. 336). Jason's malicious nakedness and lack of illusion is only his form of illusion, his particular subjective way of seeing.

Wolf recovers his balance of mind and continues his walk through the dark evening. Suddenly Christie stands in the lane in front of him, having come to meet him. In their talk among the corn shocks in the 'immense vaporous summer darkness', Christie asks with 'half-humorous dismay' (*WS*, p. 340) if their feeling for each other is 'platonic', a misused term she detests.

'Platonic' refers back to the beginning of the chapter, where Urquhart in his 'special pleading' notes, uses the phrase 'his platonic tastes' to mean 'ambiguous tastes' (*WS*, p. 317). Wolf himself erases the moral overtones from the Sir Walter story by careful application of his Pateresque style. It is doing this that makes him fearful of the loss of his 'life-illusion'; it is threatened by 'Urquhart's book and a shy, slender Christie stripped of her clothes' (*WS*, p. 414).

Not only writing Urquhart's book, but also making love to Christie would ruin his 'mythology' and 'integrity'. Although it is Christie, far more than Gerda, who embodies the wraith of his mythology, Wolf had no such scruples about making love to Gerda. Christie is certainly connected with Urquhart's book in more than one way.

Wolf's answer to Christie sounds prevaricating – he replies that their feeling for each other 'is much more mediaeval than platonic' (*WS*, p. 340). But in the next chapter, he says he can 'forgive Christie for hating "platonic"' (*WS*, p. 356). There is a parallel between Wolf and Urquhart. Wolf's relationship with Christie is 'platonic' in the sense that Urquhart's tastes are 'platonic' – in that both are a turning away from normal heterosexual love. Wolf's attitude to both Christie and Gerda and the significance of 'platonic' and 'mediaeval' bring the reader to the central meaning of the novel.

4 Gerda and Christie

A recurring early theme of Powys is of mistaken sexual choice. The male protagonist is shown between two women, the first possessing ordinary sane qualities like beauty and competence, while the second has unworldly qualities, a spiritual pathos which is also strength. Very crudely, this was the difference between Gladys and Lacrima in *Wood and Stone*, although the sado-masochist emphasis disguised it and no man in the book had to choose between them. In *Rodmoor*, Adrian Sorio loved both Nance, a sympathetic feminine woman, and Philippa, an ambiguous perverse girl whose tastes were both intellectual and cruel but with whom Sorio had far deeper affinities. Rook's choice between Ann and Netta in *Ducdame* obviously fits this pattern. *Wolf Solent* is the final full reworking of the theme as plot, although it appears in fragmented forms in later fiction.

The antithesis of the two types lends itself to symbolic purposes and Powys has attempted several. In *Wolf Solent* he shows the women not only as representatives of different psychic, psychological and even geographical kingdoms, but as fully realised characters. They are girls as well as avatars, and should rank among the best-drawn female characters in twentieth-century fiction. It is not fashionable to discuss characterisation in this way, but I think it can be said that the women in modern fiction from Ursula Brangwen to Martha Quest rather tend to sink under the weight of the representative problems they have to cart away from the supermarket of twentieth-century ideologies. Gerda Torp and Christie Malakite do not sink. Powys has achieved the creation of two women who, although they are seen and never seeing, live beyond Wolf's view of them. Although we have only Wolf's viewpoint, we are not confined to his attitudes. Powys enables us to see beyond the narrator. This can only be made clear by looking more closely at the novel.

Wolf Solent's reactions and relationships with Gerda and Christie are the real theme of the novel with the King's Barton,

Squire Urquhart, Redfern, Otter imbroglio an eccentric whispering gallery in the background. If one can paraphrase the title of H. P. Collins's book, Gerda, 'earth' woman, and Christie, 'soul' girl, are just recognisable as the women whose ghosts drift through the earlier novels.

The much greater reality of the women here is produced by far more elaborate and detailed description; the effects their personalities have on Wolf, and how the girls continue to modify these effects. Wolf meets Gerda and Christie on his first visit to Blacksod. His employer, Urquhart, sends him to do business with the bookseller Malakite and the stone-cutter and undertaker Torp. Torp's daughter Gerda is of such beauty that Wolf is thrown into an erotic trance of overpowering desire. At the bookseller's he meets Christie, a 'funny little thing' (*WS*, p. 70) who lives completely in a world of books, but with whom Wolf feels completely at home as he discusses his infatuation with Gerda. Later, after seducing Gerda among the yellow bracken of a barn, he marries her.

Chapter 10, 'Christie', shows Wolf discovering something of the nature of the two personalities he is bound up with. It begins with Wolf, newly-married, indulging in the extraordinary satisfaction he received from the performance of simple primitive actions, lighting a stove, stirring porridge. The action had necessarily to be primitive and traditional to give him 'this thrill of satisfaction'. He is caught up by a sea of impersonal memories, recollected not only by himself but by other minds as they watch their fingers perform the simple tasks Wolf was attempting (*WS*, p. 211). This awareness makes his simplest action into a kind of ritual. This 'fetish worship' and the corresponding idea of himself as some kind of protagonist, champion of all the world against the power of evil, makes him in his mind a sort of priest, one who performs before a public consisting of evanescent wisps of other people's memories. Even the cheap wooden clock is significant of all the clocks in the world ticking. The primitive significance of these simple occasions suggest a child-like mythopoeic world but Powys points out that it is Wolf's complete detachment that makes it available. Wolf is aware of the tide of group memories from a detachment seemingly 'outside both the flowing of time and the compactness of personality' (*WS*, p. 211).

This statement of Wolf's detachment at the beginning of the chapter serves both as a reminder and a suggestion for what will follow. (It is a reminder of the day when Wolf and Gerda make love in the barn. When Wolf, after a stormy evening in a pub, walks home, he sees through a window 'a human head reading by candlelight and finds such a sight touching beyond words' (*WS*, p. 168). On his walk, he recalls the grey feather that Christie used as a book mark and found that it had come to assume a 'curious importance' in his mind. He finds that his love-making and tavern-brawling 'fall away from his consciousness in comparison with that feather and that candle' (*WS*, p. 170). This is a hint as to the development of his relationships with both Gerda and Christie.)

However, in Chapter 10, Wolf seems not particularly 'inhuman' as he wakes Gerda 'lovely and sulky as a young animal', and hugs her with 'a rough, earthy, animal ecstasy'. He then leaves the house to stand in the morning air, between 'two vast provinces of leafiness and sunshine' (*WS*, p. 213), Melbury Bub and Glastonbury.

Blacksod, on the one side Dorset uplands, on the other Somerset plains, was between two 'auras'. Wolf is echoing his own situation. He is between two women, explicitly associated with these two areas. When Gerda was whistling 'it was like the voice of the very spirit of Poll's Camp' (*WS*, p. 90). Before the marriage Gerda is described by Wolf in terms of an Arcadian figure from classical myth. She possessed 'delicate Artemis-like beauty' (*WS*, p. 58) and the 'terrible passivity' (*WS*, p. 72) of Helen of Troy. She ran 'like Atalanta' (*WS*, p. 88), disappeared into the woods like 'another Daphne or Syrinx' (*WS*, p. 89). The pride of this 'daughter of Leda' (*WS*, p. 97) resembled 'that high passive nonchalance which permitted the old classical women to talk of themselves quite calmly' (*WS*, p. 100).

She is also in Wolf's mind connected explicitly with the Dorset hills among which they walk. Had the Romans changed the face of the hill? Was Gerda descended from some 'Ionian soldier' of the legionaries? (*WS*, pp. 87–8). A classical divinity, and yet a local one who evokes the bitter sweetness of an old ballad (*WS*, p. 149). Gerda does not participate in Wolf's myth of her. The image is in his mind, shared perhaps with Darnley Otter and even Christie, but this is not how Gerda sees herself. 'Yellow bracken' never seems to mean to her what it means to Wolf. In fact, she is ignorant of the importance of the symbol to him. Gerda doesn't even realise the uniqueness of her own beauty (*WS*, p. 145).

Gerda is totally unaware of Wolf's vision of her as a creature from myth and legend and folksong. He makes of her an almost literary and aesthetic creation. Wolf's view of Gerda is not simply a wilful self-delusion. The literary quality of his appreciation of her corresponds to one element in her character, 'a certain childishness' (*WS*, p. 88). She is not only Helen of Troy; she is Gerda Torp of 'rathunts and nuttings and blackberryings and mushroomings' (*WS*, p. 155), and Gerda who coaxes her father for apple pie. The intonation of her voice 'suggested the simple finery of a thousand West Country fairs' (*WS*, p. 87). She quotes local rhyme, and local fortune-tellers, but even in this, 'Gipoo Cooper told me I should never have a child' (*WS*, p. 153), there could be a hint of the extraordinary, either of the doom-laden, or of a reassurance that she will never lose her beauty and become an ordinary Blacksod woman, like her mother. Before Chapter 10, Wolf sees her in classical and primeval terms, the childishness of her nature blending naturally with the paganism he thinks he sees there.

But this vision is not something he shares with Gerda. After their first love-making, he senses her personality 'quivering and quick' (*WS*, p. 150) yet 'solitary and unapproachable'. They are silent:

> No casual words of easy tenderness should spoil the classical simplicity of their rare encounter. (*WS*, p. 151)

The vision, an encounter with an Earth-goddess, remains in Wolf's mind only. The reader's suspicions are aroused by the overdone heavy language staggering under its load of classical allusion, throughout this incident. The affected style is in marked contrast to the language with which Wolf describes Gerda's whistling:

> It seemed to hold, in the sphere of sound, what amber-paved pools surrounded by hart's-tongue ferns contain in the sphere of substance. (*WS*, p. 89)

The character of the language is a warning, a hint to the reader.

On the day of their sexual union in the yellow bracken, Wolf conjured up a rural idyll (*WS*, p. 152). But expressions like 'enchanted hovel', 'unparalleled being' and 'free from all care' are like the classical illusions; indications of the ponderous school-master he comes later to feel he has become.

In Chapter 10, while waiting for Gerda to get up, his 'enchanted hovel' is the background for his satisfied reflections on the extraordinary amount of luck he has had since coming to Dorset. A bird singing in an ash tree reminds him of Gerda's blackbird notes. He is full of physical satisfaction and mental self-congratulation. Suddenly a heart-stopping volley of shrieks occurs from the pigsty in the adjoining field. Wolf reassures himself that the farmer is only feeding his pigs and returns to his kitchen. He finds Gerda enjoying her porridge, licking her cream-clogged spoon and bidding him good-morning with 'the indistinct voice of a greedy child' (*WS*, p. 215). It is impossible to avoid the gentle and humorous hint. Gerda is the quintessence and summing up of all the natural beauty in the world, and the greed of pigs is part of this naturalness.

Gerda's peevish despair at the idea of Wolf's mother coming to tea surprises Wolf. Why should girls, themselves so mysterious, be so bound by convention? He becomes aware of Gerda's own obsessions, her private world so different from his own. Was there some 'queer inner world' of women parallel to his own? He becomes aware that her 'life-illusion' is not that of an Atalanta or Daphne, but the, to Wolf, completely strange 'reality' of a convention which remarks the thinness of bread and butter, the importance of an afternoon gown, and the cut and thrust of polite conversation. This contrasts sharply with Christie (*WS*, p. 156).

After a strange lapse into a mood of grey unreality Wolf recovers from the 'jolt to his happiness' that this realisation that Gerda's 'reality' is different from his own occasions him, but this realisation marks the close of a period in Wolf's relation with Gerda. Although she rushes upstairs 'like a young maenad' to dress, it is because Wolf wishes her to extend the conventions, so important to her dealings with his mother, to her relations with Blacksod tradesmen, with whom 'she let down every barrier' (*WS*, p. 218). Wolf thinks that her primitiveness bids fair to make their marriage a laughing stock. It is not only Gerda's inconsistency that is noted here, but also Wolf's.

(The later episode of Gerda asleep on Poll's Camp is also relevant. Wolf has already imagined some Ionian ancestor of Gerda's working at the Roman fortifications. He now has deeper suspicions. Was there some 'occult affinity' (*WS*, p. 313) between her nerves and the hill, some 'non-human eroticism' in her sleeping contact with 'this heathen soil'? This 'fantastic irritation' in which Wolf indulges, would in *Wood and Stone* have been offered as a given objective fact. Here it illuminates not only the erotic impression of Gerda asleep, but also the way Wolf's mind works. Again, there is inconsistency in his fantastic visions of her. Wolf 'invents' this Gerda, he decides she is the 'most mysterious' expression of life, and is then resentful at his own fantasy. Her 'reality' is not just that of provincial conventions, it is expressed wordlessly in her whistling. The reader can only discover this by the difference in tone of the language.)

When comforting the tearful Gerda about his mother coming to tea, he kisses her head and is overtaken by a feeling of unreality as if 'he had done this very same thing in another room, and even in another country'. He feels that he is 'acting a part', and that if he made one enormous effort he would destroy 'the whole shadow-scenery of their life' (*WS*, p. 217). Some moments later when Gerda has gone upstairs, he begins to wash up in a rudimentary manner. He catches sight of a 'stunted little laburnam tree', one of its boughs 'stretching out in a sorrowful fumbling sort of way' towards a nearby sturdy lilac. Unaccountably, it recalls Christie 'crouched in the castle lane' (*WS*, p. 219). As if a door opens 'in his mind's fortress', he experiences 'a deep sickening craving, it was hard to tell for what'. Seeing it later from the privy window,

> he got a sense of being hemmed in, burdened, besieged, while some vague, indistinct appeal, hard to define, was calling upon him for aid.

The meagre bare tree reminded him of Christie because the fit of unreality had prepared him for this. He had comforted Christie in just this way on the day of the Horse Fair when, 'he touched the top of her head with his lips' (*WS*, p. 206).

At the Horse Fair, the day after his seduction of Gerda and resolving now to marry her, Wolf is overcome by a sense of misery. His sensitivity to Urquhart's vicious misanthropy, the ludicrous idea of his mother meeting the Torps, combine to produce 'a loathing of the whole spectacle of life' (*WS*, p. 176). He tries to conjure up his psychic strength but finds it impossible. This is the first time his 'life-illusion' has failed, through not only

Urquhart but Gerda. He feels a 'terrified loneliness' which neither Gerda nor his mother could ease.

Where was Gerda now in this confused medley? She must be somewhere about; and perhaps Christie too!

'You won't care if I go off to look for my mother, sir?' he found himself saying.

Wolf's lethargy and depression vanish at the thought of Christie. He immediately becomes active, unaware however that it is the thought of Christie rather than his mother that has galvanised him. This again is one of the hints that Powys uses to show the unconscious processes of Wolf's mind.

He meets every friend, acquaintance and relation he has in the field, but his restlessness is not diminished. He is plunged in 'dangerous thought' (*WS*, p. 197), feeling a 'troubling curiosity' 'about that grey feather which he had found in that book of Christie's!' The grey feather has become an enigmatic and troubling image. Already Wolf has found that the grey feather has superseded the 'yellow-bracken' associated with Gerda. But Wolf invented the 'yellow-bracken' image himself. This grey-feather image is something outside Wolf and far more troubling than his own creation.

Wolf's sense of a 'ghastly treachery' to Gerda in the 'furtive and dangerous whisper' 'Why didn't I meet Christie first' does not stop him searching for her. He comforts her, kissing her head, while trying to tell himself that his feeling for her is pity, so 'pitifully devoid of all physical magnetism' (*WS*, p. 209) is she. This pity, but 'a pity that had a quivering sweetness in it' is aroused again by the sight of the stunted little laburnum tree. The contrasting lilac tree, sturdy and glossy, evokes the first time he saw Gerda – 'she gave him a glance that resembled the sudden trembling of a white-lilac branch, heavy with rain and sweetness' (*WS*, p. 60).

The memory of Christie at the Horse Fair, crouched under a gate, fills him with a sick craving, 'like the actual thrust of a spear' (*WS*, p. 219). The strange unreal feeling he had when he kissed Gerda prepared the way for this – he had performed that action before 'in another country'. He has a queer feeling that he could destroy 'the whole shadow-scenery of their life' if he made 'one enormous effort'. This enormous effort would be the forcing

to the surface of his mind his unacknowledged love for Christie, a
recognition of Christie as something that was part of himself.

Now the sight of the bare pathetic branch 'seemed to disturb
the complacency of his whole being'. He saw it again from the
window of their privy. These glimpses of fixed objects from
bedroom, scullery or privy windows provide him with

> a sort of runic hand-writing, the 'little language' of chance
> itself, commenting on what was, and is, and is to come.

Powys uses the 'little language' of chance himself in his style.
Wolf's senses are voracious in their appetite, but they are not
unselective. On his first train journey down to Dorset, he day-
dreams of some 'white as a peeled willow wand' (*WS*, p. 9) girl he
will make love to in the middle of a hazel wood. He decides on his
way to King's Barton that his 'life-illusion' will never be given up
'not even for the sake of the slenderest peeled willow-wand in Dorset' (*WS*, p. 25). (It is to save his 'life-illusion' that he gives up
Christie later on.) The 'little-language' comments on what is to
come.

After he had first made love to Gerda, Wolf found himself
'recalling certain casual little things that he had seen that day'
(*WS*, p. 149). One of these was 'the underside of the bark of a
torn-off willow branch that he had caught sight of in his walk by
the Lunt'.

When Christie and Wolf quarrel later in this chapter, he feels
that unless he effects a reconciliation, the afternoon.

> as perfect as a green bough, would stand out in his memory
> peeled and jagged, its sap all running out, its leaves drooping.
> (*WS*, p. 237)

These hints are like musical phrases which, scarcely noticeable at
first, return and build up until they burst above the surface of a
piece of music, with a definite character and body, become a
movement in fact, with an inevitability produced by the half-
conscious remembrance of those previous well-placed phrases.

Wolf has thought of these glimpses of certain, not particularly
aesthetically-pleasing objects before. On the 'yellow-bracken'
day, he returns to Blacksod with Gerda and Lob.

'Whom Long Thomas has taken for his leman', he repeated
in his heart; and it seemed to him as if the lights of the town,
which now began to welcome them, were the lights of a certain
imaginary city which from his early childhood had appeared
and disappeared on the margin of his mind. It was wont to
appear in strange places, this city of his fancy. . . at the bottom
of tea-cups. . . or the window-panes of privies. . . in the soapy
water of baths. . . in dirty marks on wallpapers. . . in the bleak
coals of dead summer-grates. . . between the rusty railings of
deserted burying grounds. . . above the miserable patterns of
faded carpets. . . among the nameless litter of pavement-
gutters. . . But whenever he had seen it it was always associated
with the first lighting up of lamps, and with the existence, but
not necessarily the presence, of some-one. . . some girl. . . some
boy. . . some unknown. . . whose place in his life would resemble that first lighting of lamps. . . that sense of arriving out of
the cold darkness of empty fields and lost ways into the rich,
warm glowing security of that mysterious town. . . 'Whom
Long Thomas has taken for his leman', he repeated once more.
(*WS*, p. 157)

This superb passage gives a sense of the way in which trivial
details connect with the ineffable. Here the recollections of odd
miscellaneous scrappy bits of memory are connected with what
Professor Wilson Knight has called a 'soul city',[1] some warm, rich
town glowing among cold fields. The sensation Wolf describes is
that of coming home. And this implies the 'existence' of 'someone
. . . some girl. . . some boy. . . some unknown'. 'Some boy' is a
phrase casually introduced, but it alters the meaning of the whole
passage. It takes it straight away from its context, the slow
walking with Gerda after love-making. Gerda does not suggest a
boy, or 'a "peeled-willow wand" for her limbs were rounded and
voluptuous' (*WS*, p. 63).

Christie already, on their first meeting, struck Wolf as having a
'slight and sexless' (*WS*, p. 71) figure, 'meagre, androgynous'.
The note of sexual ambivalence in Wolf has already been remarked on. At the Horse Fair this is again brought out, '"I wish
you were a boy, Christie", he brought out abruptly' (*WS*, p. 207).

Another contrast is contained in the 'frame' of the passage: the
line from Wolf's Shaftesbury ballad. The old word 'leman' and

the world of the ballad where 'the wind blew shrill and the river ran' (*WS*, p. 149), is very far from the odd sweepings and toe-nail parings of memories which tumble about his mind; things grubby and dusty and desolate, the scraps and shavings of a world moving on. What have these to do with the atmosphere of the ballad, where a single, clear, cool, understated emotion expands to comprehend a static world?

Wolf is unconscious of the incongruity of this contrast, but the reader cannot but be aware of it. The current of Wolf's sensations and 'life-illusion' is running against his conscious and literature-quoting mind. It is almost as if normal sex, natural if extraordinarily superb female beauty has betrayed him, and trapped him. Later, when talking of Bess Round and the attraction she holds for him by her very supposed perversity, he wonders if beauty is diffused throughout her whole identity, as cannot be the case where Nature 'occupied with her own enormous purposes is baiting the trap' (*WS*, p. 387) with female beauty.

This is an echo of *Ducdame*, when Ann is an agent for 'great creative Nature', and she shamelessly baits the trap for Rook to ensure the survival of the Ashover line. In *Wolf Solent*, by sharp contrast there is no such easy antithesis as between Ann and Netta. Gerda is, by implication, childless and Christie adopts a child. The mysterious city on 'the margin of the mind' is perhaps again hinted when Wolf comforts Christie at the Horse Fair. Ramsgard has 'the sort of glamour cities wear in old fantastic prints' (*WS*, p. 209).

These hints and repetitions and resemblances are the 'little language' not only of chance, but also a mode of conveying to the reader an emerging theme of which Wolf is unconscious but which is working on his mind. Despite the complacency of his soliloquy outside his house the 'little language' of hints, repetitions and resemblances ensures that the meaning of what has gone before is beginning to rise to the surface.

From the window of the privy (Chapter 10), he sees the laburnum tree again, and becomes aware of a sense of 'being hemmed in, burdened, besieged, while some vague, indistinct appeal, hard to define, was calling for his aid' (*WS*, p. 219).

This is a 'memory', a foretaste of the future, a comment on what is to come. When he has succumbed to Urquhart; when Gerda is miserable through her infidelity; when Christie is absorbed with her adopted child and has no time for Wolf; when his mother is finding new business interests in which he has no part, Wolf lays his hand on the laburnum tree and hears as if the trunk were a 'telegraphic receiver' the desperate voice of Christie crying his name (*WS*, p. 569). This telepathy is acceptable in a way that Rook hearing the triumphant cry of the Ashover tombs is not. In *Ducdame*, there is some development of the tomb image, but it is external to Rook (the vision of his son proceeds from internal pressure and is far more successful). But in *Wolf Solent*, the development of the image of the stunted tree makes this telepathy part of the internal structure. The images that represent Christie rise up from within and beneath Wolf's mind, break the surface (as in Chapter 10) and float off into the numinous, the strange. But because the development has been so subtle and natural, the strange is acceptable as perfectly natural also. This method is what makes the vision of the Grail in *A Glastonbury Romance* as real as Mr Twig's enema.

In Chapter 10, Wolf is also working in the Blacksod Grammar School with Darnley Otter. In his company, but hardly heeding him, Wolf is struck 'with a sudden question, gaping like a crack in a hot stubble field in the very floor of his mind' (*WS*, p. 221). Was he really 'in love' with Gerda? He then becomes aware that Darnley is talking of Christie. Again, another step of self-recognition has been taken, and again it is Christie in the background who has instigated it. Darnley's suggestion of taking Wolf to lunch at Christie's 'had set something vibrating deep within him'. Walking home, he 'gave himself up to his mental disloyalty' and discovers a 'curious emotional phenomenon'. He recognises that although 'Gerda's warmth gave him a voluptuous thrill of honest and natural desire' he feels that it is Christie who is 'the platonic idea, so to speak, of the mystery of all young girls, which was to him the most magical thing in the whole world' (*WS*, p. 224). Wolf now recognises Christie as part of his mental life, although their first meeting, by evoking the imagery of Wolf's mental life, had already suggested this: 'Wolf felt as though his mind had encountered her mind like two bodiless shadows in a flowing river' (*WS*, p. 72)

That 'platonic idea' is a phrase of some importance can be seen from the discussion of it when it occurred in Chapter 16, 'A Game of Bowls'. Christie dislikes the word, a feature of her character he has later to 'forgive'. During that conversation in the cornfield, Wolf prefers to use the word 'mediaeval' to describe their relation-

ship, not the meaning, but the atmosphere of the word, the
'peculiar thrill' given by 'a long trailing margin of human sen
sations' (*WS*, p. 341). He refers to his 'sensations' here, the deep
reverberations he feels behind every action, every word. He i
placing Christie in his mythology. Earlier, his mind dwells on the
syllables of 'immortal souls' (*WS*, p. 293) until they take on a per
sonality 'the shape in fact of Christie Malakite'. This personification of 'immortal souls' in Christie follows a thought-discourse
about the actual composition of his sensations. Was he
psychically sensitive enough to enter some 'continuous stream of
human awareness' which had the ability to retain all the 'frail
essences' of things:

> These emanations from plants and trees, roadsides and
> gardens, as if such things actually possessed immortal souls.

He puts Christie, therefore, in the most central and important
position in his mythology – she represents the actual ethereal
essence of what he experienced – she is the significance of those
natural objects, why they imply so much. She is, in fact, the
'platonic essence' of his sensations.

Wolf starts to realise Christie's importance in his mental life.
On his return he finds Gerda hard at work. Wolf remarks her
childishness and occasional fits of conventionality, but her inner
essence is conveyed by her music, something which he recognises
as valuable but cannot explain. Her music is her essence; a fact
recognised by Wolf when, suspicious of Bob Weevil and jealous,
he begs Gerda to climb the ash tree, so that he can hear her voice
from the leaves (*WS*, p. 358). All the moral absolutes and judgements remain in Wolf's mind, and he refuses to condemn, conscious of the dull heaviness in him which oppresses her.

But that their 'realities' are totally different becomes more and
more clear. After another argument, again brought about by
Wolf not taking enough account of her 'alien reality', he goes to
see Christie. When he reaches the Malakite bookshop, Gerda's
'stricken face' vanishes from his mind, and she becomes like his
mother, an accepted part of his life. The syllables 'a young girl'
had remained at the back of his mind like 'a precious well-
watered flower-bed, but a bed empty of any living growth'.
Nothing about Gerda had disturbed this. But now in 'the centre

of the bed', was a 'living breathing plant' (*WS*, p. 232). Wolf realises the nature of his attachment to Gerda; 'playful lust directed at some beautiful statue' bears out the impressions already received from Wolf's heavy patronising verbosities,

> I suppose you've often been told that you're as lovely as the girl who was the cause of the Trojan War? (*WS*, p. 85)

The language used to describe the feeling Christie produces in Wolf – 'diffused and thrilling feeling, permeated everything around them' – echoes a phrase used to describe Wolf's reaction to the lesbian Bess Round and her friend (*WS*, p. 387). This adds to the whole impression the reader has of Wolf's ambiguous feelings for her. One recalls Gerda's original remarks about her. ('She's for no man.... Men think too much of themselves') (*WS*, pp. 99–100).

Wolf's recognition that Christie is part of his life-illusion almost, in Jungian terminology, his 'anima', his delight in her presence is accompanied by the question 'Will she let me make love to her?' He asks himself this question in a period of shy suspense as he carefully observes a bowl of wild flowers picked by Christie. This interval of tension, and nervous mental questioning, is embodied for the reader, as it is for Wolf, by the bowl of wild flowers. The intensity of Wolf's state is conveyed by his extreme awareness of the miracle of flower petals, of the absolute wonder of this filmy vegetable fabric.

> The girl's words, 'I sent Darnley away', seemed to melt into that wild-flower bunch she had picked and placed there; and the pallor of the primroses, the perilous, arrowy faintness of their smell, became his desire for her. (*WS*, p. 234)

His mind plunges into an evocation of the 'hazel-darkened spaces' where Christie found the flowers. He knew he was incapable of 'what is called "passion"'. His feeling trembles between physical attraction for Christie and a desire for the 'unexplored regions of her soul'.

> His feeling was like a brimming stream between reedy banks, where a wooden moss-covered dam prevents any Spring-flood,

but where the water, making its way round the edge of
the obstacle, bends the long, submerged grasses before it, as it
sweeps forward. (*WS*, p. 235)

This image of his feelings seems at first sight explicable only by
inferring that the obstacle to the free play of his feelings is Gerda,
as the next paragraph would superficially bear out.

> Two images troubled him just a little – Gerda's white, tense
> face as it had looked when she left him on the street, and with
> this a vague uncomfortable memory of the figure on the
> Waterloo steps. But in his intensely heightened consciousness
> of this 'suspended' moment, he deliberately steered the skiff of
> his thought away from both these reefs.

This seems initially to be a mixed metaphor, but it is the 'skiff
of his thoughts' on the 'brimming stream of his feelings' which
steers away from the two 'reefs' of Gerda and the Waterloo face.
What then is the 'moss-covered dam'? It sounds reminiscent of the
'beautiful green mound covered with plantains' (*WS*, p. 40) of
Wolf's reverie on his first night in Dorset. Is it his life-illusion
which prevents the 'great surge of what is called passion'? Perhaps
it is unwise to follow images too far, but this image set in this short
period of intensity seems to embody such a *specialised* feeling, an
impression of creeping round something in an unaccustomed yet
enjoyable way (the sensation of long grass bending under the flow
of cool water) that it seems to imply more than an isolated feeling.
The water/moss imagery also connects up with his mystical landscape of the mind.

Wolf inserts his fingers into the bowl of flowers. It reminds him
of a 'sun-warmed pool' (*WS*, p. 235) and he feels that 'in some
occult way' he is invading Christie's soul. This has almost the
quality of a sexual act, and yet it is her 'soul' that he is invading.
The pool is generally the image of his own soul. This is another
hint of Christie's part in his 'life-illusion'. Unlike Gerda, Christie
is aware of the psychic significance of Wolf's private myth-
making, and she swiftly tidies the flowers again.

Later, in the chapter entitled 'Mr Malakite at Weymouth',
Wolf has the opportunity to spend the night with Christie. He
waits in her little walled garden, where the sight of a projecting
stone covered with green moss rings like a bell in his mind with

the echoes of a memory of certain old pier-posts at Weymouth covered with green sea-weed. He meets Christie and the 'indescribable enchantment' (*WS*, p. 399) of the sea-weed, sand and spray memory links itself with the 'delicious peace' which comes from her presence. He 'began to abandon himself to his mythology'. But Christie is a process, her presence enables his mythology to function better (and away from her). One is reminded of 'the existence... but not necessarily the presence... of some one... some girl... some boy...' (*WS*, p. 157). 'Inhumanity' is a quality they are both held to possess, but at this moment Christie's 'sigh upon the air' (*WS*, p. 399) rather tends to suggest that her inhumanity is more a part of her hieratic priestess appearance than of her character. She tells him that her father will be absent in Weymouth. The implied invitation throws Wolf into a discord of emotion. He asks himself what he feels and realises that the 'green moss... *was* happiness' but that Christie's invitation could kill his mythology if he let it.

The happiness of his vision is greater because of Christie, but is threatened by the prospective happiness of making love to her. This is in the same dangerous category as finishing a pornographic book for an evil old man. Seducing Gerda had not touched his 'life-illusion' at all. But responding to an almost open invitation from Christie would have that drastic effect. His 'mythology' and his integrity depended upon the belief that he was taking 'the side of Good against Evil' and "if Urquhart's book and 'Mr Malakite at Weymouth" killed his mythology, how could he go on living?' (*WS*, p. 411). Perhaps he does not want to sleep with Christie *because* she is so important to his 'life-illusion', too ideal to sleep with. He recognises this himself. He goes to supper with her. 'If he kept his self-respect and left Christie in peace;' (*WS*, p. 435) he would remain the 'old Wolf, the old obsessed medium for lovely, magical, invisible influences'.

Christie tells Wolf of her intention to write a book expressing an entirely feminine viewpoint. Wolf, despite his determination to turn this 'Ariel, this Elemental, into a living girl' (*WS*, p. 411), remarks to himself that this would be 'the view of a feminine Elemental, then' (*WS*, p. 438). She explains her desire to bring a Rabelaisian, even outrageous reality into her book. To Wolf's amazement, he has a great surge of distaste, a dislike of the idea of Christie enjoying any sort of 'Rabelaisianism' disassociated from himself.

He finds himself wondering whether she inherits her interest in 'shameless books' from her father and his mind returns to the 'appalling book' he found at Urquhart's the day before. This book 'which he read voraciously' was a pornographic volume 'the debased purpose of which is simply and solely to play upon the morbid erotic nerves of unbalanced sensuality' (*WS*, p. 403). It came from the Malakite bookshop. As he read he felt 'the drops of deadly nightshade' fermenting in his veins. Christie's invitation significantly gives him this sensation and is described in the same language as the effect of the pornographic book (*WS*, p. 411). The book is connected with the unsettling glimpse of a lesbian relationship, which has already been shown to be connected with Christie.

After supper with Christie, while his mind is obsessed with the thought of making love to her, he picks up her feather from the floor. He feels that the memory of Gerda makes him pause, but later, 'the conclusion he came to was that the touch of the feather had restrained him!' (*WS*, p. 437). The grey feather had come to be such a powerful symbol in his life that it was enough to break up his erotic thought-stream. It became a symbol for him very early, when he first heard Gerda's whistling which summed up all the magic of the world. When she finishes,

> silence seemed to fall down upon that place like large grey feathers from some inaccessible height. (*WS*, p. 93)

Gerda was the music, but Christie was the silence. The grey feather, symbol of something beyond the natural, the apprehensible, inhibited Wolf's natural sexual approach to Christie.

As Christie showed him her bedroom, her 'apparent complete freedom from any self-consciousness' (*WS*, p. 439) also inhibited him. And this freedom from the conventional, this inability of Christie's to be shocked by 'even the most amazing perversities' . . . was one of the things that drew Wolf to her at the beginning of their relationship.

Christie lights her lamp: 'It's not an ordinary green. It's a peculiar kind of green' (*WS*, p. 440). As Wolf sits on her bed 'the green light slowly awakening into being', he becomes intensely aware of that moment. It becomes a trance. 'He dared not move lest he should break the spell.' The sight of Christie fills him 'with a *sense* of the possibilities of *new* feelings beyond anything he had known'. The suggestion that Christie holds possibilities of new feelings beyond anything already experienced has been made before. Soon after his realisation, discussed above, that he loves Christie (Chapters 10 and 11), he ascends Babylon Hill.

He tries 'as the sun sank down towards Glastonbury' (*WS*, p. 249) to make out Christie's window, and endeavours to decide which thought/memory stream, that of Gerda or Christie, means most to him. It is interesting to note that he lets 'the double stream of memories. . . contend for the mastery of his thoughts', rather than think of the two girls in the present and future. Powys, never seeming to judge, does so in these subtle hints. Wolf realises that while 'all that poetry of his first encounter with Gerda' affected only an '*external* portion of his nature', his understanding with Christie invaded 'regions of which he himself had hardly been aware'.

The external literary quality, already mentioned, of his attraction towards Gerda is dismissed by the words 'all that poetry', and his understanding with Christie points, almost fearfully, towards something beyond even his 'mythology'. The fear involved in this is shown when, in Chapter 10, the realisation of his mistaken choice becomes conscious, and the 'very floor of his mind' seems to crack.

Christie and Glastonbury come to be connected in Wolf's mind. During the episode of the picnic on Poll's Camp, Wolf comes to feel that there is an affinity between Gerda and the heathen hill, while he connects Christie with the 'mysterious plain down there', that 'chess-board of King Arthur' which had a quality of 'old mediaeval pictures' (*WS*, p. 314). He feels Poll's Camp and its heathen atmosphere to be threatening him, 'but the valley' is 'like some immense, sad-coloured flower floating upon hidden water. . .' This strange flower and the vision of water are echoed in Wolf's trance on Christie's bed which holds him like 'some old forgotten dream' (*WS*, p. 440). The green lamp is the agent of this.

The reflections of the lamp in the looking glass (an old one, once belonging to Christie's Welsh mother) showed receding green depths 'lit up by the lamp as if by the swollen green bud of a luminous water lily'. The green water images give him a strange fear, he is moving towards some sort of crisis – 'it seemed to him to be reflecting the mysterious depths of Lenty Pond'. His desire to make love to Christie is held back by 'a fear that had unspeakable awe in it, that had a supernatural shudder in it'.

This crisis culminates in a vision of the face on the Waterloo steps; all the misery of the world looks at him from the looking glass of Christie's mother, 'of that woman who believed in spirits'. His reactions to this, away from Christie, in pain, as if his indecision somehow caused the agony of the Face, resulted in the very core of his personality splitting up. His being flows 'away in water' (*WS*, p. 444), he sinks into 'nothingness', then the will in him 'beyond thought',

> gathered itself together in that frozen chaos and rose upwards – rose upwards like a shining scaled fish, electric, vibrant, taut and leapt into the greenish-coloured vapour that filled the room.

The fish that was Wolf has already been discussed (*WS*, pp. 27, 485). It arises, despite himself, it is not willed like his sensations, but comes from 'beyond thought', like a will of its own. For this to happen, his personality, his will, must be dissipated; he must sink into the gulfs of non-existence, become nothing, for this fish to leap forth. This is very much more like a genuine mystical experience than his 'mythology' or his 'sensations' or his 'fetish-worship'. It greatly resembles an experience of J. A. Symonds described by William James in *Varieties of Religious Experience* as a 'more extreme state of mystical consciousness'.[2] I refer to William James because his book greatly influenced Powys, who frequently mentioned it. The experience possesses the four 'marks' by which William James classifies a state as mystical; its ineffability; its Neotic quality (that is a state of insight); its transiency; its passivity.[3] This is a more intense mystical experience than the one Wolf has when escaping from the School Treat (Chapter 18), when he plunges off 'to escape into the peace of his own soul' (*WS*, p. 388).

Leaving the School Treat meadow, he walks towards 'the mystical hill of Glastonbury' which rose 'like the phallus of an unknown God'. The stubble fields, the Gwent lanes, all contain memories of Christie, and gazing at the rich darkness over Glastonbury his worry over his women became as nothing and he entered a world where grass and leaf settle down 'towards some cool, wet, dark, unutterable dimension in the secret heart of silence!'

Christie, Glastonbury and Wolf's 'sensations' and 'mythology'
are all connected. Wolf's fear of making love to Christie is not
only due to his sight of the Waterloo face. It is almost a failure of
nerve, a shrinking from an approach to something beyond anything he had yet experienced, which would alter his 'mythology'
perhaps for ever. But the experience on Christie's bed, the green
lamp in the mirror, the glimpse of the green underwater world of
his own mythology, shows that his experiences would be enhanced
by Christie. It is her presence as well as the face vision which helps
the fish to leap forth from Wolf's mind landscape, and Lenty
Pond's ambiguous presence becomes in the looking glass the
underwater Vale of Glastonbury, as he imagined it on Poll's
Camp, green, chastened, magical, extended.

But he refuses to take the chance. He is convinced that his
mythology is bound up with a dualism in which he must take part
for the side of Good, but his moral sense, as he said at the Horse
Fair, his 'diseased conscience' (*WS*, p. 208) puts forward arbitrary
ideas of good and evil existing only in his mind, as Christie says.
She points out that events are 'outside any one person's mind' and
furthermore that there is something in Wolf himself that he has
'never been aware of' despite all his 'self-accusations'. 'It's this
blindness to what you're really doing that lets you off. . .' (*WS*,
p. 450).

There is no-one in the book whom the reader can use as a
'touchstone' – but Christie comes near here to isolating two
qualities of Wolf. The first, known already to the reader, that his
habit of thinking that events need only be rearranged in his mind
to be acceptable leads to an appearance, and more than an
appearance, of gross selfishness. The second, that there is something in him of which he is unaware, is less easily grasped by the
reader, who sees only through Wolf, so that he shares his obtuse-
ness. The hint that he does not know what he is doing is echoed by
similar remarks from Mrs Solent, Gerda, Jason Otter and
Urquhart, but Christie here states his lack of awareness, not of
what he is doing, but of what he is. And this casts doubt on his
version of what has gone before. And his version is the substance
of the novel. When Wolf tries to explain to her about the face on
the Waterloo steps, he himself has doubts: a 'spasm of ice-cold
integrity' (*WS*, p. 448) suddenly inhibits him. His 'mythology' –
however, dies. His 'habitual optimism' (*WS*, p. 453) falls away
leaving a furious contempt 'like a sullen, evil-looking, drained-out

pond!' Wolf tried to hold his aqueous imaginative life, but it ebbed away. He finished the book for Urquhart and accepted payment. Christie by this time has, it is hinted, had some form of sexual liaison with her father. She adopts Olwen, and her father dies, probably pushed down the stairs by Christie. When Wolf tries to explain his loss to her, she gives 'the laugh of an air-sprite for whom these human scruples were growing intolerably tedious' (*WS*, p. 531). But she adds: 'But Mother would have understood what troubles you'.

This hint of the Welsh woman who claimed descent from Merlin points forward out of *Wolf Solent* towards *A Glastonbury Romance*. The androgynous Christie with her background and hints of perversion and her affinity with Glastonbury looks forward and back. She looks back to Netta, sterile and shadowy mistress of Rook in *Ducdame* who is outside the claims of Creation and Destruction. Like Rook, Wolf is trapped by 'Great creative Nature', in this case the complete female beauty of Gerda, while Christie, the sylph, slips away. But he had the chance of making love to her.

Perhaps one of the reasons behind his inability or refusal to do this is contained in the nature of his attraction to her. Despite being the ideal of a girl for Wolf, Christie is always described as a boy/girl androgynous sylph. Wolf's feelings for her are ambiguous ('I wish you were a boy, Christie' and his dream 'some girl. . . some boy'), just as her background is sinister. Powys is getting away from normal sexuality in his depiction of the Christie/Wolf attraction. There is none of the 'equivocal male pursuer' (*WS*, p. 144) in Wolf's attitude to her, as there is with Gerda. Perhaps this is one of the reasons for the lack of consummation. Wilson Knight has written illuminatingly on Powys's interest in the 'sylphic quest'.[4]

Certainly Powys's female women, his motherly, maternal women, are overpowering with their self-sacrifice and selfishness. Mrs Solent, Gerda, Mattie, Gladys, Ann, Nell, are all creatures that weigh the Powys-persona down, drag him back, impede him. Gerda's obsession with the ritual of the tea-table dumbfounds Wolf with its suggestion of an alien world of strange growths.

This revulsion from the marrying, motherly female is not particularly uncommon, especially for those men brought up at the turn of the century. E. M. Forster is a good example of this. (Louis Wilkinson has suggested[5] that Powys's mother was self-sacrificing and masochistic and that his wife was domineering. He mentions T. F. Powys's note on John Cowper Powys's household; I won't go into a house where a woman rules'. But Wilkinson is frequently very insensitive about Powys. They had little in common.) The femaleness of women seems to have frightened Powys. He recalls in *Autobiography* how horrified he was when he discovered about the female menstrual cycle when he was at Cambridge. He describes it as one of the 'two frightful shocks' (*A*, p. 191) he received at Corpus. The other shock was sustained when he was informed about vivisection.

Vivisection, and his horror of it, became one of Powys's abiding obsessions, as can be seen from *Morwyn* and *Weymouth Sands*. Here his equation of a normal function with what he considered as the great crime and unpardonable sin (inflicting pain on a living animal) perhaps show that Powys did not escape the sometimes rather restricting effects of Victorian culture. His ignorant fearfulness is reminiscent of Ruskin's.

Perhaps *Autobiography* also sheds some light on the Christie-figure. Powys relates an episode which must have occurred in 1908 when he, his brother Llewelyn and Louis Wilkinson visited Venice in company with a beautiful girl, Wilkinson's wife, who 'insisted on dressing as a boy' (*A*, p. 406). All three were in love with 'the ambiguous beauty of our boy-girl companion'. The effect on Powys was to endow him with 'some sort of supernatural power'. This 'almost formidable power' was what he had obscurely sought 'through all lusts and my obsession' (*A*, p. 408).

The 'boy-girl' had a magical effect on Powys, similar to the effect Christie had on Wolf. J. B. Priestley in the Introduction to *Autobiography* explains it through Jungian psychology:

> He was enchanted by the magic of his own unconscious. He was under the spell of one of its own archetypes, the anima. (*A*. Intro., p. xii)

Powys's interest in the 'boy-girl' should also be seen against the whole late nineteenth-century attempt to move away from the Victorian concept of women. This can be seen in the paintings of the Pre-Raphaelites, and later, the Decadents. In Rossetti's paintings a slim pale Elizabeth Siddall looked beautiful and sad. From this model came many replicas, often heavily symbolic. Philippe Jullian interestingly traces the course of 'Romantic feminine beauty'[6] in the art of the late nineteenth century. The ambiguous androgynous qualities of Christie can be seen in the work of Klimt and Beardsley.

While a full-scale biography of Powys would be very helpful, it is not really illuminating to explain the Christie/Wolf relationship by 'Jungian depth psychology' or by snippets of biography. Christie 'works' both as a character, a component in the novel, and a disturbing symbol. Her atmosphere, 'mediaeval', 'platonic', androgynous, amoral, Celtic, points beyond the natural, and beyond the naive dualism of Wolf's home-made 'mythology'. The suggestion of Glastonbury that Wolf sees in Christie refers to a much older and more potent mythology. Wolf's personification of 'immortal souls' as Christie, the actual significance of his sensations, places her centrally as the Grail-bearer of his quest. His refusal to avail himself of this new experience, to divest himself of crude dualist ideologies, causes the vision to be withdrawn. But the mystical experience is one in which opposites mingle and dissolve, as William James points out.[7] It reconciles those conflicts which 'make all our difficulties' and 'melts them into unity'. In his Introduction (*WS*, p. v), written many years later, Powys uses language almost identical with James's.

J. A. Symonds's experience, quoted by William James, might shed some light also on the relations of dualism and pyrrhonism in Powys's work. Scepticism can be a religious experience, not just a modish agnostic attitude, it can be a religious vision, and perhaps a more sophisticated and complex one than dualism. Symonds records a feeling of reaching the 'last state of the conscious self', the 'demonstration of eternal Maya and illusion'.[8]

It is in his next novel that Powys explores this particular situation; the human consciousness on the 'verge of the abyss', beyond which perhaps lie other 'dream worlds'[9] and perhaps not. Symonds states the 'phantasmal unreality[10] of the circumstances which sustain 'phenomenal consciousness' and, consequently, the problem of which is the reality, 'the trance of fiery, vacant, apprehensive, sceptical self' or 'flesh-and blood conventionality'? Is life a dream and 'What would happen if the final stage of the trance were reached?'

It is this question that Powys undertakes to look at, though not answer, in *A Glastonbury Romance*. In *Wolf Solent*, it is Christie who could conduct Wolf beyond the natural. In the next novel, Glastonbury itself is the medium.

Discussion of *Wolf Solent*, however, cannot be left without mention of the ending of the novel. It contains the fullest statement of the stoicism to which Powys frequently returns as the only possible foundation for his 'sensations'; to 'enjoy' one must 'endure'.

Powys's particular achievement in presenting the minute fluctuations of human mood interrelating with the environment is shown most clearly in the last four chapters of *Wolf Solent*. Wolf has to come to terms with the distintegration, not only of what he has come to believe to be his personality, but with the new life he has built up in Dorset. Christie's interest in the adopted child, Olwen, estranges her; because of her adultery, Gerda has lost her essence, her ability to whistle; Darnley Otter marries Mattie; his mother sets up a business relationship with Manley; everything Wolf has relied on to structure and buttress his personality and life has let him down. His 'mythology' is dead. He has lost his sense of himself as a hero in a cosmic moral drama. He has condoned Urquhart's 'evil' by finishing his book and accepting payment. (But perhaps Urquhart's 'evil' existed only in his imagination?) He has refused to sleep with Christie to save his 'mythology'. (But perhaps Christie's love would have helped him to transcend his naive dualism?) He is left with a future of muddled drudgery.

> He had lost his breviary now, his Mass-book, his Mass! He had lost his whole inner world; and the outer world – what was it . . . (*WS*, p. 528)

At the end of the novel, Wolf has come to terms with the 'outer world', revalued his position, and articulated his relationship.

This begins when he visits Lenty Pond (Chapter 23). The purpose of his visit, suicide, is not stated but cannot be missed. Looking at the water, Wolf ponders an irrelevant question, deciding to ask Jason about it when he gets back.

> Get back? *Get back where?* So he wasn't going to utter that mandate to his panic-stricken body . . . (*WS*, p. 542)

He has made no decision, but a decision has been made. He has begun to accept his life, and even, as he walks home, begins to have an intimation of how it will be lived. Before his visit to the

Pond, Wolf had smelt poignant aromatic smoke,

> His nerves reached out invisible tendrils to respond to it; bu
> under the disturbed contact between his sensations and hi
> *enjoyment of his sensations* this motion of response only cause(
> him tantalizing discomfort.

The loss of his 'mythology' meant the loss of 'contact' betweer
what his body experienced, and how his personality responded
But after his visit to Lenty Pond, despite his numb self-disgust, h(
feels that: 'The most contemptible people are allowed to enjoy th(
stars'. His dream reinforces this tentative step. The complacen
old man with the cat representing 'an acceptance of life on it
lowest terms' (*WS*, p. 550) is pulling him away from the Waterlo(
Steps face, symbol of his dualistic 'mythology'. Wolf realises tha
he still has his body and the thoughts that hovered around hi:
body. Malakite's death cry of 'forget' reinforces this realisation
Wolf now has the materials from which he can evolve and under
stand new attitudes. In the last chapter, perhaps the most power
ful and richly satisfying of the novel, this is seen to happen.
    Throughout the novel, carefully placed mention of Lord
Carfax, Solent's rich relation, has been significant. Another moti
has been Shakespearian allusion, especially quotation from
Hamlet, Macbeth and *King Lear*. In the last chapter, 'Ripeness i:
All', they come together in ironic consummation. Wolf's Hamlet
like colloquies with 'old Truepenny' have only been interrupted
or shared with Selena Gault before, but Carfax has expressed a
desire to see Wolf's father's grave, and Wolf, full of surly
suspicious malice, takes him as far as the cemetery. When Carfax
casually refers to his old liaison with Wolf's mother, Wolf lose:
control of his high-pitched nerves.
    Carfax is an ambiguous figure. He could be regarded merely a:
a 'deus ex machina' whose power resided in his lavish fortune. O1
Carfax could be seen as successful where Wolf had failed so hope-
lessly, helped Jason and Stalbridge, encouraged Gerda and his
mother (*WS*, p. 589). However, he could be the Claudius to
Wolf's Hamlet, betrayer and seducer, whose urbane kind sophistication hid ruthlessness. His instinct was to beat down people
whose 'nerves got out of control!' By helping Stalbridge, Carfax
had carelessly and capriciously succoured the Waterloo Steps
face, and in so doing, as Wolf realises, 'stepped in between the

election and his hopes'. Unable to dramatise himself out of the situation by the use of his 'mythology', Wolf feels humiliated, impotent, surly.

Throughout the chapter, the invocation of 'Christie! Christie! my lost darling, O my true-love!' recurs like a refrain. Left alone at the grave, Wolf tries again to explain to his father that even despite the loss of his 'life-illusion', there still existed his extraordinary feeling for Christie. This leads to despair, and he curses God. As the first chapter makes evident, Christ and God are different, and Wolf finds himself talking to Christ, whom he imagines as the Waterloo Steps man, and explains what his secret life is.

'Running away from the horrors!' he had cried, . . . 'It's all right. It's absolutely all right', he had whispered furtively in the man's ears. 'You needn't suffer. I let you off. *You are allowed to forget.* It doesn't matter what your secret life is. I've told you what mine is; and I can now tell you that it can be borne. . . . Any secret life can be borne when once you've been told that you have the right to forget. (*WS*, p. 598)

In this wild harangue, Wolf faces and accepts not only the reasons and motives of his 'life-illusion', but the clue to his future life, 'forget'. He also accepts suffering by letting Christ and the Waterloo Steps face 'off'. This scene by the grave parallels the earlier one by Lenty Pond, and when Wolf moves away, again, through no action of his conscious will, he has come to some sort of resolution.

Wolf becomes aware of the loveliness of the afternoon and the blackbird song and his bitterness seems less and less part of himself.

Between his body, thus freed from his tormented spirit, and the increasing loveliness of that perfect day, there began to establish itself a strange chemical fusion.

His body was coming to conclusions, understanding and responding, while the mind was impotent and despairing. Wolf discovers that despite the 'drifting multiplicity' of his soul, his body has had a 'resurrection' and is in a state of 'exultant well-being'. This realisation of the body's integration leads him to a 'certainty beyond all logic' that the universe 'was merely a filmy, phantas mal screen, separating him from an indrawn reality into which a any moment he might wake – wake despoiled and released! (*WS* p. 604). This Platonic mystical glimpse that 'Behind the pulse beat of his body stirred the unutterable' was attained through los of dualistic mythology, loss of sense of personality, humiliation mental despair, physical well-being, and finally the incongruou vision of the dirty toe-nails of Monk.

Close to home, he feels the motions of rebirth, 'Ah! His bod and his soul were coming together again now!' It is then that Wo receives the last blow. Gerda, radiant and whistling, sits o Carfax's knee. The phrase 'Ripeness is All' comes into Wolf mind. Carfax, his 'lord from London' has ironically become on of the 'lords of life', 'They meant that the lords of life had no filled his cup – filled it up to the brim' (*WS*, p. 608). The worldly wise easy sophistication of his rich relation is the last humiliatio Wolf has to bear. The final humiliation of the probability c Gerda's adultery with Carfax has to be faced and accepted.

Again, Wolf's physical self takes control and 'by a bodil necessity' he has to enter a field full of buttercups. It is in th golden pasture that Wolf accepts that everything was negligibl 'compared with the difference between being alive and bein dead'. Again, it is his body that has forced this Homeric trut upon him. He totally and finally rejects dualism. 'To the very cor of life, things were more involved, more complicated than that (*WS*, p. 611). He is reconciled to his life, on whatever level c humiliation it has to be lived. Against the humiliations, he has h body, his thoughts and his will to 'forget and enjoy' and 'endur or escape'. The pathos of the last sentence of the novel,

> 'I wonder if he *is* still here?' he thought as he laid his hand o the latch of the gate. And then he thought. 'Well, I shall have cup of tea'

is not empty or sentimental. Even the acceptance of life on it lowest terms means that Wolf will have his bodily sensations, an these have been shown to be far more valuable than the imagina tive moral dualism of his old 'life-illusion'.

Wolf Solent is one of the great novels of the twentienth century I will not even add 'unquestionably' which implies the opposite. I is a most moving and satisfying novel. It has a very powerful effec on the reader, enabling him to be aware, perhaps for the first time, of the space between himself and the rest of the world and to understand a little of the drama that peoples this space. *Wolf Solent* contains great psychological insight displayed with an equally great tolerance, which, however, never blurs real moral issues. It suggests the emotional tones of Dostoievsky, but a relaxed sceptical Dostoievsky, if this were possible. Artistically, it has an elaborate structure of metaphor which is imperceptibly organised into unity. *Wolf Solent* alone would be sufficient to rebut the commonly held view that Powys was an unartistic or disorganised writer.

5 Place of Visions

After writing *Wolf Solent*, Powys retired from his hectic life of
travel and talk. *Wolf Solent* was the last book written in trains
and hotels. In 1930 he settled at Phudd Bottom, a lonely white
frame house near Hillsdale, a remote village in New York State.
Here Powys wrote his longest novel, *A Glastonbury Romance*,
which was published in New York in 1932. The mere physical
effort of covering so much paper in under two years is hard to
imagine. There are over eleven hundred pages in the Macdonald
London edition. Most writers would carefully husband such an
imaginative concept, bringing out several slim volumes which
over a number of years would combine to form a Glastonbury
Chronicle. Powys, in less than two years, produced a huge
visionary tale of a place and a society, which is both real and
transcended.

Both *Wolf Solent* and *A Glastonbury Romance* won acclaim and
large sales. *A Glastonbury Romance* was published in England
by Jonathan Cape in June 1933. The fourth impression was
printed in September. Unfortunately the royalties from this
success were swallowed by a threatened libel action which Powys
settled out of court. One of the Somerset readers of *A Glastonbury Romance* felt that he was portrayed in the novel. The novel
still seems to be disliked in Glastonbury, or was a few years ago
when I asked for it. Perhaps it is too much to expect that the
inhabitants of a rather dull little West Country town should enjoy
the fictional representation of their home as the 'enchanted soil
where the Eternal once sank down into time' (*GR*, p. 1063). They
had a similar reaction to another exotic intruder, Rutland
Boughton, the composer whose activities in Glastonbury may
possibly have suggested some elements in *A Glastonbury Romance*.

Boughton, composer, dramatist and socialist, is now largely
forgotten, although some of his music is still familiar. Before the
First World War, he chose Glastonbury as the site of the English

Beyreuth. He was writing *The Birth of Arthur*, supposed to be the English *Ring*. The Glastonbury Festival Committee, however, did not care for the combination of Boughton's politics and scandalous private life. (He was a socialist, an atheist, a supporter of women's suffrage and was separated from his wife.) The suggested Festival for 1913 was cancelled, but there were plans for pilgrimages, picnics and games as well as the music and dance involved in *The Birth of Arthur*. Eventually in 1915 came the "Glastonbury Festival of Music, Dance and Mystic Drama'.

Boughton set up a farming community and held festivals with 'The Glastonbury Players'. His play for them, *Bethlehem*, was innovative and interesting, and foreign intellectuals were drawn to Glastonbury, to Glastonbury's distaste. The Mayor said that Boughton was 'a very great man but too big for this little town'. His presence was felt in Glastonbury up to 1926, by which time *Bethlehem* was being played as straight Communist propaganda. 'The Glastonbury Players' went into liquidation in this year, and Boughton's influence and health declined.

What Rutland Boughton brought to Glastonbury, and what in its turn brought many other people, was a mixture of rural mysticism, Celtic revivalism, art nouveau and new English music. In its time this mixture won acclaim, both popular and distinguished.[1] It is impossible to imagine that Powys was not familiar with at least some details of Boughton's artistic/mystical/socialist ventures. As he himself points out, Montacute and Glastonbury are only ten miles apart, and although Powys was not living in Montacute, his father was the vicar there until 1918. Many of the details of Boughton's Glastonbury residence are taken up and transmuted into the texture of the novel: the Festival itself and its Arthurian material; the foreign pilgrims; the setting up of a Socialist Commune; the Commune's rather arty-crafty souvenir factory; the new genius of the poet Athling who writes for the Pageant; the scandalous anarchic and communist opinions of Dave Spear, Paul Trent and Red Robinson; the hostile opinions of some of the townspeople.

Boughton's Glastonbury ventures would provide a wealth of satiric material for a novelist – one could imagine what Iris Murdoch would do with it, or Simon Raven. But Powys succeeds in what Boughton himself was perhaps trying to do: to provide a Pageant of Glastonbury which presents mystical transcendence, 'to convey a jumbled-up and squeezed together epitome of life's various dimensions' (*GR*, Preface, p. xiv). Powys's attempt to include a political element is less successful because it is peripheral to the main theme.

Despite the speed at which the book was written, Powys read as much material on the Grail and on Glastonbury as he could get his relatives and English friends to send him. I think it reasonably probable that he read Arthur Machen's *The Great Return*, first published in 1915, which was immensely popular. (Sir John Betjeman evokes its effect on his youthful self in *Summoned by Bells*.) It describes the return of the Grail to a coastal village in Wales. The spirit world is set firmly in the Christian context; there are no pagan elements to this Grail, but angels, flying altars, miracles (the raising of the almost-dead and the reconciliation of business rivals), sweet savours and happiness. It is the nature of this happiness that interests me. The vision of the Grail gives rise to 'exquisite sensations'. The sailors who saw the Grail found that 'the average impact of the external world had become to them a fountain of pleasure': 'Their nerves were on edge, but an edge to receive exquisite sensuous impressions'.[2] It is this combination of the Grail and exquisite impressions that, despite the lack of positive evidence for it, makes me feel that *The Great Return* was, with the rest of Powys's reading, useful source material. The story may have functioned as an element of raw material for the novel, with the exploits of Rutland Boughton, and the ordnance map of Somerset pinned on Powys's wall.

A Glastonbury Romance is a novel in which the main element is the possibility of mystical experience. Mysticism and fiction do not mix happily as a rule, as Charles Williams's works show. The novels have no chance to develop because half-way through, infinity floods in and wrecks the plot. In less flippant terms, the introduction of the timeless into what is essentially a temporal mode renders it inoperative. This is the problem of the 'mystical' novelist. Once the timeless has stopped the clock, how can it be made to go again? When the vision is withdrawn, how can people live happily or unhappily ever after with any significance? Emily Brontë successfully embodied her understated sense of mystical union in the non-human, non-erotic love of Cathy and Heathcliff, and when these elemental aberrations were out of the way, life could continue, quietly, peacefully and humanly. *Wuthering Heights* is one of the great mystical novels. *A Glastonbury Romance* is another. (The brilliant achievements of Patrick White should however be mentioned here.)

Before looking closely at how Powys tackles these problems, a more general view of the whole should be gained. The first impression of it is its vast inclusiveness. Colin Wilson has called *A Glastonbury Romance* 'a God's-eye view',[3] and Powys bodies forth the psychic life of every particle of organic and inorganic matter, the secret life-motion of a louse, a tree, a stretch of waste ground, a shabby sitting-room as well as the Mayor and the famous ruins of Glastonbury. The book teems and burgeons with various aspects of conscious life, subconscious life and superconscious life. The perspectives change bewilderingly. Powys will evoke the most particular essence of the smell of Autumn sycamore leaves or the quantity of butter (half his entire ration) that Evans absent-mindedly placed upon his stale roll, and then describes the massive bursts of aggressive energy given off by the sun.

The plot of the novel is complicated. It begins in Northwold, Norfolk, where the members of the Crow family gather for the funeral of Canon William Crow. Philip Crow, the Glastonbury industrialist, expects that the will will largely benefit him; his raffish, seedy cousin John from Paris is also hopeful and on the day of the funeral begins a relationship with his cousin Mary which eventually leads to marriage. The will affronts the family as their grandfather leaves forty thousand pounds to his valet and lay-reader, the former open-air preacher of Glastonbury, John Geard.

John Crow follows Mary to Glastonbury where she has a genteel job as lady's companion. He becomes Geard's secretary and helps to promote his ideas of a Glastonbury Religious Fair, to renew Glastonbury as a 'centre of mystic influence'. John's drifting scepticism is totally alien to the Glastonbury cults, and when he has a vision of Arthur's sword falling into the River Brue, he defiantly rejects it. This is an unexpected and, to the reader who, like myself, is allergic to cults about centres of mystic influence, an extremely satisfying scene. Not enough attention has been paid to John's role in the novel as mediator between the extremely sceptical reader and the mystical elements in the novel. It is a measure of Powys's achievement that at the end, the sceptical reader feels that John Crow's sceptical attitude limits him.

The love affair between Sam Dekker and Nell Zoyland is the second theme. Sam is the son of the vicar of Glastonbury (an acute portrait of Powys's own father) and he gives up his wholly satisfying, normal and exquisite relationship with Mrs Zoyland, to pursue his religious quest. His vision is of the Grail itself.

Geard becomes Mayor, begins a religious revival, and helps, rather half-heartedly, to found a Commune. He is opposed by Philip Crow, man of action in what Powys always imagines to be a 'Norman' sense; bitter enemy, both politically and economically, of the Commune and temperamentally alien to the mystical revival. He is a well-drawn and unexpectedly sympathetic character in the same way as his cousin, John Crow, both being possessed of the self-knowledge denied to most of the Glastonbury inhabitants. They both bring a much-needed East Anglian shrewdness to the town.

Glastonbury, however, contains the possibility of the Grail, and Geard succeeds in reviving its power. Some of the town's inhabitants exist in the light of the Grail, without the necessity of its appearance. Nancy Stickles, Bert Cole, Mr Wollop – their acute enjoyment of the sensations of life is a muted mystical response. Owen Evans, the Welsh pedant, pursues the Grail experience relentlessly, for release from his masochistic prison of perverted sexuality. Glastonbury becomes a cult centre, with the Pageant and Geard's new religion. Geard, now a mystic and saint, or magician (having achieved what might be called a miracle – a raising from the dead) dies saving his enemy's life (Philip Crow is characteristically ungrateful) in the great flood that inundates Sedgemoor. It is almost as if the sea, the greatest natural symbol of the 'other' has to restore the balance, and return the old Isle of Glass to its former dormant state. Drowning, Geard sees the Grail.

This is the sketchiest of outlines. There is very much more in the novel: the Dekker household and the relationship between father and son; Miss Drew's passion for her companion Mary Crow; Persephone Spear's sad quest for significance; Tom Barter's pathetic, humiliated existence and the accidental dignity of his death; the Marquis of P., his daughter Rachel and her lover Athling; the Geard household, Cordelia's love for Evans, Crummie's love for Sam; Philip Crow's love affairs, his ambitions, his wife Tilly's delightful domestic world; the Pageant itself; the political characters and their relationships; Morgan-Nelly, Philip's bastard daughter and her 'robber-band'; and the humbler characters, Abel Twig, the servants, Mrs Legge, Elphin Cantle, and many more.

A Glastonbury Romance is startlingly different from *Wolf Solent*. The change from a 'unicentred' book,[4] as Collins has called it, to a multicentred novel releases a vast amount of liberty – the liberty necessary to encompass a particular society. The central consciousness has been divided up among several characters for an adequate presentation of Glastonbury, its inhabitants and the effect on both of the legend of the Grail. The imaginative scale is vast, and, correspondingly, so are the problems of dealing with the structure of a novel which has multiple plots and a bewildering number of perspectives.

Another problem is raised by the intention of showing a society not as the background of one or several points of view but as a whole pulsating world in and for itself. Glastonbury has to be realised through the mixture of the points of view of certain characters, and a narration which also presents the feelings of, for example, a tree, or a group of superhuman observers watching the 'aquarium' of Glastonbury, or the wraith of the crucified Christ hovering on Good Friday night. This obviously gives rise to problems with which George Eliot in *Middlemarch* or Trollope in the Barchester novels never had to cope, and which Powys did not entirely overcome.

Powys does not show the workings of a society, the manipulation of people and money, the workings of various business concerns, as, for example, Balzac does with the printing press in *Lost Illusions*. Although there are money and business concerns in *A Glastonbury Romance*, the money is generally in the form of gifts and bequests, a child's vision of the way money works. The business concerns, the Dye Works, the tin mines, the souvenir factory of the Commune, are mentioned from time to time as vague backgrounds. Powys reconstructs his social reality, as he does his other 'realities', through a series of impressions in the minds of certain characters.

This can perhaps be demonstrated by looking at the role of the aeroplane in the novel. Powys's interest in and knowledge of the machine itself seems minimal (for example, he suggests that Wirral Hill could be used as an airfield), but his interest and intention is not with the actual aircraft, but with the effect that flying, 'the conquest of the air' (*GR*, p. 144) as Mat Dekker put it, has on the minds of certain people. Mat connects it with the apocalyptic movement they all feel. But it is Philip Crow, the capitalist, for whom flying becomes an obsession, an integral part of his will to power. When he appears at the Public Hall, after Geard's failure to arrive, he stands 'in the leather jacket of a flyer, motionless and with a grim smile on his face' (*GR*, p. 340).

The ovation he receives, the applause given to the 'Authority' which he so undoubtedly contains that even John Crow admits it, shows that although Powys may have been totally ignorant of aviation, he was very sensitive to the hold the figure of the Airman had over people's imagination in the 1930s. It is almost impossible now to recapture the awe and excitement evoked by this figure, whose impersonality (eyes hidden by blank goggles), individual bravery and mechanical efficiency seemed to represent the Future. Rex Warner catches this in *The Aerodrome*. Powys, not content merely to render the effect and atmosphere of this figure, seeing further than other writers of the 1930s, represented also the sort of mind that believed this behind the blank goggles and the steely futuristic perspectives. Powys shows the springs of action, and the effects of action. The action itself claims less importance.

The Glastonbury Commune, to pick another example, is inaugurated by methods that seem particularly ineffective. A certain amount of legalistic shuffling of leases and an act of munificence by Geard and Glastonbury becomes a working socialist Commune. To anyone who has ever been concerned with local politics, this may seem laughable. But what Powys is concerned with are the motives of the Commune-makers, and below this, the source and reason for these motives. (To coin a sub-Powysian image; he is not interested in the finished plaiting of the withy baskets, but in the green shoots of the living plants, and the rich Somerset earth that nourishes them. The antiseptic passion of Spear, the Jacobinism of Robinson and the philosophic anarchy of Trent: these are the main springs of the Commune, and are of more interest than the mechanical methods of achieving it.)

Of those critics who object to the vagueness of the workings of this society, one could enquire what is the real texture of their relationship with such a society. Is it not rather composed of their reactions to buff envelopes on door mats, or stray bits of gossip about leading personalities, or vague head-shakings about the way things are going, than a thorough knowledge of the mechanics of local government? It is with this real world, so real that it is generally overlooked, that Powys deals. In this, he combines the best of nineteenth-century writing with the best of twentieth-century: the nineteenth in their achievement of rendering a society, the twentieth in psychological penetration. The constant inwardness does not exist in a vacuum, as one often feels it does in Virginia Woolf.

The question of structure is more complex. The novel builds first to the climax of the Midsummer Pageant. This movement from March to June is seen to a large extent through the consciousness of John Crow, the newcomer to Glastonbury: his preparations, blandishments and shifts to make a place for himself and marry Mary. He is responsible for the Pageant preparations, and his first impressions, largely hostile, of Glastonbury, and the reactions of the inhabitants of the town to the subject of the Pageant are used for the initial presentation of the characters.

The second part of the novel covers more time. Volume II begins in August and ends in March. Sam Dekker is used as a 'consciousness' far more than John and his vision of the Grail is central. The climax of this second part is the Flood and Geard's death and ultimate vision. The personality of Geard has come to dominate the novel. He is seen first as an eccentric intruder in Mat Dekker's church and presented by hints and gossip, and glimpses. It is not until a quarter of the way through the book in the chapter 'Geard of Glastonbury' that Geard is shown in a sustained way, when he takes Tittie Petherton's pain away, and then he is seen through Mat Dekker's eyes. The episode of Geard's visit to Wookey Cave on the day when Philip triumphs over him in his Airman guise is given from his point of view in the familiar style of memory association (*GR*, p. 333), but the episode is too short for much to become known about Geard. It is not until the Mark Court chapter when he stays with the Marquis of P., and which deals with his terrifying encounter with the anguished ghost, that Geard's consciousness is fully explored and presented. From this point, his personality is no longer that of the eccentric so often present on the periphery of the Powys novel, but the central potential of the plot. His experience of the supernatural or numinous is connected with the mainspring of his character; in the same way his exorcising the pain of Merlin in the haunted room is his exorcising the pain of Tittie.

By this time John has had a vision of Arthur's sword, an unwelcome, irritating event to him. In the second volume, Sam's vision is again different. His quest is almost that of the Arthurian knights. San had fasted, sacrificed, done penance and endeavoured to become a saint. Geard's ultimate vision of the Grail in its fifth shape is part of his own mystical personality as well as his quest.

The novel cannot be broken down into any easy discussion of structure or themes. What emerges is the question of the reality of these experiences of the 'beyond-life'. In Glastonbury a transubstantiation has occurred. It is with the experience of this that these three men have to cope, and an examination of the ways in which they do so would be a useful way to approach the novel. Mystical experience here is not anti-natural. On the contrary, these numinous experiences come about through a sensitive reciprocity with Nature.

John Crow is the most easily recognisable 'Powys-hero'[5] in the novel. Although not as stolid and heavy as Wolf Solent, he carries the Powys stick, he finds his alter ego in the dark, slim, boyish Mary, and most important, he has his 'sensations'.

But John has no sense of Solent's moral drama in which Wolf felt impelled to play so righteous a part. He does not feel the dualism that Wolf initially felt to be inherent in life. Crow has none of the 'banked-up discriminations', the mania that his actions are important in a cosmic struggle, that Wolf has.

Powys has now worked away from putting all this weight of meaning in the 'charmed consciousness' of one man, by splitting up the one man in fact into three men. The rather sluggish over-involved character of Wolf has lent its 'sensations' and coldness to John Crow, its self-righteous, self-abnegation to Sam Dekker and its 'mythology', the ability to act spiritually and alter things, which Solent felt he had and lost, to Geard.

The reader loses in this branching out a certain degree of subtlety in the language and handling of images. The images are now ready-made, Arthurian symbols. There is no need for the language to be so allusive, when so many characters can by direct speech and by thought processes give so much information, information difficult to convey through the mind of one man. The reader loses that delicate echoing and elaboration of images, that sense, almost Jamesian, of something being conveyed through a mist of filmy mirrors, or the reverberations of a whisper just out of earshot. There is corresponding gain, however. Powys has the scope to explore imaginatively the sense he always had of some world just beyond our own and probe the means by which the transcendental might enter the world of common experience.

John Crow's religious impulses are more heathen than anything else. He has pleasure in connecting himself with 'his own heathen ancestry', the Danes who so nearly sacked Glastonbury, and he rejects the whole legend-rich loamy mysticism of the West Country, the 'sweet-sickly religious lies' (*GR*, p. 122) like scum on a pond, where 'these tender false mandragoras lulled to sleep the minds of the generations!' This does not mean that Crow is a rationalist materialist. Later in the book, he is described as being 'as sceptical of materialist explanations as he was of the occult occurrences' (*GR*, p. 1046).

He carries on the role of sceptical pyrrhonist begun by Rook Ashover. He sees himself, in words reminiscent of Wolf's, as

> a hard, round, glass ball, that is a mirror of everything, but that has a secret landscape of its own in the centre of it. (*GR*, p. 370)

And, like Wolf in his 'crystal' self, John really exists in his secret landscape, savouring and luxuriating in the emanations that drift off all the visible world. Like Wolf, the natural visible world becomes part of his thought processes.

In the second chapter, when John and Mary are still in Norfolk, they row up the river. John rests in the boat, tired, responding to the sights and smells of 'fen-ditches, and fen-water and fen-peat', his old landscape. On the edge of sleep, he tries to remember his intention never to 'compete'. Through his half-closed eyes he sees a willow-shoot drooping in the water which makes tiny ripples round it. He identifies himself with the willow-shoot, while his vow about not competing becomes the slow ripples.

> He was *allowed*, he dimly felt, to enjoy his paradisiac lassitude, as long as he, this being who was partly John Crow and partly a willow shoot, kept these ripples in mind. (*GR*, p. 84)

Reminiscent of Wolf's thoughts on his first night in Dorset, this passage fuses visual images and vague thoughts in the mind halfway to sleep, thoughts random with no coherent thread. This is his 'complete world' of 'paradisiac lassitude' which he can keep by a certain trick or fetish. The 'world' he was able to preserve in this way, as well as being Rook's symbolic ditch, is the watery-green one of Wolf's mythology, but in *A Glastonbury Romance* it is not the central symbol, it is itself, seen and embraced by John's consciousness until he is 'partly a willow shoot'. The willow-shoot half-trailing in the water is given meaning and importance by John's fetishistic mind, the incorrigible human trait of apprehending the world and getting it on his side. An analogy to this is the way children will not walk on the cracks on pavements. The deep significance of Wolf's aqueous mystic world, of which Lenty Pond was the material manifestation, has vanished. Symbol and significance are elsewhere, not rooted in natural images. But nature 'sensations' are still of prime importance.

John's journeying through a landscape begins the novel. He is travelling to his childhood home, expecting that something momentous and lucky will happen at his goal. But instead of the thought-stream of Wolf as he looked out of the window of his train, registering the cow by Basingstoke church, and fusing it into his symbolism, as he wonders about his new life in Dorset, the first chapter of *A Glastonbury Romance* observes John through many widely different perspectives. The first paragraph describes a vibration passing between John and 'the divine-diabolic soul of the First Cause' (*GR*, p. 21). However clumsily this hugely widened consciousness is conveyed, certainly the rather claustrophobic atmosphere of the mind/world of Wolf is gone. Here is Powys's 'jumbled up and squeezed together epitome of life's various dimensions'. In the first chapter are 'jumbled together' the twofold divinity of the 'first Cause', the fiery godhead of the sun, the jealous soul of the earth, the idol of John's dead mother, John Crow and his cousin Mary and their respective memories of the past.

John is, from the very beginning, placed. The reader not only sees the universe through his eyes, but also sees him through the eyes of the universe. What is stressed, however, is the interrelation between the two. This is the main point of the first paragraph; that 'an exceptional stir of heightened consciousness' is, or can elicit (it is not clear which), a response from something which is beyond the material world. One of the problems of *Wolf Solent* is immediately cleared away, the question of subjective reality's relation to 'the thing itself'. The reader has been informed on this point immediately. The varying perspectives of the novel continue to inform the reader of this matter.

Reality may still be as 'fluid and malleable' as Wolf thought, but not only does *A Glastonbury Romance* enable the reader to observe the different realities of different characters, but the author deliberately comments on their versions of the 'facts', and will show the motives and reason for this. These motives may not merely be due to personal factors, but to cosmic ones also. Mat Dekker's lack of sympathy with Sam is due not only to his jealousy, but to the hostility of the Sun. Prayers may reach the Evil Will of the First Cause instead of the Good, and difficulties are therefore to be expected in the courtship of John and Mary. These cosmic influences do not make the plot fatalistic. There is still the full play of individual choice necessary for a novel. But what is lessened is the importance of moral good and evil, the problem over which Wolf pondered so long. John is shown in the first two chapters as a shifty, feckless, corrupt rogue, basically selfish. The reader is told this incidentally, just as he is told that Sam is a blundering and insensitive self-torturer. Moral worth is not the issue of the novel.

John's attitude to the spiritual is totally sceptical. But he is greatly affected by Stonehenge. John's attraction to the great stones seems straightforward, sensuous and intense. His acts of worship at Stonehenge; embracing and praying at the Hêle Stone, drinking the water at the Slaughtering Stone, and kneeling at the Altar Stone, appal Evans, his companion. They take a radically different line over the monument. John dogmatically asserts the 'Englishness' of Stonehenge.

> I think stone-worship is the oldest of all religions and easier to sympathise with than any other religion (*GR*, p. 99)

They are simply what they are; stones to be worshipped. They have no hidden or transcendental mystery. He worships them, as they are, great blocks of matter, in a state of almost drunken excitement.

Evans is horrified at what he takes to be John's blasphemy. He feels that Stonehenge keeps its Druidic 'secret to the very end', and his attitude of reverend awe combined with the air of a 'mad dissenting minister' disconcerts John. Evans's erudition is completely different to John's 'extraordinary satisfaction' with Stonehenge.

The essence of John's fluid self-delighting spirit is displayed. He longs to dance or scamper in and out of the 'enormous trilithons' (*GR*, p. 102). He feels that until now he had been concealing his weakness of character, his lack of every kind of principle, his indifference to men's opinion, and a something that was almost subhuman in him.

John's experience at Stonehenge liberated him to be 'exactly as he was', it did not initiate him into another spiritual world. The stones were just 'stones to be worshipped', and he worshipped them, not anything that they represented in another dimension. He rejected ('Damn your Druids') all the mysterious cult secrets that Evans's erudite imaginative need collected, just as he later rejects the mysteries of Glastonbury. His rituals are fetishistic and there is about them something child-like and robust;

> Three times he pressed his face against it and in his heart he said 'Stone of England, guard Mary Crow and make her happy'. (*GR*, p. 99)

His satisfaction is immediate. The result of this experience is to liberate him 'from the burden of competing with anyone'.

This refers back to John's 'sensations' in the boat in Norfolk. As Wolf's 'sensations' depended on him observing certain self-made rules, so John's depended on him 'never competing'. And Stonehenge by confirming his 'exultant protean fluidity' has liberated him from this burden of 'competing', thereby ensuring his 'sensations'. Stonehenge does not show him anything beyond himself, but allows him to be himself to the full. John rejects firmly from the start any desire to be taken beyond his own personality spiritually.

John's refusal to 'compete', to assert his will against the world, can be compared to Sam Dekker's refusal to 'possess'. They discuss this possibility in John's room soon after he arrives in Glastonbury. Sam, although unsure that he could ever practise it, defends the 'mystic life' (*GR*, p. 206). It ensures happiness by freeing one from cruelty and possession.

> if you give up trying to possess what attracts you, a lovely, thrilling happiness flows through you and you feel you're in touch with the secret of everything.

Sam states his conviction in more overtly Christian terms, he talks about 'the mystic life' in a way John never would, but there is some similarity in their positions. Sam's simplistic language, 'a lovely thrilling happiness flows, through you...', although naive, could describe John's 'paradisiac lassitude'.

But the difference between the subtle, sinuous, devious John and the naive, almost obtuse young Sam with his huge feet, is far greater than any similarity of attitude. John answers Sam's discourse on 'the mystic life' with ambiguous, almost dismissive assent. He agrees with his Christian method but it must be applied for 'heathen ends'; this is the doctrine of the Tao which only John understands.

A positively diabolic light gleamed in John's glaucous eyes and his sinuous feeble form seemed actually to curve in tiny ripples of magnetic coils, like the coils of smoke which followed his cigarette.

The philosophic quietism of the Tao with its injunction not to assert the self, certainly seems on the surface to be what both John and Sam are discussing. The Tao, meaning the Way, has two distinct meanings in Chinese philosophy. The simpler version, the Tao of K'ung, consists of a series of practical injunctions designed to achieve harmony and inner serenity: to give up self-assertion, not to resist, not to want anything. The Tao of Lao Tzu is more elaborate, not simply a Way to follow, but the underlying, controlling principle of the world.[6] (This 'inexpressible source of being' may hark back to some ancient matriarchal religion, as the power described is passive. Powys's interest in and approval of the mother goddess can be seen by the invocation of Cybele at the end of *A Glastonbury Romance*.) The ambiguity of John's reference to the Tao lies in the fact that the Tao could mean either ways of conduct to escape notice in a hostile world or modes of mystical apprehension. The Tao has this ambiguity, as does John's remark. Certainly, John, with his advice 'to freeze', to 'Turn, pro-tem, into the inanimate,' (*GR*, p.207) when trouble rose seems to refer to the more mundane version. His fluid personality seems to comprehend the Taoist injunction to be like water. But Sam could never be like John, no more different souls could have been found in Glastonbury.

Sam's dualism, his 'perpetual battle of good and evil', his lanky lumbering frame, are alien to John's trampish, sceptical, dissolving self. Because of this difference, although both begin with a similar resolve ('don't compete', 'don't possess') to give up the will, they follow dissimilar paths. John's Tao suggest a way which suits his character, to become passive, receptive, to flow like water. Sam's sturdy, more conventional mind, tends to imitate the 'mediaeval saints' and incorporates also their sexual puritanism. Sam's 'spiritual excitement' forces him to follow the path of the mediaeval saints. John does not possess it, and refuses to transcend the self in an overtly spiritual way. All he wants is to be left alone with Mary and his 'sensations'. (As Cavaliero points out with the Powys characters, 'Character is Fate'.[7])

John's reaction to his environment and to other people is a series of physical sensations, by direct contact. He is 'doomed to explore' the soul of 'every other person' he meets (*GR*, p. 329) This intense, almost feverish sensitivity is the main feature of John's character, and it was this, intensified to a morbid degree which formed his mood on the day he had his vision of Arthur's Sword (Chapter 13).

John had been retailing all the Glastonbury myths he so much hated, in his publicity material for the Midsummer Pageant. His fury with this activity, combined with the sight of a dead cat lying in the debris of the River Brue causes 'a strange vibration of malignant revolt against the whole panorama of earth life' (*GR* p. 357) to take possession of him.

The description of the episode conveys a great deal of information about the locality. When John sets out for his walk, there is a digression about whether the road is Roman or Saxon, which takes him to Pomparlès Bridge, and when there, another paragraph, in the same learned vein, discusses the derivation of the name from Pons Perilis where 'that mysterious personage known as King Arthur threw away his sword Excalibur'.

John's encounter with the dead cat, and his reaction against Glastonbury causes a spasm of intense rage and contempt. But his hatred is not felt by the 'super-consciousness of the blazing sun nor throughout the whole of the mud, clay, granite, liquid rock smouldering gases of the earth was there any awareness of John Crow's rage. The 'double-natured ultimate First Cause' was also immune to his cold fury.

But there are other Powers beside the 'great Elemental Powers' By some unconscious mental movement, John, in his 'sullen and cynical mood'', brings down 'a supernatural visitation' from 'one of these lesser potencies'. There then follows, perhaps signifi antly in view of the preceding paragraph, a discussion of the sort of personality that gives rise to legends, as for example, Arthur, who may have been one of those 'portentous' beings who appear in every generation; individuals remarkable for their abnormal capacity for emotion and 'an abnormal closeness to the secret processes of nature'. The discussion is followed by a digression on the actual locality of Pomparlès Bridge with a list of the bridges and villages on the Brue. The perspective then narrows back to John's emotion and the expression of abominable despair on the face of the cat. This tightens John's rage and hatred into 'an anger that was like a saraband of raving fury'.

At this moment,

> he distinctly saw... literally shearing the sun-lit air with a whiteness like milk, like snow, like birch-bark, like maiden's flesh, like chalk, like paper, like a dead fish's eye, like Italian marble... an object *resembling a sword* falling into the mud of the river! (*GR*, p. 361)

Powys's language deliberately gives an effect of straining after the *exact* nature of the experience. It also has an objective 'list-making' quality. John is immediately convinced of its reality as a definite, perhaps dangerous sign directed to him alone, although he has 'no reason to offer now as to how he knew what this thing was'. But he is convinced that '*something* had touched him from beyond the limits of the known'.

The episode is set in a flow of discursive comment. Although the central theme is John's hatred and pity on Pomparlès Bridge, to which the narrative returns frequently, the digressions into history, geography, geology, theology, mythology and topography serve to suggest a 'got-up' journalistic account of an incident. Despite the pseudo-explanations, the event remains personally inexplicable, as Sam's vision of the Grail does not, because Sam's is shown as subjectively inevitable.

The effect on John, after the initial shock which made him put his cap on back to front, is to confirm his belief in himself. He rejects the vision and any meaning it might have. He does not care 'what signs or omens they fling down' (*GR*, p. 370). 'They stopped those old Danes at Havyatt, but by God! they shan't stop me!'

His consciousness of himself as something 'very lonely and very cold' begins to 'congeal into a little hard round stone' and he asserts his self-hood as something impervious, and defiant. He is delighted to be wholly uncommitted to anything.

He affirms the basic Powys-persona, Wolf at the beginning of *Wolf Solent*, Rook at the beginning of *Ducdame*, the self-sufficiency of the observer and his 'sensations'; needing 'the existence but not necessarily the presence' of someone to complete their satisfaction but not finding the girl more important than their 'sensations'. His affirmation of self ends with rejection of 'occult purgations and transformations'. In this mood, he invites and exhorts the salt wave from the 'dark heathen sea' to 'sweep over this whole morbid place'.

But the chapter ends with John returning to his old pyrrhonic scepticism, accepting and rejecting not only Glastonbury but his heathen delight in stone and water. Fundamentally his chaotic fluid personality can rest with neither of these. He dismisses all the Glastonbury legends in a spirit of sceptical contempt, as things of tinsel and gilded vapour. He is no more impressed by their 'savage opposites'. John's sensitivity to all manifestations prevents him from resting in any one. It is not surprising when later in the book it is stated that

> There was more mysticism in John's Crow's little finger – for all his sceptical perversity – than in Sam's whole body. (*GR*, p. 934)

This 'mysticism' seems allied to his sensitive response to the world, his fluid and receptive spirit, to which Sam's burly simple-mindedness seems totally opposed. Powys in his Preface seems to concur with John's sense of an underlying 'completely different' reality beyond all affirmation and negation. The Grail is 'only the nature of a symbol', referring to things beyond itself and beyond language. The best approach is to accept life in a spirit of 'absolutely undogmatic ignorance'.

But, although of all the characters in the book, John corresponds most closely to the familiar Powys-persona, and is conveyed most sympathetically, he is shown to have missed something. In part, this is implied in the contrast between the love-making of John and Mary and Sam and Nell. When the latter spend the night together in Whitelake Cottage, they experience 'delirious ecstasy'. But John and Mary are baffled, tantalised, provoked, throbbing with unrealised and perhaps unrealisable cravings for a consummation that mocked them with its nearness – (*GR*, p. 312)

More important than the 'sterile' sensuality is the failure to accept the mystical. When he returns to Norfolk with Mary, they carry

the corpse of this still-born never-returning opportunity of touching the Eternal in the enchanted soil where the Eternal once sank down into time! (*GR*. p.1063)

Sam's character has already been discussed to some extent. It is as earthy and solid as John's is ethereal and fluid. In this picture of an upper-middle-class, botanising, rather simple, son of the vicar, Powys perhaps pokes sly fun at his own young self setting off on country walks with his own sturdy father. Sam takes on the clumsy, rather heavy part of Wolf Solent's character. Although he rejects his father's High Anglicanism, Sam still believes in the reality of Transubstantiation, although he rejects it in his father's Mass (*GR*, p. 146). He quarrels with Evans's manichean assertion that 'Matter is entirely evil'. The Incarnation has transformed Nature. Coming in from outside, it is *'in it*, now' (*GR*, p. 260). 'Two and two can now make five! It's the thing Outside breaking into our closed circle.' The likeness to Powys's views in *Confessions of Two Brothers*, 1916, is obvious, and is taken up again by Powys in 1946 in *Dostoievsky*.

Reality implies a world of four dimensions. . . in other words a world with a super-lunary crack in the cause-and effect logic that two and two make four.[8]

A Glastonbury Romance is the most explicit discussion of Powys's sustained interest in the possibility of mystical or apocalyptic experience, but it is not isolated.

Sam's quest for the 'super-lunary crack' has its small beginnings in the discussion between Sam and John in the latter's flat, and is carried on in his argument with Evans and John under St Michael's Tower. At the same time, and bound up with this obsession, his love for Nell has greater importance in the narrative. That the two are bound up together can be seen from his remark to John when he speaks of the 'old mediaeval saints' who gave up possession and 'let the beautiful girl go free' (*GR*, p. 208).

His decision to leave Nell crystallises on Maunday Thursday (Chapter 14). He was aware of the 'vast shadowy Image' (*GR*, p. 376) of the God-pain of Christ. He is shown as the only one at the Vicar's supper party, where he helps his father in his amiable 'priggish boy-scout' way, to be aware of the suffering that Maundy Thursday represents. This awareness seems to press him to a decision. His impression is of the spirit of Christ, 'a vast shadowy tortured ghost', hovering over Glastonbury and pressing him to make some final decision, the exact nature of which is unclear, but which, if made on this day, could never be retracted (*GR*, p. 405).

Sam is presented as part of a Christian tradition, but returning to the pattern set by, for example, St Francis, who also deliberately rejected the sophistication of his Church, or the even earlier, even more austere renouncers of the world, the devil and the flesh.

A loose parallel to Sam's renunciation of Nell can be found in Wolf's refusal to make love to Christie. However, while *Wolf Solent* by its very structure lacked objective moral judgements, although Wolf was always trying to make them, *A Glastonbury Romance* specifically states that Sam was wrong to renounce Nell. Sam's individual theology, that Christ is a God among other Gods, but '*against* the cruelty of the great Creator-God' (*GR*, p. 465), has woven a 'spiritual chain-armour' for his 'sturdy animal instinct' and converted him into 'a singular kind of saint'. But this self-abnegation of Sam's is condemned by his own God. Christ, in fact, tries in vain to reach Sam's consciousness which is madly perverting his 'secret'. It is useless since Sam's form of asceticism is an appetite related to the lust for power, a perverted delight in forcing 'its own will and its own nervous sensibility. . . against the grain' (*GR*, p. 551). The Deity who can save him is not Christ.

This sounds very much like the 'maniacal self-punishment' of the bald woman glimpsed at a window by Evans, the woman who puts out her fire the moment she begins to enjoy it (*GR*, p. 253). Very much later, Evans connects this self-torment of Sam's with his own sort of sadism, or auto-sadism. Sam says of his Christ that 'What He did was simply to use His will to kill His will' (*GR*, p. 817). This gave Evans a spasm of 'sick terror'. 'This man's Christ is a madman like I am. His will holds the rod over his will.' In Sam, Powys has represented one of the most common ways in which the desire for transcendence may be perverted.

In the same conversation, Sam shows how far he has moved from his original belief in the Incarnation. His decision to give up possession has become a denial of life. John's desire not to compete facilitates his response to life, but Sam now makes a speech which is very reminiscent of Hastings' denunciations of life and creativity in *Ducdame*. He feels 'the Tide of *life itself* is evil' (*GR*, p. 820). Redemption of matter now means 'freezing the life force in it'.

This puritanical and neurotic attitude is explicitly condemned in the novel, but nevertheless it is Sam who is permitted the vision of the Grail. This comes about not through his self-torture, but through incidental features that result from his sacrifices. Sam is described throughout as burly, clumsy, tactless with 'a dead nerve of humanity', and likened to a bear or a badger. His 'sturdy animal' self is in strong contrast to the evasive John. However, a change is brought about by his Dostoievskian humility and self-sacrifice, 'the full implications of his abandonment of the normal human desires began to unfold' (*GR*, p. 925).

Sam's sensitivity to nature (previously hardly evident, despite the botanising walks) became greatly intensified,

> What he felt was a strange and singular reciprocity between his soul and every little fragment of masonry, of stony ground, of mossy ground, . . . (*GR*, p. 926)
> . . . some subtle barrier between his inmost being and certain particular objects in Nature had begun to give way. (*GR*, p. 927)

Sam is now a possessor of the Powys 'sensations'. (What one notices here is the precision of Powys's language, a welcome relief from the cloudy and pretentious style too often associated with the mystical or transcendent. Even if the reader were not interested in the experience suggested, or even doubted the probability of its existence, he could hardly doubt the good faith of the writing, which is obviously intended to communicate something specific.)

> Sam had found out that when a person is liberated from possessiveness, from ambition, from the exigencies of desire, from domestic claims, from every sort of authority over others,

he can enjoy sideways and incidentally, . . . the most exquisite trances of absorption into the mysterious essence of any patch of earth-mould, or any fragment of gravel, or any slab of paving-stone, or any tangle of weeds, . . .

Sam has now become a sensitive receiver of those 'sensations' which John treasures, and Rook and Wolf sought. These three felt that their 'sensations' were in part due to their 'inhumanity', their freedom from too much of the personal, their refusal to participate. Perhaps this is one of the reasons for the Powys suspicion of the 'personal' female.

'The Grail' (Chapter 28) hints at these 'thrilling spasms of a quivering happiness' (*GR*, p. 934), and connects them with the 'psychic', 'spiritual' and 'mystical', saying that Sam was rather below than above the normal level as far as these attributes were concerned. But now 'his whole being seemed caught up and transfigured'. The thrill and exultation released in him by the familiar sight of an old post in the River Brue makes him try to work out the 'mystery of all these experiences'. Sam's 'inarticulate craving' (*GR*, p. 936) draws forth a response from the atoms of 'inorganic substance'. 'Matter itself' stirs.

> He could actually feel a magnetic power pouring forth into his fingers from this post. . .

The feeling occasioned by the post was greater, more intense than previous 'spots of time' experienced lately by Sam. The feeling became associated with 'that little dead fish that his father had taken out of the aquarium'. Matter assumes a definite shape, 'electric with animation'. 'Ichthus, the World-Fish'. He has not picked up the expression from his father's books or the sermons of Mr Simeon. That the 'mystery of matter' which 'shivered through him in so many accidental contacts' should take the form of a fish was natural to Sam, with his upbringing.

> Did he actually see in his mind's eye, then, the red fins, the greenish markings, the black stripes, the silvery tail, of any real fish? No! It was more subtle than this. But he did feel as if the solid matter all round him had become porous, so that some essence of life could move swiftly through it. In the mute balancing of this finny life-essence, passing through the

primeval watery element that existed in all things, lay an inexplicable clue.

The mention of Mr Simeon, the famous Cambridge preacher of the early nineteenth century, is no doubt intended to suggest how remote this inward experience is from the Christianity of moral exhortation and spiritual strenuousness.

The image of the fish, already discussed in *Wolf Solent*, has also recurred throughout *A Glastonbury Romance*. As Wolf said, 'It's the best symbol for the unutterable there is'. The Dekkers' aquarium has had its counterpart in the reference to the aquarium of Glastonbury into which other invisible viewers peep (*GR*, p. 622). Tewsy's extraordinary catch of the giant chub brought to fruition an old Glastonbury superstition (*GR*, p. 736). The fish at Harrod's Mill were part of John's consciousness (*GR*, p. 69). Powys has chosen the symbol of the fish which contains many meanings. It refers to the 'primeval water element' from which life came. The mention of 'uprisings from the pools of silence' perhaps hints at this, as it certainly echoes Wolf's experience. 'Ichthus', the sign of the fish, used by the early Christians as a symbol for Christ, and a sign for other believers, refers to the God-man, the human personality that was also Divine. It also refers to Pisces, the last sign of the Zodiac, a negative, mutable water sign signifying mystical disintegration and rebirth, the most mysterious and inexplicable Zodiacal sign and one which astrologers claim has ruled for the last two thousand years, as Powys knew.[9]

Mr Evans, excited by Tewsy's chub, and his excitement breaking out in a string of literary allusions, speaks of the Celtic Fisher-Kings fishing for 'more than a fish' (*GR*, p. 740),

> not only the Mwys of Gwyddno and the sword of Arthur, but that which exists in the moment of timeless time when these two are one!

Evans carries on to speak of this as the 'self-birth of Psyche', and the 'stone without lichen', but from this quotation it is evident that he is speaking of wholeness, completion, the being at one with itself, opposites reconciled. This is then one explanation from the novel of the symbol of the fish.

Sam is driven to consider 'the ultimate dilemma' (*GR*, p. 937), the existence of pain. This 'dilemma' is one which Powys returns to throughout his career, symbolising it, not very effectively, later on, as vivisection. It is the existence of pain which has caused Sam, in his hypersensitive sympathy, to reject the whole life force. But he now begins to accept it. Without a limit to pity '"Ichthus the World-Fish" would float dead upon his back!'

Sam's excitement increases, he becomes intensely aware of his actual position – 'about half a mile north east of Cradle Bridge Farm and about half a mile south west of Cold Harbour Bridge where Young Tewsy had showed him that fish'. The reader was informed of John's topographical position before his vision, but in an objective way. Both were standing by the River Brue.

After this, 'the earth and the water and the darkness *cracked...*' Sam is stricken with hideous 'crashing' pain as if a spear had pierced him from beneath, and the vision appeared: 'a globular chalice' (*GR*, p. 939) with two circular handles, 'clearer than crystal,' with 'dark water streaked with blood, and within the water was a shining fish'.

The 'gigantic spear' he felt is also part of the Grail, the sexual symbolism of the spear and cup suggesting, as Powys remarks in the Preface, a Pagan ancestry. That Sam's pain is integral to the vision is perhaps shown by the blood mixed with the dark water, and perhaps, as the Grail is also a Christian symbol, it also refers to Christ's blood mixed with water at the Crucifixion.

Critics[10] have connected the enema that Sam on the following day gives to Mr Twig with the vision, and the text seems to indicate this at one point. They perhaps also follow the hint given by Powys in the Preface. Far more important, however, is the connection between the growth of Sam's 'sensations' and the appearance of the vision. 'The Grail' chapter shows a specific growth of sensitive awareness suddenly becoming mystical vision. The fish and its significance grow from Sam's imagination. The experience is achieved by concrete, specific methods which anyone might imitate. Powys effectively insists on the connectedness of natural with supernatural, and it is for anyone to achieve such a connection in their own consciousness.

John Crow's cynical reworkings of Arthurian legend may have precipitated his vision, as it seemed, almost by accident, but Sam's vision had been worked for and invoked. He had begged Christ for the smallest sign to show 'you are really *there*, behind it all' (*GR*, p. 909). It becomes the culmination of his life up to that point. Both visions occur when sensitive awareness, pain and pity mingled and intensified. John rejects his vision. Sam is changed by his. 'This change was nothing less than a coming together of his body and soul' (*GR*, p. 954).

His soul now accepted his body, and its presence within him seemed to 'make Sam's flesh feel porous and transparent, as if large, cool, undulating waves were sweeping through it'. This receptive medium-like quality is one shared by John. His sexual puritanism falls away and he no longer has any scruples about making love to Nell. The fact that she has gone back to her husband is a bitter irony. But Sam's last thought is 'I can endure whatever fate can do to me, for I have seen the Grail!' (*GR*, p. 986). In the Flood, he is reunited with his father in their joint fight to save the people of Glastonbury from drowning. 'Endure' is one of the maxims Wolf and John find they have to obey.

If John and Sam have an element of the 'case-history', this is certainly not true of Geard. The Nonconformist open-air preacher is a character not immediately recognisable as Powysian. But one recalls in *Autobiography*, Powys's early ambition to be a magician (*A*, p. 7), and one finds certain similarities between Geard and the more obvious Powys personae.

From the beginning he is further from the narrative main stream than either John or Sam, and his subjective thought-processes are far less evident. The first hint of spiritual magnetism comes when he relieves the pain of Tittie Petherton. He speaks of himself as a medium for Christ's spirit: 'Through me, at this moment in Time, the Eternal is breaking through' (*GR*, p. 287). When he hears Tittie's groans, his face twists into 'a spasm of physical pain' so grotesque that the nurse expected to hear from him the same agonised cry as from Tittie. The receptive medium-like qualities of Geard are so great that he 'becomes' what he sees or hears. In the Flood he touches a dead woman and becomes as if dead. After his death, a psychological treatise was written about him stressing Geard's 'hyper-sensitised and super-porous sympathy' which laid upon him 'the curious pathological necessity, under which he was known to labour, of actually sharing with all his bodily nerves the physical suffering of those around him'. After Powys has offered this explanation, he goes on to warn against total acceptance by saying that the pamphlet's 'pathological technical terms' (*GR*, p. 1105) distracted intellectuals from 'the religious aspects of the problem'. Powys, though not taking an obscurantist line or exalting irrationality, indicates doubt as to the value of such a framework. Its main use, he suggests, is in a substitution of terms; enabling people to avoid the religious problems which embarrass or puzzle them.

It is then, on the religious leader that the emphasis should fall. Geard is shown as regarding himself as such, his Noncomformity a thing of the past. His intention is to inaugurate a new religion, to dig a new course in which humanity could flow. This intention is allied to an enormous force that seemed to be pouring through him. The occasion of this is Easter Sunday (Chapter 15) when after he had celebrated his own Mass in his suburban garden, he goes to Mark's Court, where the Marquis of P. makes him welcome. The Marquis's daughter, Rachel, and his illegitimate son, Will Zoyland, are present.

> It was beginning to become for Bloody Johnny, as he drank cup after cup of strong tea and withdrew more and more into his secret thoughts, one of the great ocean-wave crests of his conscious life. (*GR*, p. 426)

This imaginative upswelling of Geard's is interrupted by an altercation which becomes a dialogue of the 'Two camps' of Glastonbury, the camp of Philip Crow and his capitalist common-sense, and the camp of the religious and political idealists whom Geard, somewhat reluctantly, seems to lead.

The argument with Will Zoyland comes to this head over the figure of Merlin. Although Zoyland scoffs at 'Merlin, forsooth', he suggests to Geard that if he were willing to spend the night in the haunted Mark's Gallery, he would rethink his attitude to the 'cranks'.

The episode in the haunted Gallery is one of the great climaxes of the book. In the room with its legendary connection with King Mark, Geard becomes slowly aware of its atmosphere, although most of his thick, heavy nature was

> absorbed by day and by night in his contact with Christ, which resembled, though it was not identical with, the physical embrace of an erotic obsession. (*GR*, p. 442)

Significantly, Geard has a combination of the heavy, earthy nature of Sam and the receptive psychic qualities of John.

The strange cry of the room, juxtaposed in Rabelaisian manner with the two servants passing water in the room beneath, renders him almost senseless with terror and pity; an unbearable pity relieved as he himself shouted 'Nineue', taking on the role of 'the great and lost magician'. Great pity in the face of great pain is something that both John and Sam feel at their moment of vision. But Geard, by contrast, is not a passive observer of or listener to his psychic phenomenon. He acts with great physical strain, he gives a benediction, 'Christ have mercy upon you', and blesses the great lost Merlin. The effect is similar to the Ancient Mariner blessing the water-snakes. After the deathlike reaction, a great peace and delicious sleepiness descend upon Geard. He has achieved something in a psychic sphere and established his right to be called a magician.

After this experience, he works out a clearer conception of the Grail. Geard comes to the conclusion that 'certain material objects can become charged with supernatural power'. Thought is a living thing with the power to create and destroy. The Grail has been 'attracting thought to itself' for a thousand years because of the magnetism of Christ's blood'.

> I now know what the Grail is. It is the desire of the generations mingling like water with the Blood of Christ, and caught in a fragment of Substance that is beyond Matter! (*GR*, p. 457)

His earlier realisation that there was something in his mind, or the human mind, completely beyond Matter, perhaps hints that Geard is a medium for supernatural power that comes from the human mind, perhaps from some collective unconscious.

But Geard goes beyond receptivity. He also acts. When he exorcises the cancer in the flesh of Tittie (Chapter 23) he commands it to come out, using the psychic power of Chalice Well, a spot 'charged with the desperate human struggles of five thousand years to break into the arcana of life'. His will becomes a spear 'the bleeding lance of the oldest legends of Carbonek' which he plunges into 'that worst enemy of all women' (*GR*, p. 709)

Geard is a magician because of his twofold nature. His passive receptivity to the psychic power poured into the Grail gives him powers he can use positively. He incorporates the spear as well as the Grail, reconciling Evans's 'knot of opposites'. Glen Cavaliero

has said that after the episode at Mark's Court, Geard 'does in a
sense become Merlin himself'.[11] Geard's firm refusal to have
Merlin represented in the Pageant suggests perhaps that Merlin
was present in Glastonbury already.

Geard's sermons on Chalice Hill are undertaken to inaugurate
a new religion (a religion powerful enough to enable him to raise
the dead). A clue to the nature of this new faith is found in the
contrast of Geard's views with those of Sam. Geard, unlike Sam,
accepts both the good and evil in the First Cause. Equally important is their attitude to St John's Gospel. This, the most
mystical and neo-Platonist of the Gospels, is the Mayor's 'favourite book': 'He says it's the whole Bible of his new religion' (*GR*, p
815). Sam, however, rejects the Fourth Gospel in his life-denying
quest. But this hint is taken up again, after Geard has established
his Saxon Arch on Chalice Hill and worked his miracle. His
religion is described again as his 'new, mystical, Johannine and
Anti-Pauline cult' (*GR*, p. 1040).

Geard's last sermon is more explicit. His acceptance of the
holiness of all life, with even slugs and snails possessing souls
leads him to formulate a world on the margin of this, an 'invisible
dimension' beyond which are other dimensions, other 'dream
lives'.

> Into this sequence of dream-worlds our souls drive us for-
> ward, drinking up Life and struggling with evil, seeking rest
> and peace. (*GR*, p. 1085)

From this deeper dream came the Grail, and its touch 'is to drink
up Life at its source'. And this is what men and women should do:
'drink up Life'. Geard's speech dies away as he tries to pass the
border-line between what may and what may not be expressed.

> The sole meaning, purpose, intention, and secret of Christ,
> my dears, is not to understand Life or mould it, or change it, or
> even to love it, but to drink of its undying essence!

This not only refers to physical and sexual union, Geard
mentioned this particular form of 'drinking up Life' earlier. It
refers to the receptive savouring of sense impressions, the felt
significance of those 'spots of time' that seem to have

amifications in the eternal. Geard here states that they do have amifications in the eternal. These are the 'sensations' of Rook nd Wolf and John. Glen Cavaliero points out the sense of a louble world in Glastonbury, and that 'awareness of that world is he true blessedness'.[12]

He cites the simple exponents of this awareness, Mayor Wallop, Bert Cole and especially Nancy Stickles. The all-embracing nature of this kind of diffused nature mysticism indicates an .cceptance so total that to concentrate on any one part is to reject he whole. This is why Geard speaks of a multiverse, a 'sequence of dream worlds'. In this way, total scepticism equals total icceptance and lies become truth, as Geard points out (*GR*,). 891). 'Any lie' that a multitude of souls believes 'to the cracking point', '*creates new life*' while the slavery of so-called truth drags is down to death. By 'lies', Geard is referring again to the creative power of thought. This extreme relativity can only be sustained by complete rejection of the world of action.

This perhaps is one of the reasons for Geard's suicide, his desire to meet the 'Living Being', of whom he had 'personal experience', ace to face, satisfying all his erotic desire, both mystical and ensual. His suicide is not undertaken in weariness of spirit, but as a continuation of his quest. Early in the novel Evans ponders on he death of Merlin, brooding over the 'mysterious word used in one of the Grail books about his final disappearance', 'Esplu-neoir'.

> It is inevitable from the context to interpret this as some 'Great Good Place' some mystic Fourth Dimension, or Nirvanic apotheosis, into which the magician deliberately sank or rose; (*GR*, p. 179)

This strange evocative word had a significance for Powys. It is mentioned as early as 1930 in the short story 'The Owl, The Duck, and – Miss Rowe! Miss Rowe!'[13] where the white horse 'alada utters this word. In doing this, he transports the sentient clutter of the room, ornaments and dolls, away from the pain of he world of matter into some other dimension. 'Falada' the horse is a borrowing from 'Grimms' story of the Goose Girl, where he Princess's horse, though killed, and its head nailed to the gateway, will still speak the truth and discriminate between the true and the false'. Powys's attraction towards this image of th truth-uttering head can be seen again very much later in *Th Brazen Head*.

'Esplumeoir', the act of sinking into another dimension, is wha Geard undertakes by his dying. In his willed death, he sees th Grail (*GR*, p. 1116). The vision is shown to be incidental t Geard's 'Esplumeoir'.

> In calm inviolable peace Mr Geard saw his life, and saw hi death, and saw also that nameless Object, that fragment of th Absolute, about which all his days he had been murmuring.

The Grail is only a *fragment* of the Absolute. It is not the whole Geard's attitude to it is one of almost irreverent familiarity. Gear has the abnormal power, capacity for emotion, and closeness t the secret powers of nature which Powys had earlier attributed t Arthur. Geard is something new in one sense, but he is not unlik the familiar Powys persona. His 'drinking up life at the essenc recalls the receptive 'sensations' – seeking qualities of Rook, Wo and John. But he rejects the intellectual self-involvement whic Wolf has to lose at the end of *Wolf Solent* and John clings to. (A Brebner has remarked, 'John's vision is turned on the pivot of hi ego, selfishly examined and rejected').[14]

He has their detachment and closeness to nature, but he is abl to act in the world of Matter. It is as if Wolf's mythology, wher he feels that his actions are of importance in some cosmic dimen sion, has become objectively true. Sylvanus Cobbold, Urye Quirm, Owen Glendower, and Merlin follow in this line of mages real or self-deluded.

A Glastonbury Romance is a vast novel and much will b neglected in any critical approach to it. But I hope to have show how the path from nature 'sensations' to mystical apprehension has been opened.

Quite apart from the unusual imaginative distinction of Glastonbury Romance, the book offers the satisfaction of thorough intellectual coherence; the positing of a certain kind o experience and the detailed exploration of the different ways i which all of the main characters fail or half-achieve it or full achieve it. By no means the chief of Powys's virtues, it adds to th pleasures offered to the reader of this extraordinary book.

6 Last Look Back

Both *Weymouth Sands* and *Autobiography* were also written at Phudd Bottom and published in the USA, in 1934. *Weymouth Sands* is the last of Powys's novels to deal closely with a rich, textured, contemporary environment. Publication of it in Britain was delayed as the novel had to be abridged and its locations disguised. Weymouth became Sea-Sands, Portland Shell-Back and the novel was published in London in 1935 as *Jobber Skald*. This was to avoid the possibility of more libel suits.

Weymouth Sands is an intensification of the sustained discovery and discussion of self that gave rise to the Wessex novels. *Autobiography* is the culmination of it. It is generally simplistic to look at a writer's personality and life for clues to his novels, and could be very misleading, but with Powys, as with D. H. Lawrence, it is almost inevitable. Powys's novels, his autobiographical writings, his philosophical books, his literary criticism all seem to throw light on and expand the reflection of certain abiding and central preoccupations that are taken up and fully dealt with in *Autobiography*. Powys returned to England in 1934. *Maiden Castle* was his next novel, published in the USA in 1936 (London, 1937). This was his last novel to deal, however vaguely, with the real present but its thin, undetailed background and its Celtic mythical theme show a marked change of direction. *Autobiography* was the last of a series.

Weymouth had been the home of Powys's grandmother and much of his childhood had been spent there. From *Wood and Stone* onwards, Weymouth had occupied a persistent place in the novels, one of cleansing, escape and rebirth. It was the birthplace of Wolf Solent's mythology. In Powys's own imagination 'every aspect of the Weymouth coast sank into my mind with such a transubstantiating magic' that 'it is through the medium of these things that I envisage all the experiences of my life' (*A*, p. 151). Transubstantiation is a word not used lightly by the son of a clergyman, but it is this solemn religious word which conveys the real power of Weymouth in Powys's imagination.

Weymouth Sands is an ecstatic rendering of the experiences Weymouth gave him as a child, overlaid by adult reminiscence and philosophising. The plot is correspondingly weak. The subject of the novel is the atmosphere of Weymouth. It is evoked by constant incantation of its features; St John's spire, the stucco façade of Brunswick Terrace, the Jubilee Clock, the Nothe forts, the statue of George III, Chesil Beach, Hardy's monument, distant Maiden Castle, Sandsfoot Castle, and the looming bulk of Portland.

Magnus Muir, a bookish bachelor, is the most recognisable character. He is an older, more timorous Powys-persona, experiencing 'sensations' and living with the memory of his dead father. His sad, inconsequential love for the unfaithful Curly is one of the plot strands. More central is Perdita Wane's love for Skald, the 'jobber' from Portland, whose hatred for Cattistock, a business man, turns into a murderous obsession. There are many interesting scenes and characters in the panorama of *Weymouth Sands*. One of the themes is the familiar quest, stated by Skald, 'I can't tell what it is about this view that stirs me up so!'[1] Perdita asks him if it has that effect because he has known it from infancy. This is the simplest level on which this question is asked. Magnus Muir's ponderings are more complicated. He feels that 'these simple things' (*WSds*, p. 40) are of inexplicable significance; the outward 'accidents' of some interior 'substance', a life independent of his ordinary humiliations. Muir connects this significance with his childhood. As he thinks of the crowded sands – the adults sitting on the dry sand, the children playing nearer the sea,

> he began to be aware that when he thought of the 'wet' sand – ... there arose in his memory some saying, like the 'logos' of an oracle, that must have been uttered by his father when he was too young to comprehend it. (*WSds*, p. 308)

This 'logos', this great truth, escapes the grown man completely, but the significance of it remains with him and this memory of it calms him. Muir's 'sensations' are not enjoyed easily. The first chapter describes him intently looking at the sea, strained, grim and concentrated as a priest occupied with liturgy.

A less central, more humorous level of questioning is represented by Richard Gaul, the young philosopher who is writing the *Philosophy of Representation* (which owes much to Jung). The argument of the book is that all concepts are true, not in a literal sense, but in a 'representative' sense. Behind every creed and mythological figure 'lay a quite definite human craving' (*WSds*, p. 98). This is a familiar argument from the earlier books and is taken up again more specifically in *Maiden Castle*. Gaul also, however, veers towards Platonism – 'there is something in the deep places of life – though doubtless outside the material world – representative of such things'. This seems to me to be direct contradiction, very symptomatic of Powys's ambivalence. Is the true significance bestowed by man and his mental and emotional cravings, or does it come from outside the 'material world'? Do we create or do we discover? Gaul sums up this problem.

> For what was beauty if not a manifestation in the midst of objective reality of something half-created and half-discovered by the cravings of our human organism? (*WSds*, p. 99)

This quest for the point at which we stop creating and start discovering is surely the central one of all religion and philosophy. It cannot be resolved artistically through the self-involved Wolf Solent persona. In *A Glastonbury Romance*, Powys presented a magician or saint to take over the quest. Sylvanus Cobbold in *Weymouth Sands* pursues it in a far less dignified manner than Geard, but both are open-air preachers. Geard, however, preaches from his own temple on Chalice Hill, while Cobbold is harassed by the police for the obstruction he causes when he preaches from the Esplanade.

Cobbold is an eccentric 'character' in a sea-side town. Although the brother of the famous clown Jerry Cobbold, he has 'declassed' himself, living simply, in a cottage by the sea, mixing with down-and-outs, sand-entertainers, gypsies. He is a vulnerable, almost pathetic character who is described quite simply by Powys in his list of characters, as 'a mystic'. Sylvanus Cobbold's effect on the lonely and the spiritually lost is first stressed. The neurotic misfit, Peg Frampton, hears his voice and feels that the individual speaking had broken some barrier, and was uttering simple words that nevertheless seemed to come 'from a level of life that was outside ordinary experience' (*WSds*, p. 243).

Sylvanus seems at first to be a more powerful Muir, someone

who can 'escape' into nature. But his 'Cimmerian' detachment is stressed.

> His whole life now consisted in the self-pleasing enjoyment of a curious mystical contemplation... (*WSds*, p. 271)

His 'sensations' are shown as more deliberately religious than those of Muir, but the religion is, by design, left vague and allusive. References to it suggest rather than explain. But one of Sylvanus's 'revelations' was that

> the Absolute was to be found in the concrete and not in the abstract,... But it was... in thought *first and last*. (*WSds*, p. 402)

Power and satisfaction came to him though the establishment of a 'certain rapport between himself and the cosmos' (*WSds*, p. 271). This is achieved 'by reducing the sensations of consciousness to the most primitive elements'. This is attained or accompanied by a ritual set of fetishistic exercises that are reminiscent of a child's game, or a priest's hieratic gestures. His morning ritual is described in great detail (Chapter 11). He buries his refuse in a hole and puts his tools away. As he does these simple things, he elevates them into sacramental acts, accompanying them with religious but unchristian chants: 'Rise to life, Human Beings. Rise to life, animals', 'Rise to life all other Souls of the dead' (*WSds*, p. 386). He next chants a 'Homeric litany to all his tools', with particular propitiation to his wheelbarrow. After his sacramental total acceptance of the ordinary, Sylvanus's sensation as he strides along is as if 'Nature were returning to God, as if the Relative were returning to the Absolute'. This is the effect of his ritual. Another is the sight of the dazzling glitter of sun on sea which 'was the nearest revelation of the Ultimate Being that man can attain' (*WSds*, p. 392). Sunlight on sea is an obvious symbol, but it is its profound effect on Sylvanus that is stressed, not its symbolic qualities.

Sylvanus needs young women to help his mystical quest. He feels that they are more receptive to the world's mystery. Quirm, the would-be magician of *Maiden Castle*, also believes that women will help him 'break through'.[2] Common to both is a belief in unsatisfied desire as a force to use on this quest. Sterile sex is a theme recurring in the novels. For the first time, Powys suggests that it could lead to transcendence. Although Sylvanus sleeps with his girls, he does not consummate his love with them. Quirm says that 'the grand trick of all spiritual life' is to 'Stir up sex until it would put out the sun and then keep it sterile' (*MC*, p. 252).

But for his 'debauching' of young girls, and his refusal to stop preaching, Sylvanus is confined in the Brush Home. This rather unlikely place combines the practice of animal vivisection with the care of lunatics. Powys connects a number of preoccupations here in a perfunctory way; sadism, vivisection and madness.

Sylvanus's desolation at the end of the novel can only be supported by two things; the first is the stirring of his spirit, when reminded of his own private liturgy, to resist 'even though his fighting is all done in the circle of his own mind' (*WSds*, p. 520). The second is the sense of restoration he feels when in contact with the simple and homely that continue to exist despite the evil inherent in the Universe. It is this sense of the ordinary that sustains his fight and soothes him.

Despite the sadness of the plot strands – only Perdita and Skald achieve a satisfactory union after being parted – the effect of *Weymouth Sands* is a happy one because of the rendering of the radiant atmosphere of Powys's memories of Weymouth. I have been summarising the intellectual elements in the book, but emphasis must finally fall on its ecstatic, visionary quality. Town, sea and island are more vividly present than Glastonbury in the earlier novel. They have a radiance by which the characters, however individually sad, are irradiated. The characters are weak, isolated, depressed, insignificant. There is more explicit reference than in earlier novels to neurosis, madness, promiscuity and sadism. Powys shows how difficult it is merely to live one's life and keep one's inner world in some sort of order. Outward circumstances are not favourable; neither are they particularly tragic. Powys shows the grey, unheroic elements of life. Cattistock's heroic act (a foolish rushing into the sea to save a non-existent victim of a storm) was a calculated risk, undertaken to impress the Portland Quarrymen and induce them to withdraw their pay demands. It is not acts of heroism but heroic attitudes that the characters of *Weymouth Sands* have to learn.

All are contained in the mellow light of Weymouth. Magnus's childhood home contains and embodies his life's experiences:

That difference, for instance, between the *dry* sand and the *wet* sand, which had remained in the memory of Magnus as a condensation of the divergent experiences of his life . . . (*WSds,* p. 456)

The sands become an understated and inclusive symbol. The raucous shrieks from the Punch-and-Judy booth become the 'strident brutality' of man, or of the cosmos,

> but perhaps it will only be when the Original Jester himself repents Him of His joke, and ceases to cry Judy! Judy! Judy! across our shining sands that that look out of the void will melt away. (*WSds*, p. 519)

That look is the 'ghastly vision of things' that Sylvanus has to face in his scientific prison. It is Wolf's 'face on the Waterloo Steps', the suffering of individual men and women. If Powys does not present evil adequately in his image of vivisection, he shows its effect on his characters, with unbearable vividness. He can never gloss over or come to terms with the suffering of others because he can never objectify them, never make a person into a thing. This sympathy is shown in the smallest details. Gaul asks Muir whether he feels it would be safe to sleep with Peg Frampton, given her reputation. He is ludicrously concerned about VD. Muir is ashamed, 'Her life's in her soul, after all, just as ours is!' (*WSds*, p. 541). Powys's pervasive compassion, humour, and inclusive wisdom is nowhere more evident than in *Weymouth Sands*.

When *Weymouth Sands* was written, Powys turned to even deeper examination of himself and his past. He wrote to his sister in July 1933,[3] that his next book would be a strange, unprecedented queer 'sort of original, mental autobiography'. The first thing that strikes one when reading *Autobiography* is its intellectual lucidity; the second, its extraordinary candour; the third, its no less extraordinary reticence. The gossip which seems so inevitable, and to some so welcome, a factor in most autobiographies is missing. This is partly due to Powys's deliberate refusal to write about particular women, and his concern not to hurt feelings. It is mostly due, however, to his own complete lack of interest. He overlooks that portion of social life which is the currency of gossip. Perhaps the very personal quality of the book renders it ultimately almost impersonal.

It is not a chronological account of his sixty years. To use his own phrase, the book 'hovers' over his life's country so that chapters are blocks of land seized upon and described. Powys moves from his Derbyshire birthplace to South Dorset; from the landscape of Sherborne and Montacute to Cambridge. From the fenlands he moves to the depressing Brighton and Hove coast, and then to the South Downs. His trips to Europe are described, his tours of the USA. The war has a chapter title to itself, but the background of this is again the United States and particularly New York. The last chapter describes Powys's New York State retreat where his retirement was temporarily set. It is impossible to visualise an incident in the book, without also remembering, not its 'setting', but what Powys's emotional, sensuous attitude to that environment was at the time. The minute particularity of the novels is still present.

By the end of *Autobiography*, Powys is ready to return to England, and at sixty-one, now feels it has taken

> half a century merely to learn with what weapons, and with what surrender of weapons, *I am to begin to* live my life. (*A*. p. 652)

It is this sense of the arduous difficulties to be faced, the almost impossible efforts to be made, that Powys stresses. It is a nineteenth-century emphasis on the refining of the personality, the paring away of inessentials, the conscious making of a soul. He does not speak of natural goodness, at least, not his own. He describes the human soul as a fountain, choked with rubble and invaded by the sea.

> Not until the fountain has banked itself up with great stones against this dead-sea invasion, not until it has pushed the sticks and leaves and gravel and roots and funguses and mud and cattle dung out of its way, can it draw upon the deep granite wells of its predestined flow. (*A*, p. 39)

Autobiography records this process. But this image could have occurred in one of his father's sermons, or in the novels of George Eliot. There is a serious, almost solemn strain in Powys which is frequently disguised by his humorous throw-away tone, or grandiloquence. He clearly saw the necessity for spiritual hard work.

Powys begins by naming the elements which he feels have

helped to form his 'life-illusion'. They are a number of seemingly
contradictory desires which he has had to curtail, appease,
indulge or propitiate. They are

> a desire to enjoy the Cosmos, a desire to appease my Cons-
> cience, a desire to play the part of a Magician, a desire to play
> the part of a Helper, and finally, a desire to satisfy my Vicious-
> ness. (*A*, p. 7)

The desires to enjoy the Cosmos and to play the part of a
Magician are evident in the Powys figures in the novels. As Powys
points out, the two are not entirely compatible. A Magician must
act, while the enjoyment of the Cosmos requires passivity and as
few practical problems as possible. In Geard, Powys shows that
the role of Magician can coincide with the *cult* of the enjoyment
of sensuous feelings. But there is a recurrent tension between the
need for mythic drama and 'letting it all go' to experience selected
sensations.

Powys's Conscience was, he remarks, a trouble to him. He
states that the grand struggle of his life was between his Conscience and his desire to live a life of sensuous-mystical sensations.
This is Wolf Solent's situation; his 'diseased conscience' orders
him to do arbitrary and ultimately inhuman things. It is less of a
conscience than a fetishistic robot operating away from the life-
flow of its owner.

Powys distinguishes between his Conscience and his desire to be
a Helper. The impulse to help came from his imaginative
sympathy and led him to do all in his power to enhance the 'life-
illusion' of everyone he met. (People said of Powys that he made
them feel important.) The same impulse made him a vegetarian
and anti-vivisectionist. Vivisection became a symbol of evil: both
as a symbol or a reality, it seems trivial beside the Russian mass-
acres that were taking place as he wrote in Phudd Bottom, or the
Nazi atrocities of a few years later. One cannot blame him for not
coming to terms in fiction with the huge state evils of the twentieth
century. Few people have. But there are worse things than vivisection, and as a symbol it seems very naïve.

Powys's desire to satisfy his Viciousness is one of the major
themes of *Autobiography*. It seemed to take the form of a desire
for sadistic images (which he managed to confine to the pages of
his pornographic reading matter); and the obsessive need to stare

t the legs of very slim young girls. The first he regarded as harm-
ul and he managed to root it out. The second he accepted as
omething which gave harmless pleasure. Either would be
atisfied to satiety by an evening's television viewing today. V. S.
'ritchett comments with modern sophistication on how rural
'owys's 'Viciousness'[4] seems, but Powys shows good reason for
ighting it. If it is possible that obsessive brooding thought can
reate palpable atmosphere, then his pornographic cravings
night be harmful to others. It is certainly harmful to oneself, as
ny monomania is, by reducing other elements of life to dust and
shes. The sadist Evans in *A Glastonbury Romance* is intolerably
ored when he cannot brood on his overriding vice. All legitimate
leasures, all delicate intimations are meaningless. To give one-
elf up to this sort of obsessive vice is to become less of a human
eing. It is wasteful.

Powys's discussion of the elements in his nature that helped to
orm his 'life-illusion' is an important aid to understanding the
ovels, as well as being fascinating psychological self-analysis. He
ery humorously charts the amount of eccentric needs and greeds
hat go to make up a human being's life drama.

Childhood experience is, as one would expect, important in
Autobiography. Here it is obvious that *Autobiography* followed
Weymouth Sands very quickly. Many features of the novel are
expanded in *Autobiography*. Magnus Muir's dead father still
holds a central position in his consciousness. So it seems to be with
Powys. The 'sturdy begetter' is explicitly connected with Powys's
life-long fetish-worship. In the first chapter, he describes the
glamour and enchantment of his father's laurel-axe. Like the
'logos' of Muir's father, it would have been 'a mystery that would
have guarded me all my days' (*A*, p. 3).

Fetishism is a subject on which Powys had spent a lot of
thought. He discusses it at some length in Chapter One. He does
not avoid the humour implicit in endowing the most mundane
objects with transfiguring significance. The 'real significance' (*A*,
p. 5) of the soles of his father's boots contains the 'secret of the
cosmos'. The 'enormously thick soles' emanated 'inscrutable
ecstasy'. With full awareness of the ridiculous element, Powys
seriously discusses the reason for its significance. He speaks of 'an
under-tide of life-reaction' and proceeds throughout the *Autobiography* to expand on this.

In this first, very important chapter, Powys emphasises the

power of the creative imagination, beginning with the impor
tance of the 'symbolic world' of a child's games. (In *Maide*
Castle, little Lovie's games with her doll are brilliantly presented.
'Real reality is entirely of the mind' (*A*, p. 28) and holds the lowe
material reality in subjection. Powys stresses the importance o
both will and imagination. Imagination is not mere idle fancie
and day dreams. There is a Coleridgean emphasis on Imaginatio
as opposed to Fancy. Powys's sense of imagination involves cons
cious hard work.

But Powys cannot find in his memories of his childhood an
trace of his 'conscious embracing of Nature with a psychic
sensuous ecstasy' (*A*, p. 29). What I think is obvious in this firs
chapter is the unbounded capacity for fetish-worship which
underlies Powys's embracing of Nature. It can also be seen as a
separate phenomenon – Powys 'christening' his sticks in a
particular river, or making a cult object of a particularly large
stone – but it is this sense of the extraordinary significance o
material phenomena, whether boot soles or Somerset views,
which supports the conscious embracing of nature. The capacity
for 'inscrutable ecstasy' released by chance 'omens of the way' i
surely necessary before the adult could make a cult of it, deliberately refining his sensations, bringing contrasting memories to the
present image until he experiences a moment of 'ecstasy'. These
moments are likely when in contemplating some scene or object,
one recalls 'some *other* deep cause of satisfaction' (*A*, p. 41),
totally independent 'and *not in the same plane of feeling*'.

Powys's deliberate pursuit of what he calls 'totally useless, pur-
poseless, unprofitable feelings' (*A*, p. 167) involved a number of
factors which he specifies fully in *Autobiography*. He stresses the
'rapport' (*A*, p. 169) he feels with the objects at which he looks.
He emphasises the contemplation of their 'precise physical
appearance', and yet at the same time, stresses the stream of
memories and literary reminiscence that are necessary for the
culminating ecstasy. The sensations he ascribes to inherited race
memories. Man's fulfilment lies in them.

> Human sensations are Nature's self-expression. They are the
> earth's awareness of herself. (*A*, p. 238)

This is achieved only after hard mental and physical work –
although the term 'self-expression' does appear to suggest the

opposite. Powys had no regard for what he called 'this whole
modern tendency to disparage the will and the imagination in
favour of letting yourself go' (*A*, p. 275).

The deliberate choosing, limiting and refining of certain
particular sensations involves the jettison of so many seemingly
important aspects of life that it seems as if Powys recommends the
life of a desert hermit. The abandonment of time-wasting
ambition is readily understandable. But his recommendation to
avoid human responsibilities seems alien to readers familiar with
the liberal literary tradition of human relationships. But Powys
states the fact of the solitariness of the human being who has to
adjust his 'God-given peculiarities' to his 'chance-given environment' (*A*, p. 564). This environment may or may not include
human relationships and responsibilities. Those who, like Powys,
find that their 'peculiarities' include the necessity for mystical-
sensuous sensation, would be wiser to avoid too much responsibility. Powys emended 'Thou shalt love thy neighbour as thyself' to
the more inclusive, and less personal commandment 'Thou shalt
be merciful, and pitiful and considerate *to all living organisms*'.

The reward for this spiritual, mental and emotional hard work
is 'that feeling of exultant liberation from the immediate pressure
of practical life'. With this somewhat prosaic phrase, Powys describes the aim of the whole of his life-flow. He hoarded his
memories of 'beyond-sensation' deep in his consciousness 'like a
sunken ship, full of fathom-deep treasure' (*A*, p. 199) which he
could haul up when required.

Autobiography is not merely a full account of Powys's cult of
sensations. It is an amusing, ludicrous and profound account of a
personality that thousands found fascinating. For it is in *Autobiography*, far more than in the literary essays, that one gets an
account of Powys the lecturer. His combination of shameless
revelation and impressive peroration, scatalogical reference and
learned allusion, direct invocation and poetic parenthesis make
this the book of all books to read to recapture not only Powys's
personality, or as much as he wishes to present, but Powys as a
lecturer. Llewelyn Powys found the second half of the book
insincere while J. B. Priestley's Introduction to the 1967 edition
states that Powys's accounts of his friends are boring. Certainly,
the chapters dealing with his childhood and youth are written
with more freshness and immediacy. But the second half of the
book, the American half, deals with his adult purposes and in-

tentions, not unimportant subjects. The American chapters are rhetorical, public and general in a way that reflects his America occupation. His whimsical conversational generalisations seem t wish to provoke debate in an audience. The ending of the book builds up to a grand climax; a peroration of great effect whic should be read aloud. Short, simple, contrasting sentence increase the tension until the final paragraph, long, slow an solemn, beginning 'And thus it comes to pass, even while we ar still in life. . .'. This is the ending of an impressive old-fashione lecture, or sermon.

Powys took his role seriously. Characteristically, he says of hi lecture tours that they were entertainment, not a cultural stunt but his forty-year-long task of bringing and upholding privat and poetic values was to him a very sacred trust. He was no simply a public lecturer. He was always on the side of the original poetic, introverted and he told them that they were right, and th poets and novelists of his lectures were on their side, against th 'clever, fashionable Herods'. He had no time for the cultura establishment, and wasted none with the formal academic worl or literary milieu. What does emerge from Powys's account of hi lecturing is his concern for those often isolated and oppresse individuals and unregarded minorities who sustain their 'life illusions' on very little. Jews, negroes, women (although Powys di not regard women in the political terms of today), the poor, th overworked, the imaginatively-starved: his intention was t encourage them, to help them to live, in his phrase from Goethe 'in the Whole, in the Good, in the Beautiful' (*A*, p. 501).

Again, the image of the preacher comes to mind. It is in *Auto biography* that he explicitly connects his imaginative and sen suous creativity with religious feeling – 'To endure joyfully is to see God' (*A*, p. 361). 'Pseudo-science' and 'pseudo-realism' are hostile to the 'up-mounting spring of life-acceptance in us'. In the past, this 'stoical' habit of drawing 'life-energy' from within, was called God. This now lacks historical justification: 'But *that* is no reason for deserting the living well-spring of mysterious magic within us'. The creative powers of the imagination are religious. But it is a religion without ultimate salvation, not to everyone's taste. What it offers is enlightenment. But in the end this religious note is not insisted on, and falls into place with the rest of the suggestions, allusions, quotations and reminiscence that make up *Autobiography*. Powys's desire to be a Helper found its

fulfilment in his role of preacher. His need to describe his sensations was allied to a desire to help others to the independent and
ecstatic existence his sensations enabled him to live. His 'philosophical' books are practical manuals to this end. *Autobiography*
finishes the series that began with *Wood and Stone*.

7 The Welsh Novels

Powys returned to England in June 1934, living for a short time near his brothers Llewelyn and Theodore in South Dorset, then moving to Dorchester, where he worked on *Maiden Castle* and *The Art of Happiness*, before removing to his new home in North Wales in July 1935. Sir Mortimer Wheeler and Colonel C. D Drew were excavating the Neolithic hill-fort of Maiden Castle between 1934 and 1937, and the local interest stimulated by these archaeologists was incorporated by Powys in his novel.

One of the themes of *Maiden Castle* is the efforts of the Welsh man Uryen Quirm to reawake the old gods once worshipped there. He has some occult powers and believes himself to be a reincarnation of a Welsh mythical figure, but he fails in his quest. Dud No-man also fails in his romantic relationship with a circus girl. He 'buys' her from her employer and lives with her for a while but, tiring of his impotent or selfish love-making, she leaves him. Dud is Uryen's son, and despite their temperamental differences, they share many characteristics. Both seek goals set ultimately beyond ordinary humanity: Uryen to revive the old gods; Dud to experience Powysian sensations in the context of his own myth-making. Both use sterile sex to accompany and accomplish their quests. Their courses run parallel and both fail. Quirm is searching for the secrets of Welsh gods, and his occult Celtic knowledge is given prominence. Powys's interests were moving towards the mythology and landscapes of his new home.

Powys's home in Corwen was a cottage set in the side of the Berwyn range of mountains. It overlooked the town, the river Dee and the Snowdonia range to the north. Here he lived for over twenty years. The companion of his last years in America and his Welsh years was Phyllis Playter, daughter of an old Kansas friend, whose mother and aunt also moved to Corwen with them. Powys records the reasons for his move in *Obstinate Cymric* (*Essays 1935–47*): not love of solitude, but a stirring of some longing, or obscure destiny, 'hiraeth' in Welsh, 'to return to the land of my remote ancestors'.[1]

In Wales he felt he had found the 'particular psychic aura' towards which he had been groping for years and which *A Glastonbury Romance* and *Owen Glendower* showed. He describes his new home in Corwen; its prehistoric hill-city, its old carved pillar associated with the cult of the Earth-Mother, King Eliseg's monument, the ruins of Valle Crucis Abbey, the ruins of Dinas Bran.

> Bards and Gods and Demons and Druids have all left indelible impressions on the landscape of my new home. ('Welsh Culture')

This landscape he transformed in *Owen Glendower* and *Porius*).

It was these 'indelible impressions' left by history and myth on a particular locality which Powys responded to so intensely. Wales, far more than England, resembles Greece, in that story and landscape are fused. King Arthur's court may or may not have been at Cadbury, but Dinas Bran has always been regarded as the castle of Bran the Blessed, one of the pre-Christian gods, just as the spot where Oedipus killed his father, the meeting place of three roads, can still be seen at Delphi.

Another feature of Wales which Powys mentions in the essay is the continuity and widespread knowledge of Welsh culture. A railway freightman who brought up Powys's parcels was a learned antiquary, interested in Llywarch Hen and a friend of several living bards. Here, then, was the world that Powys had created in his fiction; a world where landscape showed the print of history and mythology and literature and where ordinary people were aware of the forces inherent in these remains. Powys also found in Wales 'a deep tradition of understanding between the mountains and the people' ('Welsh Culture'). In fact, Powys found in Wales traces of most of the characteristics he advocated and approved in his writing, for example, pluralism. He tries to prove that 'a communistic matriarchy' is the secret ideal of Welsh family life. He also attempts to show that something resembling the Chinese Tao 'is at the deepest heart of Welsh psychology'. Other familiar themes are present: the 'intense pleasure and infinite interest in little things' of the Welshman and his power of 'escaping into his soul' ('Welsh Aboriginals').

In *Visions and Revisions*, when Powys writes of Keats or

Shelley, he is really talking about himself. Again in these much later essays, it is clear that it is his own personality and obsession that he had discovered among his ancient countrymen. Artistically, however, this rediscovery of his imaginative landscape was very fruitful.

Owen Glendower, 1940, is the first great fruit of his Welsh experience (*Morwyn*, 1937, is a rootless fantasy about vivisection and descents into Hell. It is very disappointing after the Wessex novels). Powys displays the 'Welsh' characteristics he describes in *Obstinate Cymric* in an objective historical setting in *Owen Glendower*.

The historic setting of *Owen Glendower* brings about some changes in Powys's accustomed themes and style. The young Rhisiart, while superficially behaving like the accustomed Powys personae, disappears for much of the novel. In the familiar mode *Owen Glendower* begins with a journey undertaken by a man with a 'life-illusion' which he intends to preserve. But Rhisiart's 'life-illusion' is important in the first few chapters and then dismissed. It centres on the imagined landscape of Dinas Bran, the fortress of his ancestors. Obstinacy, passionate obsession, frenzied patriotism and 'vague fairy-story hope':[2] all these are elements of Rhisiart's feelings about Dinas Bran.

This is an essential clue to how *Owen Glendower* differs from the earlier novels. Private myths have become part of the public realm, the historical matter of the novel. Rhisiart's obsessive dream is political: to restore the 'lost glories of the old chiefs of Powys'. Descriptions of Rhisiart's attitude towards Dinas Bran could also sum up quite well the political atmosphere of the novel; its obsessive quality, its patriotic politics, and yet its mythical derivations and, underlying all, the half-rejected reliance on magic. At the same time, the psychological roots are touched on: Rhisiart's adolescent desire to revenge himself on the Hereford world of his childhood and the teasing of his frivolous mother.

In the first chapter, he is faced with the possibility of the 'loss of his life-illusion'; that the real Dinas Bran would dissolve the ideal. This is not given the tragic potential of Wolf Solent's loss and in fact, the sight of the fortress is more significant than he could have hoped.

Its foundations are
sunk in that mysterious underworld of beyond reality whence

rise the eternal archetypes of all the refuges and all the sanctuaries of the spirit, untouched by time, inviolable ramparts not built by hands. (*OG*, p. 12)

This early vision of the Platonic refuge of the human spirit is less important to Rhisiart than it is to the development of the novel. It could be said that it is the secret landscape of the theme rather than the character. Rhisiart's 'life-illusion' is more concerned with action and revenge, as his old Crusader sword and horse signify, than with refuges and sanctuaries. This landscape is at odds with his patriotic fervour.

The landscape symbol of escape and refuge is set at the beginning of Glendower's campaign of aggressive action against the English. Glendower breaks his magic crystal and becomes a man of action. The landscape symbol functions as a warning against this choice of action. The warning is given and completed early in the novel. Partly for this reason, the symbol seems less important as far as Rhisiart is concerned. Although attached to him, it does not seem integral. Rhisiart's feelings about Dinas Bran soon become merged into his feeling for Glendower. Both place and hero partake of the same 'mystic enchantment'. After this, Rhisiart becomes less and less of a mythologiser. He becomes secretary to Glendower, using his cunning 'Norman' legal knowledge to aid the Welsh dream of nationalism. Glendower is the centre of the novel.

Glendower's 'psychic withdrawals' (*OG*, p. 121) are rather different from the superficially similar mental actions of other Powys heroes. They are not entirely under the control of the will. They are described as 'attacks', 'prolonged reveries' (*OG*, p. 410) or 'fits'. But they have this in common with the conscious sensation-seeking of other characters; they always leave him feeling powerful, confident, secure. He vaguely feels that his soul 'went somewhere', but where 'in a world like this' to return refreshed and strengthened? These 'escapes of consciousness' aid his willingness to wait upon the event, to accept the sacrifice of those he loves. They enhance his passive impersonality. But from them, also, he gains his mistaken certainty of the success of his revolt, and towards the end of the novel, an 'attack' renders him incapable of preventing the atrocities of his French allies in a Worcestershire village. In the world of action, trances of the soul

are of as much practical use as an epileptic fit. They are part o
Glendower, the magician, the dreamer, the poet. They connec
him with Merlin and his 'esplumeoir' (*OG*, p. 889). They are ne
help in dealing with Henry IV.

Throughout the novel, there are suggestions that Glendower'
successes depend more on evasions, retreats and surprise attacks
and that his policy to besiege castles and send large armies on the
offensive is a failure. Glendower's hesitation at Worcester whex
his troops far outnumber the King's shows him his true nature
'His chance had been given him and something in his own natur
had balked' (*OG*, p. 821). He could not act as an aggressor
deciding that he and his people could afford to wait. 'He knev
how his own soul could escape, escape without looting cities ano
ravishing women'. At the end of the novel, the image of escape
and evasion is returned to and harmonised with the politica
action. Glendower, hermit among the rocks of Mynydd-y-Gaer
refuge of the old pre-Celtic Welsh, has long given up his dream o
a Welsh prince upon the London throne. The Welsh soul and the
Welsh landscape lend themselves to 'the mythology of escape
(*OG*, p. 889).

> Its soul is forever making a double flight. It flees into a
> circuitous Inward. It retreats into a circuitous Outward.

This is familiar from the earlier novels, but it has been made par
of the historical matter of Owen Glendower. Glendower'
personality is the clue to his campaigns. The ambiguity of hi
character, his magic and his vanity, his scholarship and hi
magnetism, his nationalism and his impersonality; all can be seer
as parts of a diverse and complex man who made the wrong
choice. He should have chosen the 'mythology of escape' rather
than the rhetoric of action. The rhetoric was misleading. The
prophecies were misinterpreted. Glendower dies, willing his sou
to sink into the landscape, a perpetual exteriorising trance.

After Glendower's death, the novel ends with Rhisiart (now a
Judge) and Meredith, Glendower's surviving son. Rhisiart know
'with Welsh knowledge' that 'the things which are seen are un
essential compared with the things which are unseen (*OG*, p
934). To Meredith is given the last Powys injunction – 'to forget'
After spending the night at his father's funeral pyre, the sight of a
stag at dawn brings 'a random crowd of kindred impressions from

he misty shores of memory' (*OG*, p. 937). The significance of
hese images is overwhelming: 'What were they, what did they
ave in them that they could bring such comfort?' The novel ends
vith this experience of comfort and release.

Owen Glendower is a fascinating novel. It is also a very learned
ne. It shows that Powys was no amateur in the academic world,
ut could master and deploy a vast amount of historical material.
t reveals great understanding of the late mediaeval world in all
ts aspects. The account of Glendower's uprising is not only
actually correct; it provides an answer to a historical puzzle: why
e wasted so many opportunities when he had resources in Wales
and French aid. The purely military side of Glendower's policies
s mysterious, as indeed Shakespeare represents it in *Henry IV
Part I*. Powys provides a rationale in his 'mythology of escape'.

Powys has transformed the landscape and history of his new
home into a mythic world congruous with historical fact and
eopled with real heroes that are nonetheless Powysian. He has
pened out his private world and found a place and a tradition
or it. The result is a most impressive novel.

Wales had provided a place and a tradition. For a time and a
mythology, Powys presented his home fifteen hundred years
efore in his most experimental novel, *Porius*, published in 1951,
leven years after *Owen Glendower* was finished. Most of this
ime was spent in the writing and revising of the novel, that Powys
regarded as of great importance to his whole work. It describes the
eactions of the dwellers of the Vale of Edeyrnion (his home of
Corwen) to a Saxon raid in 499 AD. Porius, the central consciousness, is a prince of the Brythonic Celts, and his role is to find some
ort of place for himself and security for his people among the
alarming fragments of religious civilisations, ideologies, races and
magical forces that surround them. The Modrybedd, matriarchal
rulers of the more primitive tribes, enlist Saxon aid because of
their objection to Porius, heir through the male and not the
female line. News of the raiders brings a very unglamorous
Arthur with his soldiers to the forests. They are accompanied by
Merlin (Myrddin Wyllt) and his enchantress, Vivien (Nineue).
Despite Porius's dynastic marriage to his cousin Morfydd, he is
intensely drawn to the old aboriginal giants of Cader Idris, the
Cewri. Powys also uses the story of Blodeuwedd, from the
Mabinogian. In this novel, Welsh myth enabled him to synthesise
all his ideas, themes and sensations. (But it should be noted that

the *Porius* that was eventually printed by Macdonald in 1951 is a truncated version of the original. Some of what seem imperfectly conceived characters, whose roles and subsequent careers are mysterious, would probably be amplified and explained in the full text. Nevertheless it still remains Powys's 'great revolutionary contribution to the novel'.[3] Colgate University, New York State has the uncut version of *Porius* and Churchill College, Cambridge, has a copy of the missing portion.)

Powys has chosen a setting which is undoubtedly the 'multiverse' about which he wrote so frequently. All sorts of mythologie contend among the trees; decayed Roman imperialism, Druidism, Pelagianism, the Aboriginal paganism of the Cewri giants Medrawd's nihilism, the cults of Mithras and Christ, the Matriarchy of the old tribes, the brutal warmongering of the Saxons the private mythologies of individuals, and the powerful nature magic of Myrrdin Wyllt.

Against the social stability of the Edwardian rural scene (which is really the setting of *Wolf Solent* and *A Glastonbury Romance* despite their aeroplanes), only an outsider could detect and propose a multiverse. John Crow, Wolf Solent, Rook Ashover were eccentrics. But the disintegration of the classical world, the spread of redemptive and mystery religions and the onset of the Dark Ages, provide an example of a 'multiverse' which many historians would accept, and which is much better suited to Powys's purposes than small towns in the West Country at the turn of the century. Consequently, the debates on mythologies mythologies as atmospheres, are more confident and less private than in the earlier novels.

Dualism is confined to the cult of Christ, with the hysterical Priest inciting the murder of atheists and heretics, and the nihilism and black despair of Medrawd (Modred). In the novel both Christianity and nihilism find their being by opposition to something else, and enforce this either by love or hate. Christian 'love' is deceptive.

> What the world wants is more common-sense, more kindness, more indulgence, more leaving people alone.[4]

Myrddin Wyllt is the perfect spokesman here, with his natural affinity with and respect for all living things, for Powys's deep suspicions of the polarised nature of the deeply personal. He saw love as 'too involved' with sex, nerves, hate, and 'other dangerous and unstable things'.[5]

The 'multiverse' is an appropriate term for the worlds in collision that are presented in *Porius*. Powys also gives a reason for this fragmentation which is closely allied to Myrddin Wyllt's disappearance at the end. He uses the astrological division of Ages ruled by zodiacal signs.

Powys's use of influences and atmospheres has been extended to include astrology.

'Pisces must rule for two thousand years,' the Henog had said, 'and then Aquarius must take its place.' (*P*, p. 497)

It is suggested that it is the change to the new zodiacal era which precipitates this fragmentary chaotic multiverse. The following age, after Pisces, will be Aquarius, and it is implied that this will ensure the return of Myrddin Wyllt and the onset of the second Age of Gold. In this way, Myrddin Wyllt's disappearance or 'esplumeoir', a word not used in the novel, is seen, not as an individual, almost inexplicable act as is Geard's drowning, but in a tradition of magical hibernations when the king or mage leaves his people for some island or cave to return either at a more propitious or more dangerous time. After two thousand years, Neb explains (*P*, p. 661), Merlin will return and banish both 'the god of thunder' and the 'god of hell'. Peace between men and beasts will return.

Myrddin Wyllt will drive away the dualist religion (God and the Devil) and a Golden Age will ensue. Here, and throughout the novel, the magician is connected with Cronos, or Saturn, the disinherited Titan of the Age of Gold, whom Powys has used before as a symbol for the inauguration of a new sort of world and a new sort of sensibility. (Professor Wilson Knight has discussed the meaning of this in *The Saturnian Quest*.) Powys offers these interpretations of the situation with the same non-dogmatic humour that he offers Rhun's Cult of Mithras. He is not committed to any of them. This is shown in a contemporary remark on the age and consequent 'poetical authority'[6] of astrology. These hints and 'explanations' are put into the mouth of minor, even ridiculous characters as, in *A Glastonbury Romance*, Evans rather pedantically lectures on the significance of the fish.

The novel contains more Powys-personae than any other.

Porius himself with his mythology of the ancient Cewri giants and his sensation-hungry 'cavoseniargizing' is the main protagonist and it is through him that most of the action is revealed. Secondary characters, however, also possess this faculty. Brochvael, the erudite traveller, is cited as a sensitive sensationist. Nineue, the witch, is suspected by Porius of 'cavoseniargizing'; Cadawg, the ancient warrior of the cave, has the sensation when he touches an old pierpost that it would take him to 'an enchanted embarkation'. Taliessin, the young bard, is another example. Both his nature and his poetry are recognised by Myrddin Wyllt as given wholly up to 'an almost babyish abandonment to pure unadulterated sensation'. His poem is almost a manifesto of the pluralist sensationism that Powys had been attempting to describe for so long. Even the dead Christian Father, Pelagius, is described as a teacher of the creative powers of the imagination, although a survey of his surviving writings does not support this view. Myrddin Wyllt himself is connected with this, but in a somewhat different way. He is always described externally, never from the centre. His thought processes are rarely displayed and his personality remains mysterious, despite his connection with Cronos. This affinity or reincarnation, it is not clear which, reminds one of Uryen Quirm in *Maiden Castle*, who believes he is an ancient god. Their claims are neither justified nor rejected by Powys who presents them as one more aspect of personality.

The number of Powys-personae in *Porius* is paradoxically both a weakness and a strength. The chief danger, that of repetition, is mainly avoided. The characters themselves are very different and they display the Powysian cult of 'sensuality' in its varied aspects. Taliessin's use of it results in his poetry while Cadawg's ecstatic sense of another dimension is part of his feeling that something important is going to happen in a practical sense. The weakness is mainly in the impression given that the Dark Age forests of North Wales were full of extraordinarily complex and thoughtful individuals. (That this is a prejudice need hardly be stated. The twentieth century does not have the prerogative of complexity. However the characters in *Porius* possess a self-awareness which is more modern than antique; a generalisation which the comparative rarity of autobiography before the eighteenth century tends to support.)

The strength is in the rich texture of the novel, provided by the narrative strained through these individuals. Every path through he forest, every moss-bed and rock, the barbaric Druid mound, he dark corridors of the Gaer fortress; all are conveyed intensely as they fuse with the stream of thought and feeling and sensation of the characters. This stream is conveyed minutely, so that, almost literally, every minute of Porius's troubled night out, in the first part of the book, is presented. This enhances the sense of reality, but it also frustrates it as the plot has a tendency to become submerged under the slow weight of sense impressions described. Powys has never so amply demonstrated that the real event consists in the individual's sense impressions of it and reflections upon it and not in mere reported action.

The central consciousness, Porius, shows that Powys has moved away from exclusive use of the nervous, literary/intellectual eccentric as the central figure in the novels. Rhisiart in *Owen Glendower* is one of these, but Porius is the son of a Romanised Brythonic chief, a giant, the strong man of the tribe, and one who is intimately and crucially concerned with great events. He ends by freeing Myrddin Wyllt from his rock tomb. The rather déclassé ineffectual anti-hero is absent. Porius is not an outsider. One of the reasons for this has already been given. Porius could be both the hero in the world of action, as for example when he kills Saxons, and the sensation-lapping pluralist because of the time and setting of the novel. The primitive strength and integrity that enables Porius to be Prince of his Brythonic tribe was not antithetical to his sensitivity. Powys had found the perfect vehicle for his imaginative world by creating his home at Corwen fifteen hundred years before. The qualities that made Porius Prince made Wolf Solent, Sam Dekker and John Crow outsiders in a very different society.

Nevertheless, Porius still retains the passivity of the earlier central figure. It is the women who take the decisions and even inaugurate the war.

But it is not only through the old matriarchal rule of Modrybedd and other powerful women (as for example, Porius's mother and wife) that the importance that Powys attached to the feminine principle is shown.

Passivity and receptivity to all forms of life and time; that is the secret of Myrddin Wyllt's magic. When Porius supports him (Chapter 111), he becomes aware that this 'captured god of time' (*P*, p. 59) was a medium for a multiplicity of impressions, 'as far flung and telescopic as they were concentrated and microscopic,' which include 'battles and migrations' and 'millions of infinitesimal insect lives'. Myrddin Wyllt's personality, like John Crow's, has the quality of yielding and evaporating, of 'conscious recession' into 'primordial beginnings'. Myrrdin Wyllt has a 'multiple identity composed of many separate lives'; of birds, beasts, even plants rocks and stones. Although weak and helpless, he is at the same time vaster and older than Porius, who feels 'a rich, deep, dangerous, sensual pleasure' in the 'yielding' of 'this tremendous entity', this 'huge composite earth creature'.

The 'half-sexual pleasure' Porius derives from supporting the magician, which now seems like 'power over this captured god of time', reinforces Myrddin Wyllt's association with the female principle. But the physical description suggests an ancient earth-goddess while Porius's discovery hints at a Jungian collective unconscious which the magician could tap at will, enlarging his identity until it embraces other identities, escaping at will 'into others' (*P*, p. 60), discovering beneath its own 'obstinate opacity', a virtual identifying with others.

This idea, that the individual could escape from the personality and all self-projections into the collective psychic life of the animate and inanimate world, has been suggested before by Powys. It is a factor in the Wessex novels.

Normally, the penalty gladly paid for such experience is total rejection of the world of action. If a sensitive of this sort tries to act positively as well as receive, his sensations and unique claims are driven away, as Quirm felt that his were after he had displayed his occult Celtic knowledge in journalism. Geard is exceptional in being able to act positively, as well as receive his intimations, and for this reason he is a magician.

Myrddin Wyllt, despite his weakness and his submission to Nineue can also act as well as receive. He is not only a 'medium for unseen forces' (*P*, p. 105) but a magician who works magic. His act of magic is the restoring of Blodeuwedd to her own shape (Chapter XXVIII). This story from the *Mabinogion* is used in *Porius* to assert Myrddin Wyllt's association with the female principle. In the *Mabinogion*, Blodeuwedd, a girl created from flowers to be the wife of Llew Llew Gyffes, is unfaithful to him, and Gwydion, the magician, punishes her by turning her into an owl.

In *Porius*, the white owl is drawn to Myrddin Wyllt as indeed all animals and birds are, and he restores her to her former girlish shape. Cavaliero has pointed out[7] that in the original unabridged version of *Porius*, the freeing of Blodeuwedd is firmly anti-Christian, with 'acid reference' to the young priest's praise of Gwydion's 'noble morality' in punishing Blodeuwedd's 'murderous infidelity to the man whose desires she had been created to satisfy'. Enough is left in the published version to show that this magic act is in direct contrast to the Christian ceremony that directly preceded it, the burial of Porius's father, Prince Einion. The independent, adulterous Prince is sealed underground by broken rocks and Christian ritual. The independent, adulterous flower-formed girl is released from her prison of beak and feathers by Myrddin Wyllt's earth-magic. Morfydd's reaction of out-rushing sympathy for this strange being is to do with her certain knowledge that 'every feminine creature' (*P*, p. 656) had found a champion at last. Powys here explicitly connects Myrddin Wyllt's magic with the female principle and shows both to be in direct contrast to the cult of Christ. His magic is earth-magic; he is sustained by his affinity with the earth and its animals. After prophesying wildly he is restored by the sight of horse and cow. Animals flock to him.

The magician's connection with Cronos is shown most fully in Chapter XV when his mind journeys back through time. The nature of this excursion is obscure. It is more like 'ponderings over obscure memories (*P*, p. 280) than a 'mystical trance', but the dreamer himself is unsure whether he remembers or imagines it. The trance takes the form of a 'memory' of the 'first Golden Age, when he, as Cronos, had driven away the monstrous Titans, Briareos, Cottus and Gyes', and stood 'on the misty ridge at the end of the world'.

The landscape of the fantastic spot is rendered in a way reminiscent of Turner's painting which brings out the essential atmosphere of a locality by great swathes of watered colour, and with a few strategic details. Powys evokes the mist, the 'ice-cold gusts', the rocks, the greyness and the 'Tartarean winds', and makes this fantastic landscape real by concentrating on one detail, the changing frost patterns on the rock. The eddies of ice-cold air created

all manner of fantastic scrawls and curlecues and hieroglyphs, all of them to be dissolved as soon as they appeared, but only to be re-formed again in endless and infinite succession. (*P*, p. 283)

This comparison, with its suggestion of life forms continually dissolving and reforming, belongs to the same world-view which sees Myrddin Wyllt as the incarnation of fluid and infinitely varying forms of life.

Myrddin Wyllt/Cronos catches a glimpse of 'the face of Styx herself (*P*, pp. 284–5). The effect of this face on the onlooker produces 'a sense of inescapable doom'.

It is the constant reference back to natural details which prevents *Porius* from becoming empty fantasy and gives the book its sense of exciting strangeness and possibility. Myrddin Wyllt is jerked from his doom-laden trance by a homely physical sensation, that of

a bright-eyed water-rat, assiduously and with absorbed and intense concentration licking his knuckle. (*P*, p. 286)

This sensation restores Myrddin Wyllt immediately, and it seems an answer from all the 'doomed creatures of the earth to the eldest daughter of backward-flowing Oceanus'. The physical sensation of contact with this precisely-balanced water-rat suffuses him with such satisfaction that it more than adequately answers the cosmic despair of this 'strange Being'. (It is the details of the precisely balancing feet that saves the description of the rat from being sentimental.)

This, the certainty and importance of physical sensation, is the only reality upon which Powys will rest. The tiny tongue of a water-rat is more real and more satisfying than the possibility of being a god. Everything is a possibility in a 'multiverse'. Only one thing is a certainty, physical sensation.

It is Porius who presents this certainty in the strange clash of atmospheres, ideologies and mythologies. Like other Powys-personae he is not only very sensitive to sensations but has evolved a mental process which is allied to this sensitivity. He visualises every crisis or personality in terms of 'some particular physical sensation' (*P*, p. 32). The more frequently they recur, the more definite the physical image grows, mysteriously and apart from his will. The image always has some curious connection with the thought or circumstance it represents. The 'mysterious mental process' was something that fused together physical image and incident or personality as, in *Wolf Solent*, Wolf's 'yellow bracken' conjured up Gerda for him.

Porius's habitual mode of awareness was in this mode of associative sensation. The process, not of symbol, but of association, was first noted in its early, crude manifestation in *Wood and Stone*. It is a psychologically accurate observation of the way chance-seen or chance-felt objects are swept up and synthesised by the memory or the imagination into a vibrant image, fusing with some incident, or character, to become, not a symbol, but a sort of memory bank which functions as a psychic sensation. It is these that Wolf Solent is described as hunting 'like a mad botanist' and they are 'indescribable, indescribable' because they are store houses of sensation and memory.

In *In Defence of Sensuality*, Powys describes this process as 'the bread of old memories dipped into the milk of new sensations',[8] a good description as it brings out both will and appetite, two qualities that characterise this 'sensation-seeking'. Its suffused sexual element is brought out in *Porius* also. Porius uses this 'characteristic mental peculiarity' to 'cavoseniargize', a deliberately grotesque and ridiculous word used to detract from any leanings towards the mystical (*P*, p. 403). This is referred to as a 'particular form of lotus-eating' (*P*, p. 82) and a 'secret game' (*P*, p. 84), and it involves a detached immersion in the physical world almost impossible to describe:

> to feel this first and last sensation of the human body and soul in harmony you had at once to unite things and isolate things, to immerse yourself in things and to escape from things. It was anything but easy.

This is a willed action, but its practice involves passivity, detachment, escape. Porius's 'submissiveness' to his mother, Morfydd, and his duties is stressed. His willingness to wait upon the event, however, does not render him incapable of dealing with it. It is just not important. He simply feels in his 'blood and bones' rather than his conscience that if his pleasure is found in the 'indiscriminate impact of inanimate elements and inanimate objects upon his senses', then it is foolish to plan for anything that does not further his 'cavoseniargizing' (*P*, p. 403).

The fact that 'Nature' had given him 'such responsive senses' was enough. Powys uses the reciprocity between these responsive senses and the elements as a mode of conveying the matter of the novel. Porius realises that the dominant urges of his interior life take on, not an 'intelligible symbolic shape' (*P*, p. 41) communicable to others,

> but rather some accidental, chance-bestowed pattern of form and colour that in itself was quite meaningless and very often absurd.

Porius is remarkably clear and methodical in his analysis of the experience and careful to discriminate between alternative interpretations of it. Powys has used this fetishistic response to nature as a narrative technique before, most notably in *Wolf Solent*. In *Porius*, however, this method is most fully explored.

Chapter I shows Porius on the watch-tower of the Gaer fortress. A vast amount of information and a complex plot is introduced through this centre of consciousness and his reaction to the mist of that late October afternoon. The pictorial, topographical and historical setting is presented through this interaction. The mist, however, takes on other qualities, bestowed on it by Porius's mind.

> Wavering and fluctuating in its advances and retreats, and only tangible to the sensitive skin by a faint impact of wetness and chilliness, the mist rises, it would appear, by its own volition, or by the will of the divine water, straight out of the river, and unaffected by wind or sun assumes, weak creature as it is, the dominant and mastering control of a whole unreturning day. This rape of a day by the weakest of her children was more significant of that spot than any other of Nature's methods. (*P*, p. 5)

Chapter I also stresses the particularly submissive and peace-loving temperament of Porius, who hated to make decisions. The affinity between the 'weakest' of natural phenomena and the submissiveness of Porius is not mentioned, but cannot be missed. Its 'mastering control', therefore, is a pointer in the novel, much as Wolf's use of heavy classical allusion about Gerda is a clue to their subsequent relationship. There is also a suggestion of

Powys's Taoist interests here; in the weak conquering the strong.
It has an effect, a personal, conscious one, on Porius. The
ambiguous colour from the stubble spreads towards him like a
presence.

Porius himself provides the significance of the stubble-mist, a
purely private one rising from his consciousness of impending
problems and personalities, and a little later gives it an overt
symbolic meaning which is dismissed as soon as uttered; that an
inscrutable power from the 'stubble of the world's past' was
threatening his future. Porius's contemplation of the recent past
continues. He remembers the murder of Morfydd's brother,
incited by the Christian priest, the Modrybedd's despair, and the
strange rumour of 'gigantic footprints' after the disappearance of
the body.

Porius now changes his imaginative use of the mist image. Its
significance now is to isolate and make prominent the dwellings of
those who affected his life; the Modrybedd, the priest, Morfydd.
But while Porius's mind is playing with the external natural world
in this way, the image of the mist is becoming more dominating in
the novel. Next, it reminds Porius of Morfydd. When moved by
anger or tears, there always appeared on her forehead 'a livid
patch of just that precise tint' (*P*, p. 10). This rather pedantic,
detached memory connects the mist even more closely with
Porius's concerns. Soon the mist is associated with the past, with
the childhood that Porius shared with Morfydd and his cousin
Rhun.

Porius has endowed and then extracted from this natural
phenomenon of mist and stubble field different types of
significance; a passive but powerful sexuality, a slow human per-
sistence, an oppressive arbitrary power, an isolating spot-light, a
reminder of Morfydd's face under stress, the comforting memory
of their joint childhood.

Porius is reluctant to leave the watch-tower, and the 'liberating
obscurity of this immense catafalque of mist' which, while it did
not heal or solve problems, gave him an 'inflow of strength' to
view humorously 'conflicting currents of fate' (*P*, pp. 10–11).
Strength flows from this natural phenomenon, which Porius has
endowed with so much of himself. The significance is from
himself not from the natural environment. But the image is
significant to the reader as well; the 'confused and conflicting
currents of fate' and his 'desire as to the issue' 'remained wavering

and uncertain'. It is the mist also which is confused, conflicting wavering and uncertain. In this way the mist becomes, for the reader, an objective correlative for the whole state of Porius at the beginning of the novel. This is due not only to all the meaning that Porius has been pouring into it and extracting from it, but to a significance that has been built up from this and aided by subtle hints from the author. Apart from the significance of the mist image itself, its function in the first chapter is to provide a unifying factor to pull together the complexities of what could well be a very muddled and diffuse plot.

The image of this Autumnal mist recurs throughout the novel. The night before the wedding of Porius and Morfydd, Brochvael connects it with sex.

> And with this sense of the piling up of mountainous vast earth-ridges of dead leaves, from whose decomposition emanated a deadly sweet sexual longing that seemed to be diffused through the whole approach of this unnatural mist from the precipices of Cader Idris. (*P*, p. 448)

By this time, the image contains more meaning. Cader Idris was the home of the almost legendary aboriginal giants, the 'Cewri'. Porius's great-grandmother had been 'a giant-waif from Cader Idris' (*P*, p. 14) and his enormous strength he felt to be inherited from these 'prehistoric aboriginals'. This was vital to Porius's sense of inmost identity; a consciousness of a 'Titanic brood' (*P*, p. 125), older than Troy or Argos in his veins. (The mention of 'Titanic' connects the Cewri with Cronos and Myrddin Wyllt.) Later, when the Christian priest is inciting the crowds to kill Myrddin Wyllt, and the magician is crouching and muttering into the earth, the atmosphere changes, not only physically but psychically, and the mist arrives as if in answer to Myrddin Wyllt's invocation from the direction of Cader Idris (*P*, p. 485). Its arrival causes, or coincides with (it is not clear which) the death of the priest,

> his eloquence died down under the corpse-like chill of this unnatural niwl or 'death-fog', the shock was more than any life-force could bear,

and in the mist, Brochvael glimpses 'two gigantic figures passing

ɔy' whose smell left behind a 'desperate unspeakable craving'.
The mist departs as quickly as it comes, and Brochvael and the
ʒewish doctor indulge in one of the many nervous, pedantic
ırguments which Powys uses as a bulwark against total
ıcceptance of the numinous and other-worldly, as he used the
ɔsychological treatise about the death of Geard in *A Glastonbury
Romance*.

The doctor rebuts Brochvael's talk of hallucination by a string
ɔf analogous examples, two oxen seeing a Behemoth, or two
ɖesert men glimpsing 'the sons of God' or two conger eels
suddenly conscious of a sea serpent. This switch from religious to
ınimal metaphor ends with the ambiguous 'men not made as we
ıre made'. What is evoked is a picture of primitive, almost god-
ike monstrous beings.

The normal world of Edeyrnion is an uneasy tension between
ɖifferent races and religions. So at first the Cewri giants seem to
ɔe merely the last of a barbaric species, ogres to frighten civilised
settlements. But, as the novel progresses, it becomes clear that
:hey are, like Myrddin Wyllt, part of the lost 'Age of Gold'. This is
ıot a spiritual other-world but a physical, magical older world.
[ts image is the mist, water vapour rising from the earth,
ınglamorous but overwhelming. Porius's 'life-illusion', a word
ɳot mentioned in the novel, shows his awareness of this older
world. There are none of the interior self-dramatisations in which
Wolf Solent indulged. But as Solent had his aqueous green world,
so Porius has a vision and a myth which is from his inmost being.
[t involves no dualist and moral imperatives, except to continue
'cavoseniargizing'. It centres on the Cewri giants. The fact that he
is descended from them through his great-grandmother gives rise
to the atavistic myth that these Titans practised
'cavoseniargizing'. He feels that his barbaric ancestress taught his
family

> some old Cader Idris trick of lifting this jealous past and crazy
> future off their feet while you hugged the present. (*P*, p. 139)

There is an explicit sexual element in this (*P*, p. 146).

Although Nineue, Morfydd and Bloddeuwedd are of the
familiar boy/girl type, the real avatar for Porius is the young
Cewri giantess. As Christie personified Wolf's ideal, so the
giantess is

the very Creiddylad of his secretest broodings, and yet a real living, breathing, goddess-like young girl. (*P*, p. 517)

Porius glimpses the Cewri giants, father and daughter, on hi wedding day (Chapter XXII). He leaves Morfydd's bed when h hears that the Cewri are carrying off corpses and eating them (They are shown as ogres rather than noble savages. Powys doe not sentimentalise them. He also mentions Cronos/Myrddir Wyllt eating his children.) The meeting of Porius and the giantess is immediately followed by their sexual union. He is completel satisfied by this fulfilling of his inner myth. He is in essence aboriginal and realises a coming together and wholeness of hi inmost identity. There is none of the intellectual unity of though and feeling between the lovers which Wolf and Christie show, o John and Mary Crow. Personality is not important. The lovers are described as 'primeval forms of matter'. Porius and the giantess have a primordial bond.

Close on their union 'on that day of stubble-coloured mist' (*P* p. 517) comes the death of both the giantess and her father. Sh saves Porius from her father's blow by taking it herself. The gian seizes her body and leaps into the tarn. After this, the centra symbol of Porius's mental life is changed; it is not the giantess but the mysterious lake in which her body lay. It exists as a 'portion of his consciousness' (*P*, p. 525). This lake image recur with the stubble-coloured mist as a significant symbol. Eventuall it becomes for Porius a kind of Grail vision:

a chasm opened into something deeper yet, an ecstasy of life worship indescribable in words, (*P*, p. 538)

This mental image, 'a sight which from henceforth he could cal up at any moment', becomes a key to another dimension, a signi ficant and numinous experience.

That sight and his eternally varying reactions to it would from henceforth be *his* voyage into another world, *his* visit t Caer Sidi!

Myrddin Wyllt's earth-magic and his Titanic origins; the primitive Cewri; Porius's muscular strength; the two Cewri sentences of gnomic wisdom 'Tread the earth amorously. Endure and Enjoy to the end', and the passivity of both Myrddin Wyllt and Porius which enables them to follow these precepts and plunge their senses into nature until a sense of another dimension is reached; all these aspects are contained in the image of the stubble-coloured mist. This mist encloses a world where all Powys's themes and obsessions meet and are dealt with at greater length and with greater tolerance than in earlier novels.

The obsession of *Wood and Stone* about the weak and strong is here dealt with definitively, without any sado-masochistic overtones. The Dostoeivskian 'ill-constituted' are shown to be, as in *A Glastonbury Romance*, the magicians and the bards whose sensitive response to nature gives them great power. The 'psychic bond' (*P*, p. 551) of Porius and Myrddin Wyllt works on behalf of the weak. Porius is the

> formidable protector of the imaginatively eccentric, the emotionally weak, the mentally disturbed, the nervously deranged. (*P*, p. 536)

This is made particularly clear at the end of the novel when Porius, after struggling through a landscape of rock and icy mist similar to Myrddin Wyllt's Tartarean waste at the edge of the world, frees the trapped magician from his rock tomb. Porius hears, 'like a mist among mists' (*P*, p. 681), a vast, indescribable, multitudinous murmur, of all the weak, terrified, unbeautiful, unconsidered, unprotected creatures, for whom Myrddin Wyllt is plotting 'a second age of gold'. The weak are brought into this unifying image of the mist and connected therefore with the passive strength and sensitivity of Porius, the magic of the primitive Titan and the sensitive reciprocity they both have with the natural world.

It is the weak and disturbed boy-bard, Taliessin, who voices the sensationist pluralism Powys had come so fully to endorse. He is described as an 'elemental' (*P*, p. 414) devoid of all sex instincts and characteristics. His poetry is the artistic expression of the Powys cult of the sceptical sensationist in a multiverse. In his poetry, he 'plunges' into the essential being of the thing described, carrying his impressionability into what appears to the uninitiated (*P*, p. 415) to be a drop of lifeless water.

Powys spent some years working on a life of Keats, and was probably influenced by Keats's letter describing the 'Chameleon

Poet'.[9] This Keatsian sensuous absorption in the present pheno
menon is allied to an attitude of total undogmatic scepticisn
rejecting all religions and philosophies, and this attitude is learn
from nature.

> The 'I feel' without question, the 'I am' without purpose,
> The 'It is' that leads nowhere, the life with no climax,
> The 'Enough' that leads forward to no consummation.... (*P*
> p. 417)

Cavaliero's comment that 'to celebrate the significance o
everything is to assert the significance of nothing',[10] can b
challenged by reference to the pantheist doctrine which cele
brates God in all things, or Hinduism which asserts that everythin
is a fragment of the Absolute. Powys is not verging on nihilisr
here, and this can be seen by putting the verse in its context wher
it is seen as humorous and tolerant. Taliessin sits down and con
templates some straw, until a relation is formed between the two
'though of course the chances were entirely in favour of it being
one-sided affair, (*P*, p. 418). The parenthesis is a strategy typica
of Powys's management of tone in a difficult context, a 'mystica
experience'. What is so often associated with pretentious utter
ances is lightened by a touch of casual humour. Yet what is des
cribed is a serious mode of meditation. When Taliessin lets 'hi
whole soul sink into a multiple consciousness of the material o
our planet in its various immediate manifestations' (*P*, p. 419)
Poeys anchors his meditation in the real and homely by recallin
the boy's fondness for honey.

Brochvael's prayer to 'Chance the Saviour' (*P*, p. 218),

> left all the doors of mystery so wide open that the crafties
> denial of anything beyond the senses was betrayed in the utter
> ance.

To believe in any one thing beyond the senses would be to close al
doors but one. To deny that there was anything beyond the sense
would be to be instantly belied by the draught through all th
doors. To leave all the doors of perception open in this wa
permanently would require a 'super-porous' receptive sensitiv
who could sustain and heighten sensation by an effort of the will
Another parallel with Keats can be drawn, his theory of Negativ
Capability.

A contemporary essay in *Obstinate Cymric* shows the difficulty Powys had in adequately expressing this sensation.

> What it really amounts to is an attempt to use in some kind of psychic synthesis, all the senses together, in a mysterious fusion of the ego with the non-ego[11]

The clumsiness of this, which Powys himself admits, rather disarmingly calling himself a 'quack', is obvious, despite the fact that Powys for many decades had been attempting to describe his habitual mode of consciousness. In some of his works of fiction he succeeded. The rejection of dualism and all imperatives, whether social, sexual, or religious, enabled him to cultivate a multiverse, and his detached ironic scepticism enabled him to sustain and present an ecstatic perception of the world reminiscent of Wordsworth's in *The Prelude*.

Powys speaking of *Tintern Abbey* differentiates between the perception and the meaning of it; pantheism;

> The mystery of life unrolls itself before us in sufficient majesty and tragic beauty to need no turning of the organ-grinder's handle of holy rapture to increase what we feel in its presence.[12]

Bertrand Russell's definition of mysticism;[13] that the experience is no doubt valid, but the meaning or philosophy cannot be deduced, would no doubt be acceptable to Powys here. Powys stresses his admiration for Wordsworth, describing himself as an 'old Wordsworthian' and remarking that he has nourished his inner life on his poetry for more than sixty years. But he rejects Wordsworth's larger spiritual framework.

Powys's proposition, 'We're here because we're here'[14] is a flippant reduction of a serious theme he was struggling always to present without reducing, a theme that could so easily emerge in the repetitive boredom of the existentialist. The experience of the human race is present in the individual mind. Powys's view is joyously anarchic.

> We're here because we're here. 'Hallelujah! I'm a bum'. 'Bums' indeed of a pluralistic, strung-along irrational multiverse are we; and yet in our hornless skull are the great gods and little gods.

Powys, in the same essay, emphasises the fluidity of his soul as 'wavering mist'[15] that can assume the shape of anything.

The humorous self-deprecation, 'I'm a bum', cannot entirely hide the achievement, in merely personal terms, of emerging from an upper-middle-class Somerset vicarage through the glaring single vision of Victorian moral imperatives, troubled with the obsessions outlined in *Autobiography* and ending on this mature, humorous note of sceptical acceptance.

The fear of the female, so apparent in *Ducdame*, has been transmitted into a reverence for the 'female principle'. (Without discussing the truth or falsehood of this concept as psychology or philosophy, it is clear that Powys produces fascinating character studies and explorations of individual women, and the process culminates in *Porius* where the 'female principle' is shown convincingly in fictional terms to be the means of true wisdom.) The obsessive need for moral categories outlined in *Confessions of Two Brothers* is replaced by a sunny anarchism, a humorous acceptance and liking for individuals, however diverse and odd, and a celebration of their foibles, fantasies and indignities. The desire for revelation has been replaced by the possibility, never denied, never overtly stated, of experience of other dimensions. The quest to understand the meaning behind his experiences of Nature becomes a desire to express as precisely and as subtly as possible the significance of these experiences, leaving Words-worthian metaphysic well alone.

At the end of the novel, Porius releases Myrddin Wyllt from Y Wyddfa, the rock tomb on the summit of Eryri. Powys blends the element of fairy tale: the strong man who rejects the temptation of the bad fairy (Nineue) and saves the good magician by his huge strength; with idiosyncratic psychological accuracy: Porius's distaste for Nineue's large nipples, or the way that thinking of Morfydd made him drop the magician's thunderbolt.

The next morning, Porius finds himself at Harlech, hearing through the mist, the waves breaking nearby. Myrddin Wyllt has gone, having presumably undertaken his magical hibernation. Porius, warm and comfortable, decides to enjoy the mist and the smell of seaweed. 'There are many gods; and I have served a great one' (*P*, p. 682). This final confirmation of the reality of sensation in a pluralist multiverse ends the novel on the same note of comfort and release as the ending of *Owen Glendower*. But the multi-verse is more comprehensible, more obvious in a dark age setting than a mediaeval one. Powys connects the political multiverse with the personal one. A 'chance-ruled chaos of souls' (*P*, p. 681) with some touches of kindness and fellow-feeling is better than a world under the blind authority of Caesar or God. A multiverse could be merely terrifying flux, but Powys's anarchic vision has an ample tolerance and imaginative freedom which mitigates its loneliness. Powys shows the 'world of blind authority' in the Christian priests and Myrddin Wyllt escapes until Christian monotheism has disintegrated. (Henry IV's sadistic Archbishop in *Owen Glendower* with his passion for burning Lollards is an example of this 'blind authority' at its most humanly powerful.)

In *Porius*, Powys displays most fully his preferred qualities of tolerance and a passivity which is receptive to all the intimations of the natural world and beyond. Even in its present imperfect form, *Porius* is the most complete philosophical and artistic fulfilment of Powys's life-work. It is a perfect synthesis of his themes and preoccupations. His interest in mythology and history and his obsession with the individual's response to Nature are brought together and unified in *Porius* far more fully than in *Owen Glendower*. The Age of Gold is shown to be concerned with personality rather than a particular, even prehistoric time. The Titanic Eden of the Age of Gold is present in Porius's every response to the natural world. It is present in the Cewri and in Porius's memory of the Cewri. This tolerant receptivity becomes magic in the figure of Myrddin Wyllt who is the bridge between the remote mythical past, the Dark Ages of Porius, and the modern reader. The Titanic personality, primitive, atavistic, receptive, protective and creative, contains the Age of Gold.

8 Summing up

Powys's writing career did not end with the great achievement of *Porius*, but it is hard not to feel that with *Porius* his work had its culmination. Although *Atlantis*, 1954, replaced *Porius* as Powys's favourite book, there seems to be an absence of tension, the presence perhaps even of self-indulgence in the novel. This relaxation is a common factor in his last works, of which *Atlantis* is certainly the best.

These last works, partly novels, partly extended allegories, partly dialogues between familiar Powysian concepts, are of great interest to the many confirmed Powys readers, but it must be confessed that they demand a knowledge of Powysian themes and a delight in Powys's personality which the new reader is not always able to or willing to give. With the partial exception perhaps of *Atlantis*, Powys seems less and less concerned with artistic considerations.

The Inmates, 1952, explores Powys's interest in mental illness, more especially the sanity of the insane. It is set in a madhouse peopled with some very improbable mad people. These, as Powys makes clear from his Preface, are symbols of a truth which Powys calls 'the Philosophy of the Demented'.[1] This philosophy is William James's Pluralism. Powys admits to 'a shameless exploitation wherever possible of my own personal manias' and this is perhaps one of the reasons why the novel seems almost entirely whimsical. Powys had used self-projections before, but had set against them an alien reality or realities with which the Powys persona had to come to some sort of terms. Sylvanus Cobbold in *Weymouth Sands* is an eccentric figure but his incarceration in the Brush Home has a tragic force brought about by the careful presentation of Sylvanus's reality, set against the different realities of those personalities who make up Weymouth. To present a believable multiverse takes more time and artistic care than to create a universe, and this time and care is not bestowed on *The Inmates*. The Glint Asylum is an unrealised background, peopled with eccentric caricatures, from which John Hush and Tenna

Sheer only just emerge as slightly more rounded characters. That Powys was no longer interested in creating an embodied fictional world in the conventional sense can be seen from the sensational ending, where magic, Tibetan adepts and a giant helicopter, combine to release the group of mild eccentrics from their prison.

Atlantis, 1954, continues Powys's search for a world which resembles his mythical landscapes. He embodies it in Ithaca, a world partly Homeric, partly Hesiodic, wholly Powysian. The landscape of one man's mind, set in tension against other realities in the earlier 'realistic' or historical novels, has now spilled out and the magical, animistic and mystical perspectives completely absorb the action. The central Powysian hero, sensuously involved with his responses to the environment, is no longer important or necessary. The result is curiously disappointing. The tension of adjustments and the questioning of issues is absent, and urgency is lost.

However, *Atlantis* is a particularly rich and fantastic fairy-story, with rather more animistic licence than many fairy stories can take. The mood is leisurely, comprehensive, static and visionary. The allegory contains familiar themes. The old Gods of the Age of Gold, Titanic and Matriarchal, have returned to threaten the New Olympians. Atlantis, a sophisticated civilisation, has been drowned because its impersonal and mechanical science will subvert all human values. Religious bigotry and inhuman, intellectual science are shown as evils. The old Odysseus sails west with his son Nisos, whose youthful clarity of vision and desire to see clearly are made use of as narrative devices, and Zeuks, perhaps the most interesting character of the book.

Zeuks, son of Pan, is the spokesman firstly for 'Prokleesis',[2] a defiance similar to John Crow's against

> whatever it is that calls itself the cause of life, or imagines itself to be the cause of life, or is supposed to be the cause of life.

This robust, sceptical, challenging attitude is modified later into a philosophy, or rather an 'essence of living' (*AT*, p. 284) which combined 'forget' and 'enjoy'.

> For by the Styx, it's a question if we can enjoy anything till we've forgotten almost everything.

Zeuks retains his scepticism and his humour, and it is his laughter
that ends the novel. It is not the laughter of a Thersites, cynical
and mocking. Zeuks 'dies laughing' at Zeus, the hard-pressed
tyrant. This may be the last challenge that the rebel makes
against authority, but it also suggests the humorous simplicity of
his resolution:

> Why should I laugh at life rather than challenge it or defy it
> when all I've really got to do is just to enjoy it. (*A T*, p. 285)

The Brazen Head, 1956, is set in a strange, ostensibly thir-
teenth-century but partly mythical West Country. It is far
removed from Wolf Solent's territory. The novel is a debate-
fantasy, using, but hardly characterising, such historical figures
as Roger Bacon, St Bonaventura and Albert of Cologne. The evil
of total negativity, the downward destructive drive first seen in
Hastings in *Ducdame*, is symbolised by Peter Peregrinus whose
magic lodestone or magnet possesses a powerful sinister force.
Theological debates within Christianity are contrasted, not only
with Peregrinus's malicious nihilism, but with Sir Mort Abyssum's
willed appetite for both sensation and lack of sensation. Sir Mort
is also the spokesman for the 'invisible Dimension'[3] of thoughts,
dreams, emotions and sensations which exist independently of the
generations of thinkers and dreamers whose emanations make up
this dimension.

The Brazen Head contains many figures and themes, but they
are not marshalled with any sense of artistic urgency. The book is
episodic and the parts, although interesting, seem unrelated.
Here, Powys definitively turns away from presentation and interrelation of character and environment and shows his interest in
the movement of ideas and concepts in an allegorical setting. It is
hardly surprising that his last works use the mode of science-
fiction, although science has no part in them, and fiction as style
or form is disregarded. In these last works, Powys seems to be
having long discursive arguments with himself, playing jokes with
philosophical concepts, setting one intellectual counter against
another, while introducing as 'characters' those forces and
symbols which have been of great significance throughout his
work.

Up and Out, 1957, shows Time as a slug being swallowed by
Eternity. God, the Devil and the human protagonists decide to

commit suicide, having seen that the stars have already done so.
The companion story, *The Mountains of the Moon*, is less overtly
symbolic, but still full of philosophical disquisitions. *All or
Nothing*, 1960, returns to the dualist theme of the early novels.
Destruction and Creation are symbolised by Bubble and Squeak,
seemingly a 'fossilized skull', and a 'petrified flower bowl', on
either side of an overhanging rock.[4] Upon the 'fossilized skull'
blobs of earth were forming a pillar, while on the 'flower-bowl'
water drops were bursting bubbles. In this humorous way, Powys
discusses the dualism of creation and destruction.

After a series of space travel adventures, in one of which they
encounter the Cerne Giant, the young protagonists meet Queen
Boadicea, the imprisoned matriarch, who reconciles the duality.

> All is not Nothing, neither is Nothing All, but both of them
> have one home-star, where they can sink to eternal quiescence,
> or mount to ever-lasting activity, and that home-star, my
> children, is the heart in everyone of us. So goodbye, my dears.[5]

You and Me, *Two and Two*, and *Real Wraiths* were written
during the last few years of Powys's life and published posthu-
mously in 1974 and 1975. They bear the marks of extreme old
age. In a sense they are a grotesque shorthand of Powysian
beliefs, attitudes and inevitable questions. *You and Me* and *Two
and Two*, as the titles suggest, are concerned with different kinds
of dualism. *You and Me* begins with an essentially Powysian
sentence,

> I was born outside this whole bloody Universe; yes, outside
> all the Universes that were or will be.[6]

This is sporadically about the dualism of the self and the not-self,
and 'Um', the creature from outside matter, caricatures the
Powysian outsider of earlier novels who feels he comes from a
different planet. *Two and Two* follows a wandering magician
'Wat Kums' through known and unknown Infinity on the back of
the Titan Typhoeus.

There is an abundance of scraps of ideas and themes in these
three stories, but the recurrent motif is 'space travel' into nothingness. They could be described as meditations on death and what
it might entail. *You and Me* emphatically denies the possibility of

survival after death, and the author seems to have no great desire
for it. In *Two and Two*, Wat Kum's journey takes him steadily
deep into Nothingness.

> What a comfort not to have the voices, the encounters, the
> intimacies, the walls and ceiling, the arches and stairways, the
> corridors and towers, the doors leading to balconies, . . . [7]

Later, the wanderers, having decided that they created them
selves, leave their bodies behind and plunge into bodiless Mind
where they further ponder the questions raised by existence. The
essence of life lies in 'individuality', created by the pressure of
infinite Nothing. Powys seems to be echoing the views of modern
physicists when he goes on to conclude

> Your view is that our present life never ceases, *not* that some
> thing called our 'soul' goes on living when our body is dead. [8]

There is, in these two books, a real sense of an author, who,
never 'a passionate life-lover', [9] is ready to give up the exhausting
'encounters' and 'intimacies' of an over-busy world to sink into
nothingness. Their tone is not sad or resigned but matter of fact
and humorous, if necessarily low in vitality.

Real Wraiths has more vitality. The style is denser; there is
greater characterisation, and the plot has some interest, despite
many incidents and ideas that are not developed. Tang and
Wang, young sister and brother ghosts, leave North Wales to
travel. Their party increases as they journey through Europe.
Perhaps the most interesting addition is Mr What-Not, the ghost
of a collection of heterogeneous objects flung down on a table.
Inanimate objects can have ghosts. Even a 'fallen tree or
shattered hut' [10] has 'its ghost hovering over it'. It is touching that
Powys's pursuit of the significance of some aspects of the natural
world ends after ninety years in a joke.

The party also includes the Devil, now out of a job since the
death of God, and some classical Gods and Goddesses. Instead of
the journey into Nothingness, the story ends when King Hades,
late of the Underworld, is persuaded by Hecate to 'plunge' and
become 'the living soul of the whole material world' (*RW*, p. 96).
(One is reminded of the end of *Owen Glendower*, when the dying

Prince is described as willing his soul to sink into the Welsh landscape.)

The girl ghost Tang reduces Powys's 'philosophy' to its barest bones, when she says

> I tell you the secret of all human life lies in day-dreaming. Yes, the secret of the universe is not in men fighting and labouring nor in women cooking and dressing-up. It is in men's day-dreams and women's day-dreams. (*RW*, p. 28)

The last works of Powys are of significance to any thematic study of the author, as he collects all the themes of his career and, with various degrees of seriousness and commitment, rearranges and redeploys them. But here, if anywhere, is support for Walter Allen's contention that one can be thoroughly dissatisfied with what Powys has done with his genius (Appendix). But after what Powys had already achieved, such criticism seems captious and ungrateful. His last writings are the intellectual toys of an old man.

In 1955 Powys moved to Blaenau-Ffestiniog where he lived until his death in 1963. Many English writers have settled in Wales, but acceptance by the Welsh has not always followed. Powys was completely accepted. His desire to learn Welsh, his friendliness and interest in others, his knowledge of Welsh mythology and history, his love of the mountains, his continuing energetic and austere life: these made him loved and respected by the Welsh, and he is now regarded as a 'Writer of Wales'. This is quite a personal achievement for an upper-class, public-school Englishman.

Blaenau-Ffestiniog is a town composed of equal parts of slate and rain, set high in the Snowdonia range. Its landscape is dramatic and fantastic rather than pretty: walls of rock and mounds of slate; snaking rows of houses clinging to steep inclines; waterfalls in the back garden. Powys moved there when the slate-quarrying industry was dying and before Blaenau-Ffestiniog was attracting tourists interested in industrial archaeology, and steam trains. This was Powys's final, chosen home, his preferred landscape, very different from Montacute. Perhaps another expatriate writer, Philip O'Connor, provides a clue about the attractions of the mountains.

It is, vis-à-vis English scenery, an abstraction... But it i
abstract in the proper sense (of a refinement of material) and
not in the false anti-material: it would not do to dream it away
into transcendentalism... [11]

To use a metaphor from art, Powys had found the 'Cubist'
expression of Nature after the rich glow of 'Impressionism' in the
West Country.

Powys seems to stand isolated and apart from his contempor
aries, and an attempt should be made to set him in the context of
the writers of his own time. Here we encounter a paradox. In
many ways, Powys's techniques and strategies from *Wolf Solent*
onwards were brilliantly original and experimental in an age of
literary experimentalism. Powys was a contemporary of James
Joyce, Virginia Woolf and D. H. Lawrence. He was working at a
time when the phrase 'stream of consciousness' was not a cliché
but an exciting new discovery, and would surely apply to the
creator of Wolf Solent's internal monologues. The discussion of
sexual relationships was undertaken quite as fully by Powys as by
Lawrence.

The paradox lies in the fact that Powys combined a range
which probably equalled the most advanced techniques and
avant-garde interests of his time with the ample grace of an old-
fashioned littérateur. The title of *The Pleasures of Literature*,
1938, and many of the essays in the volume suggest the world of
Augustine Birrell or George Saintsbury in what was the age of
Leavis's *Scrutiny*. Powys never disowned the tastes of a cultivated
nineteenth-century gentleman; 'The Bible as Literature', Mon-
taigne, Cervantes, Goethe, Homer, Greek Tragedy. Yet he was
more than this. *The Pleasures of Literature* includes Nietzsche,
whom Powys had read with interest before 1914 when he was
virtually a preserve of the Orage circle, it includes Dostoievsky
whom Saintsbury had dismissed; it includes Proust. At a time
when the name of Milton aroused iconoclastic passions, he
prompts Powys merely to a balanced and humane assessment.

Powys saw no need to disown large parts of his cultural heritage
to produce work startlingly unlike anything that had gone before.
Inclusiveness is a vital word in defining Powys's attitudes; his
literary inclusiveness is only a part of his general human inclusiveness. This is where he differs from Lawrence. Powys, it is clear,
felt a narrowness in Lawrence and in much other contemporary

writing. He resisted the fictional tendency to lose the essence of a
particular individual in 'these representative and symbolic sex-
reactions'.[12] He was concerned with a wholeness which he felt
contemporary novelists had lost sight of; they had forfeited a
solidity and all-round credibility.

> They do not *stand out*, these dissected perambulating
> pathoids. They puke and pine, they mime and mow at each
> other, they reveal to a wonder their 'stream of consciousness',
> but their loves and hates are the loves and hates in fish-ponds
> and aquariums.

In the same essay on Dickens, he remarks that the moral
shibboleths had changed since his day but the moral slave-drivers
with their 'unrelenting self-righteousness' were still active. Powys
resisted their attempt to

> take the whims and the fancies, the vagaries and the wanton-
> ness, in a word the *heart*, out of the lives of men and women.

It is difficult to avoid the feeling, especially from its context, that
this criticism is aimed at Lawrence. Powys dislikes what he feels is
an attempt to break up with the stick of moral imperatives the
delicate web of idiosyncracies and fancies that make up a personality. The 'sublime irresponsible mystery of being alive at all'
must not be diminished by being lived to any ulterior purpose.
The word 'irresponsible' is significant. Powys differs from
Lawrence in his belief that humour is one of the guardians of
precious human individuality. He sees the mechanical processing
of modern industrial civilisation as only one of the enemies of life.
He is suspicious of all moralising ideologies.

This is one of the reasons why one cannot helpfully compare
Powys and Lawrence despite what seem areas of superficial
similarity, and despite Powys being, as he said, very much impressed by Lawrence. There is a difference of tone and attitude
which can be seen in the calm lack of engagement in Powys's
reference to his great contemporary;

> I can understand D. H. Lawrence's 'dark gods' which are
> simply erotic attractions and repulsions. (*A*, p. 376)

Both are concerned with inner states of being, but a comparison, for example, of Wolf Solent's sense of the loss of his 'life-illusion' with Lawrence's description in *The Rainbow* of the way in which Anna undermines Will's religious sentiments would be mainly a list of differences despite some superficial similarity in the situations. The Lawrence passage would typically describe extreme states of feeling, of people forced, in intense passion, to understand the truth about themselves and others. Language is pushed to the limit, and sometimes beyond the limit of what it can express. In Powys there is none of this frenzied tension of insistence. Thought processes may be mysterious but they unfold with quiet inevitability. Both Cavaliero and Brebner have pointed out this basic difference between the two writers. Here were two contemporary writers, both dealing with the inner life and the intricacies of sexual experience, but with little light to throw on each other. One simple point is perhaps worth making. Lawrence wrote *The Rainbow* and *Women in Love* in his early thirties. Powys's major novels were written in his sixties. The more meditative, detached and deliberate tone is not altogether surprising in a much older man. Indeed, Powys's age is possibly a factor in his standing outside the literary movements of his time. He was not a youthful iconoclast of the 1920s. He simply went his own way.

Powys was certainly interested in contemporary 'stream of consciousness' writers. He wrote a book on Dorothy M. Richardson, paid generous tributes to Joyce, acknowledged that Proust had taught him

> a certain trick of taking the unpoetic details of daily life as if they were just as extraordinary... as any Venetian palaces or Alpine peaks.[13]

Yet despite his interest in and enjoyment of these writers, he saw them as offering only one facet of literary experience and not the most significant. Speaking of Joyce and Proust, he remarked in 1938:

> Neither a gnomic style throwing alluring and tantalizing stumbling blocks before un-erudite and unphilological minds, rousing snobbish satisfaction in some and infuriated facetious-

ness in others, nor long-winded struggles to find the secret of
the Eternal in our Memory are absolutes in the art of writing.
Neither literature nor philosophy began with these discoveries;
nor will they end with them.[14]

He then sets against this Rabelais' question; why did men think
they were so wise now, and others so foolish before? A man of
wide culture and enormous reading, he felt no incongruity in
setting Rabelais against Proust since for him literary experience
covered hundreds of years. Similarly, in setting Powys in his context, one must use, if one can, the whole Humanist tradition of
European culture. But ultimately one must rest with Jeremy
Hooker's suggestion that it was not Powys's provinciality or
eccentricity which distanced him from contemporary literary
currents but

> his questioning of all theories and catchwords in the remorse-
> less process of thinking for himself.[15]

But Powys's particular quest is the quest of the Romantic poets
– to understand the significance of personality through its
relationship with Nature. That he came to see his environment as
flux is one of his strengths. To be a Romantic in an existentialist
world; recognise it for what it is, and still carry on as a Romantic,
enduring and enjoying and endowing Nature with the same
numinous significance requires an enormous feat of the will and
imagination. It is almost as if Coleridge, on one of his wilder
flights of fancy, wandered into a production of *Waiting for
Godot*, and while enthusiastically participating in the conversation, found the significance of the experience in his sensitive
response to the aged look of the boots set against the bare tree.
 There is much in Powys that reminds one of the first-generation Romantics. Coleridge's ponderings on the creative process of
the Imagination in *Anima Poetae* are an obvious example of this.

> In looking at objects of Nature I seem rather to be seeking, as
> it were asking for, a symbolic language for something within
> me that already and forever exists, than observing anything
> new.

Coleridge saw that his joyful perception of natural thing
depended on what his 'Soul' was capable of bringing to the
experience.

> Ah! from the Soul itself must issue forth
> A Light, a Glory, and a luminous Cloud
> Enveloping the Earth!
> > ('Dejection A Letter')

In this poem, Coleridge states that his 'shaping spirit of Imagina
tion' is suspended because of his loss of 'Joy' which is

> The Spirit and the Power,
> That wedding Nature to us gives in Dower
> A new Earth and new Heaven.

His creative imagination produces a particular vision of life with
out which natural things are 'lifeless Shapes'.

> I may not hope from outward Forms to win
> The Passion and the Life, whose fountains are within!

In *The Prelude*, Wordsworth also stresses that the mind is no
merely a passive recipient of visionary visitations but 'a sensitiv
being, a creative soul'. He also discusses 'spots of time', distinctiv
memories which can be revived to 'nourish' the mind. The role o
memory in Powys's sensations is very important, as is the nature o
contrast. They were important also for Wordsworth. In Book XI
of *The Prelude*, he describes a childhood ride to an ancien
gibbet on the 'rough and stony moor', which frightened him
Afterwards he saw a girl carrying water; an 'ordinary sight', bu
one of a 'visionary dreariness' which he lacked words to describe
The significance of the contrasting experience was somethin
outside the normal. He goes on to describe his youthful sel
revisiting the scene with 'the loved one' at his side. Agai
contrasts of emotion heighten experience; the remembrance o
'visionary dreariness' gave 'radiance more sublime' to 'youth
golden gleam'.

Powys's cult of the 'sensations' has a willed, purposeful qualit
about it. He deliberately used memory and contrast to produc
them. He also cultivated some particularly Keatsia

characteristics; absorption in the present physical moment and undogmatic acceptance of mysteries without 'any irritable reaching after fact and reason'.

This deliberate cultivation of sensations also places Powys with the Aesthetes. The preoccupations of, for example, Walter Pater have obvious parallels with those of Powys. The sensations of Marius's 'Cyrenaicism' in *Marius the Epicurean*, his 'visionary awareness of everyday life'[16] are similar to those of Powys. Marius also deliberately cultivated himself for the reception of sensations. Assuming "Life as the end of Life',[17] it was desirable to be

> refining all the instruments of inward and outward intuition,... till one's whole nature became one complex medium of reception,...

But Pater shows that this 'vision' raises moral issues. The place for a 'principle of conduct'[18] must be found. This question is brought up again in two stories, 'Denys l'Auxerrois', *Imaginary Portraits*, 1887, and 'Apollo in Picardy', *Miscellaneous Studies*, 1893. In both, Pater uses classical and pagan personifications to depict natural forces. Their effect is amoral, Dionysian, life-enhancing and destructive. Pater sees the ecstatic apprehension of the surface of life as pagan and issues a warning; it might be dangerous to return to a 'condition of life' in which 'the values of things would, so to speak, lie wholly on their surfaces' unless we could also regain a childish unconsciousness, an 'appropriate lightness of heart'.[19]

The beauty of the natural world, Pater saw, was something outside the laws of good and evil. The moral laws of a later Christian age are at variance with the fluid natural exuberance of paganism. Pater was a very solemn sort of hedonist, a worried epicurean. Similarly, his vulgarisers, Oscar Wilde and the poets of the 1890s, sought lugubrious and murky sensations among the fragments of their public-school classicism. Wordsworth's apprehension of 'unknown modes of being' became by the end of the century a self-consciously naughty hunt for a nude Pan in a suburban shrubbery. The minor literature of the Victorians and Edwardians contains several of these Pans. The first poem to appear in John Cowper Powys's *Odes and Other Poems*, 1896, is 'To the Great God Pan'. Pan enters the caustic stories of Saki and even the delightful riverside world of *The Wind in the Willows*.

Perhaps the most familiar Pan stories today, because of their continued publication, are those of E. M. Forster.

Arthur Machen's *The Hill of Dreams*, 1907, is a direct heir of Pater and the Aesthetes, and could, if better known, make a far better comparison with Powys than Lawrence. It deals with material very familiar to the Powys reader. *The Hill of Dreams* is partly autobiographical and shows the author's passionate and sensitive response to the hills of Wales. The early chapters set the rather familiar scene of the lonely boyhood of a bookish outsider, Lucian, son of an impoverished clergyman. Lucian was continually rapt by his vision.

> And there were moments when the accustomed vision of the land alarmed him, and the wild domed hills and darkling woods seemed symbols of some terrible secret in the inner life of that stranger – himself.[20]

Lucian's ambition was somehow to describe this intense affinity. Poor and shy, his contempt for the society which has no place for him helps him to evolve 'a certain process... partly mental and partly physical'[21] to escape into his own mind when he has to encounter other people. He excapes into a fantasy world of paganism. His sensations are fuel for this inner vision, a 'mystic town', a splendid golden Roman city where he and his sweetheart could live.

His love is an extraordinary religion of pain, ritual and passion, rather loosely based on a couple of encounters with a farmer's daughter. The effect of his responses to her is incalculable, evolving into a masochistic liturgy of contrived and fantastic sensation. She herself is unimportant.

> She had been the key that opened the shut palace, and he was now secure on the throne of ivory and gold.[22]

(The way Lucian uses Annie as a 'key' to imaginative sensations is very similar to Wolf Solent's attitude to Christie; she is necessary to his 'life-illusion' but would be denied to save it.)

Lucian refined and exalted sensation until it produced a strange consistent day dream of an ideal paganism. He had

> the philosopher's stone transmuting all it touched to fine gold; the gold of exquisite impressions.[23]

But the Huysmanesque solution brings him to drugs, madness and death, leaving a manuscript full no doubt of exquisite impressions, but unreadable. The detached self-involved sensation-seeking consciousness could perhaps leave nothing else.

Machen points a horrifying moral at the end of *The Hill of Dreams*, which is oddly at variance with the whole drift of the book. The author seems wholly to endorse Lucian's ecstatic mode of apprehension and then shows its terrifying disintegration. The effect is remarkably depressing. But the book has an importance in literary history. How, it implies, can a sensitive aesthete cultivate his ecstatic vision of the world without drowning in his own subjectivity? What about a 'principle of conduct'? These are questions of which Pater was aware. They are questions that Powys answers in his novels. Powys's rejection of moral categories did not result in vulgar paganism but in a liberation and refining of the spiritual understanding. His pluralist sceptical awareness gave rise to a strange blend of phenomenalism and Platonism: that things were essentially as he perceived them but that they had a significance beyond this.

Powys is not a prisoner of his subjectivity. In his novels, subjective reality is set against other realities. Although he brilliantly presents the centre of reality; the self, the creative imagination and the receptive senses, he shows that it has to make many shifts to accommodate itself to the alien reality of other people and the physical world. He bridges the gulf between the inner and outer world. His subtle use of nature imagery fuses the outer world of objects with the inner world of consciousness, creating a significant new reality. Powys stresses the significance of the natural and inanimate outer reality until the texture of the novel is dense with Dickensian solidity, but he also shows that it is the creative imagination which bestows this reality.

In following my argument, I have, of necessity, been obliged to neglect subjects which lay out of my way. Unfortunately it is this dense surface texture of the novels which has suffered neglect. I have not said, and it should be said loud and long, that Powys is an outstanding comic writer, entertaining and diverting on a number of levels. This in itself opens a wide gulf between him and the Aesthetes, despite his use of their themes. The great novels contain not only great themes, like the myth of Glastonbury, tragedies like that of Wolf Solent or the working out in fictive art of the 'multiverse'. They are very pleasing aesthetic objects in which fundamental matters are surrounded by a brilliance of surface detail. Powys's novels are never theses. Although the reader is drawn to the depths of his work, the surface glitters with extraordinarily enjoyable incidentals.

There are many types of comic effect in Powys. The simplest is his revelling in the bizarre and incongruous; Mrs Legge's sitting-room next to the brothel in *A Glastonbury Romance*, with its portraits of ancient civic dignitaries; the many eccentrics of the novels, whether creators of private fantastic worlds or simply exponents of elderly dottiness, hinting at dark secrets or unmentionable preoccupations. Powys frequently uses the gnomic utterance as a comic device, and the deeper currents of the novel are frequently heard behind a stream of half-understood, disconcerting remarks of the aged, the rustic and the mad.

Powys also juxtaposes comedy and tragedy for incongruous effect. In the painful or tragic moments of Powys's novels, little undignified incongruities keep obtruding themselves. Magnus Muir sums up the loss of his love in this vein,

> 'She wins,' he thought, 'I lose. But I am the one who can swallow Bath buns'. (*WSds*, p. 561)

Powys's mixing of modes contains a multitude of nuances; irony, pathos, farce in subtle combinations which suffer in analysis.

The love of incongruity is accompanied by a love of individuality and quirkiness. Powys catches accents, tricks of expression, the particular eddies of personality: the mixture of the gentlemanly and the lubricious in Malakite; Miss Drew, gentlewoman and obsessive, a combination of refinement and lesbian passion at once painful and ludicrous. He explores the world of children, their games, rituals and conflicts; or the world of the very old, their memories and physical exigencies. The attention to the individual, without false dignity, is serious but it is also a rich source of comedy. Sam's mystical vision is accompanied by the necessity of administering an enema to Abel Twig. Whatever philosophical or mystical speculations this may give rise to, it is certain that its chief effect is amusing, and that this is what Powys intends. The vivid particularity and intensity of character is important beyond any thematic considerations.

Powys's sense of the private world of the individual is so marked that it is possible to overlook the role of social comedy in his novels. His fidelity to a forgotten middle-class world of personal austerity, self-discipline and sexual puritanism has been confirmed recently by Angus Wilson.[24] It may be that here, as in the often criticised rustic characters, the reader is missing many subtle effects of social comedy through ignorance. However, enough comes across to suggest that the Dekkers, for example, are brilliant delineations of social types, as well as individuals. The combination of a sense of leadership and social responsibility, self-denial, priggishness and repression, deep love for each other, inarticulacy and wrong-headedness is poignant, convincing and very public-school.

Powys is also adept at catching the interaction of people of different backgrounds, a traditional prop of social comedy, but in his case without the faintest trace of snobbery. Sam's visit to the Geard household, and Geard's relations with the Marquis of P., are good examples of this. Apart from the humour of class and background, Powys is keenly aware of irritable cross-purposes between the sexes, and the mental elbowing between men, the treacherous sympathy between women.

There is no cruelty in Powys's comedy. There is no exclusive satire, there are no sneers. There is room for everyone in his humane, humorous vision. Powys had a strong sense of the world left over after any philosophical statements he may have wished to make about it and it is this feeling of pleasure in the lumber of his vision which makes the surface of his writing so very pleasurable

His greatest achievement, however, is his combination of philosophy and technique. His 'philosophy' suggests a mode of living: to enjoy nature, to simplify and forget problems, and to will the return of pleasant memories. ('Tread the earth amorously. Enjoy and endure till the end' as the Cewri put it.) He advocates a self-conscious 'condition of complete simplicity', which few could attain. Its disciplinary use of the will to control and regulate memory and contemplation makes this mode similar to that of a strict religious contemplative. The result is an ecstatic apprehension of things as they are.

This mode of contemplation, bringing memory to new sensation and savouring the experience, is instrumental in the formation of Powys's style. His alertness to all stimuli of sense, and his sensitivity to the way in which sense experience affects the movements of the mind, produces a prose which imitates the action of the mind, where a sensation gives rise to a memory which forms itself into a complex, significant and vibrant image of sense and thought. One is referred again to the Romantics and particularly Coleridge. (Look, for example at Humphry House's brilliant elucidation[25] of Coleridge's style.) Powys is in the tradition of the first-generation Romantics and his preoccupations are the same; not only minutely to record impressions of the visible world, but also to show its interaction with the creative mind, and to ensure in some way that this interaction, whether it be Powys's 'ecstasy' or Coleridge's 'joy' is continuous.

Appendix: Criticism

Before one considers the body of literary criticism on John Cowper Powys, one has to bear in mind the tone that some critics have used about him. One would not deny that there was a case against him which needed to be answered, however many of the adverse views rested on misapprehensions and misreadings. There is certainly room for debate. What makes such discussion difficult is the flippant and dismissive manner critics have adopted, largely, one feels, to disguise a fundamental absence of sympathy, even incomprehension. It is hard to pin down or to argue with a process of belittling innuendo, which may nevertheless prove extremely damaging.

V. S. Pritchett's review in *the New Statesman*[1] of the Penguin edition of *Wolf Solent* in 1965 may serve as an example of this kind of criticism. It may well have delayed the growth of Powys's reputation at an important stage. Essentially, Pritchett refuses to take Powys seriously at all or even to pay him the compliment of an indignant dislike. His attitude is one of mildly amused dismissiveness and superiority.

> Whether admirers really go for the poet novelist or whether they get most out of the elliptical essayist who appears to be tramping on some solypsistic walking tour in which Dorset and the Welsh border blend with the psychic mysteries to make an ever-dissolving topography I do not know. Perhaps they hear echoes of *A Shropshire Lad* and of the effort to keep the Folk going. Wolf Solent always carries an intensely symbolic walking stick, an object of trust or perhaps also of sexual support.

It is disappointing when a critic will not bother to undertake the job of serious criticism. He offers instead irrelevant jibes at Powys's admirers. Pritchett, certain of the political and social response of his readers, merely touches certain switches designed to provoke automatic laughter: 'walking tour'; *A Shropshire Lad*;

'effort to keep the Folk going'; 'perhaps also of sexual support'. (Powys made the joke about the sexual significance of his walking stick at least forty years before Pritchett did.) A little later, Pritchett speaks of 'scholar gypsy charm', 'calling for ale, collecting and naming wild flowers'. He employs a series of expressions certain to have ludicrous connotations for his audience, in order to denigrate Powys. The expressions themselves are not found in the novels, and represent importations of Pritchett's own. He has turned complex questions into the material for cheap jokes. Pritchett attacks a 'clique', Powys's admirers, but he appeals to the humour of an even narrower clique.

The innuendoes themselves rest on certain assumptions.

> The game of the mystic novelist is a dangerous one, yet (among others) Dostoievsky, one of Powys's masters, showed how it can be played. He turned his questioning and conflicts, and even some of his journalism, into crowds of extremists who are entirely acceptable and at home in their fantastic habitat.

In other words, 'mysticism' in the novel is acceptable if, in some way, it can be made politically and socially 'relevant'.

The easy and flattering assumption of a shared superiority ('One smiles at the rather absurd period charm of these novels') does not disguise a fundamental lack of sympathy or comprehension. Insensitivity is shown in small matters as in large. Pritchett asserts that Powys has no 'comic sense', a view which could scarcely survive even the most cursory reading of the major novels. (One need only point to the 'robber-band' of Volume 1, Chapter 7 of *A Glastonbury Romance*.) Pritchett's final impression is

> that some lettered prehistoric pachyderm was trying with learned pathos, to get in touch with the village grocer, and was distracted by the village girls' garters.

This may be amusing journalism, but it does not begin to be criticism. Pritchett cannot come to terms with the unfashionable Powys and uses jokes to cover his retreat. They are funny jokes, and it may seem that I have made too much of what was meant to be lightweight ephemera. Entertainment, rather than bookselling, is the purpose of newspaper reviews. But whatever the intention, the effect of this article was probably to retard the development of Powys's reputation.

There are more honest attempts to approach Powys. Walter Allen, in his survey of twentieth-century British and American fiction, *Tradition and Dream*, 1964, states the difficulties that arise.

> *A Glastonbury Romance*, for instance, is scarcely shorter than *War and Peace*. Its length is justified by the enormity of Powys's ambition; his vision of man is apocalyptic. It is this that makes him so extraordinarily difficult to get to grips with. It seems to me possible to recognize J. C. Powys's genius and at the same time to be thoroughly dissatisfied with what he has made of it. Being interested in man only in his relation to the universe and to universals, he has set him in a vast mythology of natural forces so alien to the temper of the age as to be impossible for many people to take seriously.[2]

This reaction, part admiration, part irritation, part incomprehension, is an honest description of the feelings of someone reading J. C. Powys for the first time. Allen stresses the difficulty of initial acceptance of Powys's inclusive universe.

Pritchett mentions Powys's 'admirers' and hazards guesses as to what they 'go for'. Perhaps the prevalent notion that J. C. Powys has a fanatical clique of readers lobbying public opinion impedes his recognition as a major novelist. Whatever the truth of this, it is surely irrelevant to Powys's worth. The admirers of Powys include Angus Wilson, George Steiner, J. B. Priestley, George D. Painter, P. J. Kavanagh — hardly fanatics. What is it then about John Cowper Powys and his readers that seems to provoke the contempt so evident in Pritchett's article?

It is certainly true that extravagant claims have been made. Powys's earliest critics emphasised his work's religious significance. Lloyd Emerson Siberell in 1934 hailed him as a sort of philosophical magician,

> John Cowper Powys leads us through the shadows and the stormy surge of confusion that prevails in contemporary literature into the eternal realms of light that lie beyond the gold of his art. Through the gamut of conceits and artifices of

our day comes the voice of the modern Plato uttering truths
that resound against the hills and touch the heart.[3]

This large, but ultimately rather meaningless, critical claim is
perhaps typical of Powys's early admirers, who sometimes knew
him, and were indignant at the response of established criticism.
This 'small group of discriminating followers' who 'resolved that
his influence and wisdom shall not pass on unheralded' have
probably done Powys's critical reputation some harm by
extravagant claims of this sort. They saw him as more than a
novelist, as a sage with a wisdom to communicate.

It is not unknown for poets and novelists to be regarded in this
way. This is how nineteenth-century readers saw Wordsworth,
Browning and Dickens. Before it is dismissed as the inarticulate
yearnings of people who have lost a faith and not yet found an
ideology, it should be borne in mind that serious critics have
suggested that D. H. Lawrence should teach us how to live, and
were doing so at about the same time as Siberell was saying the
same thing about Powys.

These admirers, however inflated their prose, were numerous
enough for Powys to be able to concentrate entirely on novel
writing in the early 1930s, as he himself says in the Preface to
Siberell's book. He certainly had a following of partisan
enthusiasts, and this may have been due, not only to his writings,
but to his personality. Unfortunately they concentrated almost
entirely on what must be called Powys's 'philosophy'. Richard
Heron Ward stressed this in 1935, 'His philosophy, as of course it
must, forms the real stuff of his novels...'[4] Although Powys
called himself a propagandist in *Autobiography*, he did not
intend his works to be regarded entirely as propaganda.

> I should flatly refuse to two classes of persons any claim to be
> regarded as genuine lovers of fiction. The first are those who
> want nothing but moral support and encouragement.[5]

Ward looked on Powys as a religious teacher, calling him the
'logos-utterer', 'displaying a kind of elemental eternity'. That
Ward was not really concerned with Powys's artistic achievement
can be seen from the remark,

> Where John Cowper Powys is concerned there is very little to

distinguish between 'Wood and Stone', published in 1915 and his latest novels.

Ward felt that *Wood and Stone* has 'none of the immaturities of the first novel' because Powys's 'personal conception of life' had already taken place. In this, he totally ignores not only the artistic growth and achievement of that twenty years, but also the intense refining of thought and attitude that accompanied it.

Ward's rather fierce exclusiveness deals summarily with establishment intellectuals,

> It is easy for them to consider something such as 'Glastonbury Romance' which they cannot apprehend, necessarily 'bad', and to condemn it as such, while it is in reality too good for them, and deals with a state of being, a state of spiritual evolution, quite above them.

One can understand a hostile reaction to this. But Ward's book was published in 1935. Several studies have followed, and they show none of this rather touching, totally uncritical euphoria.

Early commentaries tended to include John Cowper Powys in a discussion of the Powys brothers. Louis Wilkinson's several writings on the subject,[6] while providing many interesting anecdotes, do not show any particular sensitivity to John Cowper Powys's novels. The British Council pamphlet[7] discusses the three brothers together. Individual articles and reviews, however, continued to stress the importance of Powys. In 1963, Angus Wilson said:

> there is little doubt that he will stand with James, Lawrence and Joyce in the eyes of future literary critics.[8]

G. Wilson Knight's *The Saturnian Quest*,[9] published in 1964, just after Powys's death, was 'pioneer work'. He traces 'a pattern' of 'deepest meaning' throughout Powys's work and no study of the novels can be completed without acknowledging this original and profound presentation of themes. Wilson Knight purposely avoided judgements of values, however, and this was something still needed.

Kenneth Hopkins in *The Powys Brothers*[10] 1967, discusses him very perceptively, but a 'biographical appreciation' of the three writer-brothers was obviously not the large-scale study and general guide that seemed so necessary after Powys's death. H. P. Collins's *John Cowper Powys: Old Earth-Man*,[11] 1966, is also biographical but is a much larger scale survey of the work. Again the claim is made,

> He must emerge as one of the most challenging and formidable – as he is certainly one of the strangest – figures of our age, and it is as a novelist he must emerge most powerfully.

Derek Langridge's *Record of Achievement*,[12] 1966, traced the development of Powys's reputation as well as listing the editions of his work, and as he says in his 'Introduction', his bibliography was primarily for the 'ardent body of admirers for whom Powys is likely to be their "one of all"' writers. This is an invaluable bibliography as are the Additions to it in Appendix II of *Essays on John Cowper Powys*.

Some small pamphlets were also printed. James Hanley's *John Cowper Powys: A Man in the Corner*, 1969; *John Cowper Powys The Solitary Giant* by Richard Breckon, 1969; and Ellen Mayne's *The New Mythology of John Cowper Powys* in 1968. In 1971, G. Wilson Knight's *Neglected Powers: Essays on Nineteenth and Twentieth Century Literature*[13] included several discussions on Powys.

In 1972, the centenary of Powys's birth, *Essays on John Cowper Powys*,[14] edited by Belinda Humfrey, was published. The editor's Introduction stated the intention to 'begin or provoke more of the close critical study which this generous writer merits', and this is certainly fulfilled in the contents, which by means of individual essays arranged to cover the work chronologically, closely scrutinise aspects of Powys's work. These are augmented by some very useful Appendices, including some unpublished letters and poems by Powys.

In 1973, three more studies came out. *The Demon Within*[15] by J. A. Brebner and *John Cowper Powys: Novelist*[16] by Glen Cavaliero are both full-scale studies of the novels. Cavaliero's critical work places the novels in a literary context and perspective and this is very helpful. Both Brebner and Cavaliero discuss Powys's style and examine its language in some depth. Jeremy Hooker's *John Cowper Powys*[17] in the *Writers of Wales* series is a long essay, that is all too short. I would recommend both Hooker and Cavaliero as excellent critics for those hoping to engage seriously with Powys's fiction.

Morine Krissdottir's *John Cowper Powys and The Magical Quest*[18] is one of the most recently published works on Powys. It is a highly specialised study of mythological, religious and alchemical themes and their parallels in the novels. It is an interesting examination of esoteric and occult matters which are engaging the attention of an increasing number of readers.

Powys Newsletter, published by the Colgate University Press, Hamilton, New York and edited by R. L. Blackmore, was started in 1970. In this country, *The Powys Review*, the journal of The Powys Society, is edited by Belinda Humfrey from The University of Wales and is an important addition to studies of the three Powys brothers.

Powys is a writer who evokes both massive contempt and near idolatry. The truth does *not* lie half-way between the two extremes. There is no golden mean here. Powys is a very great writer. Hooker has said that 'he is a great liberator from ideas which cripple the human being's sense of his potentiality'.[19] The effect of reading his novels is exactly this. It is heady, liberating – it lets you off, but in no light way.

Notes

INTRODUCTION

1. Glen Cavaliero, *John Cowper Powys: Novelist* (Clarendon Press, 1973) p. 183.
2. George Steiner, 'The Difficulties of Reading John Cowper Powys', *The Powys Review* (Spring 1977), 7.
3. Glen Cavaliero, quoted in *The Powys Review* (Spring 1977), 11.
4. Steiner, op. cit., p. 9.
5. Belinda Humfrey (ed.), *Essays on John Cowper Powys* (University of Wales Press, 1972), p. 24.

CHAPTER 1: BEGINNINGS AND ECHOES

1. Llewelyn Powys, *Somerset and Dorset Essays* (Macdonald, 1957). (A selection from two books of essays which were published separately in 1937 and 1935.)
2. John Cowper Powys, *Autobiography* (first published 1934; Macdonald, London, 1967), p. 629. Hereafter cited as *A*.
3. Frederick Davies, 'John Cowper Powys and King Lear: A Study in Pride and Humility', *Essays on John Cowper Powys*, B. Humfrey (ed.) (University of Wales Press, 1972).
4. Louis Wilkinson (ed.), *Letters of John Cowper Powys* (Macdonald, London, 1958), p. 338.
5. Thomas Hardy, *Tess of the d'Urbervilles* (1891, Macmillan, London, 1968), p. 104.
6. Dorothy Van Ghent, *The English Novel: Form and Function* (Harper, New York, 1961), p. 201.
7. Hardy, *Tess of the d'Urbervilles*, op. cit., p. 145.
8. John Cowper Powys, *Wood and Stone* (G. Arnold Shaw, New York, 1915), p. 141. Hereafter cited as *W&S*.
9. John Cowper Powys, *Confessions of Two Brothers* (The Manas Press, Rochester, New York State, 1916), p. 13. Hereafter cited as *CTB*.
10. Roderick Mawr (John Cowper Powys), *The Hamadryad and the Demon*, republished in *The Powys Newsletter Two* (Colgate University Press, 1971).
11. Kenneth Hopkins, *The Powys Brothers* (Dent, London, 1967), p. 38.
12. John Cowper Powys, *Visions and Revisions* (first published G. Arnold Shaw, New York, 1915; reprinted Macdonald, London, 1955), p. 186. Hereafter cited as *VR*.
13. Charles Dickens, *Little Dorrit* (Penguin, London, 1971), p. 70.
14. Fyodor Dostoievsky, *Crime and Punishment* (1866; Penguin, London, 1960), p. 71.
15. Ibid., p. 132.

CHAPTER 2: THE OUTLINE

1. John Cowper Powys, *After My Fashion* (Picador, London, 1980), p. 29. Hereafter cited as *AMF*.
2. John Cowper Powys, *Ducdame* (Grant Richards, London, 1925), p. 301. Hereafter cited as *D*.
3. Louis Wilkinson (ed.), *Letters of John Cowper Powys* (Macdonald, London, 1958), p. 155.
4. John Cowper Powys, *The Pleasures of Literature* (Village Press, London, 1975), p. 131.
5. G. Wilson Knight, *The Saturnian Quest* (Methuen, London, 1964), p. 28.

CHAPTER 3: WOLF SOLENT

1. George Dangerfield, *The Strange Death of Liberal England* (first published 1935; Capricorn, 1961) p. 432.
2. Peter Green, *Kenneth Grahame, a Biography* (London, 1959), p. 116.
3. Dangerfield, op. cit., p. 432.
4. Richard Jefferies, *The Story of My Heart* (1886), quoted by F. C. Happold, *Mysticism* (London, 1963), p. 360.
5. Ibid., p. 356.
6. John Cowper Powys, *Wolf Solent* (Macdonald, London, 1961), p. 95. Hereafter cited as *WS*.
7. Walter Pater, *Marius the Epicurean* (Dent, London, 1963), p. 243.
8. G. Wilson Knight, *Neglected Powers* (Routledge & Kegan Paul, London, 1971), reviewed by Cyril Connolly, the *Sunday Times*, 7 February 1971.
9. Virginia Woolf, *To the Lighthouse* (1927, Penguin, London, 1965), pp. 32–3.
10. Ibid., p. 35.
11. F. W. H. Myers, quoted by Basil Willey, *Nineteenth Century Studies* (1949, New York, 1966), p. 204.
12. John Cowper Powys, *In Defence of Sensuality* (Gollancz, 1930; reprinted Village Press, 1974), p. 7.
13. Ibid., p. 6.

CHAPTER 4: GERDA AND CHRISTIE

1. G. Wilson Knight, *The Saturnian Quest* (Methuen, London, 1964), p. 33.
2. William James, *Varieties of Religious Experience* (1902, Collins, London, 1971), p. 371.
3. Ibid., p. 367.
4. G. Wilson Knight, *The Saturnian Quest*, op. cit., pp. 59–60.
5. See Louis Marlow (Wilkinson), *Welsh Ambassadors*, (Chapman & Hall, 1936) pp. 24, 145.
6. P. Jullian, *Dreamers of Decadence* (Pall Mall Press, 1971), p. 39.
7. William James, op. cit., p. 374.
8. William James, op. cit., p. 372.
9. John Cowper Powys, *A Glastonbury Romance* (first published New York, 1932; Macdonald, 1966), p. 1085. Hereafter cited as *GR*.
10. William James, op. cit., p. 372.

CHAPTER 5: PLACE OF VISIONS

1. I am indebted to a Radio 3 broadcast on Boughton's centenary for drawing my attention to him.
2. Arthur Machen, 'The Great Return', *Tales of Horror and the Supernatural* (Panther, London, 1975), p. 188.
3. Colin Wilson, *The Occult* (Mayflower, St Albans, 1973), p. 65.
4. H. P. Collins, *John Cowper Powys: Old Earth Man* (Barrie and Rockliff, London, 1966), p. 65.
5. G. Wilson Knight, *The Saturnian Quest* (Methuen, London, 1964), p. 36.
6. Ninian Smart, *The Religious Experience of Mankind* (1969, Collins, London, 1973), p. 212.
7. Glen Cavaliero, *John Cowper Powys: Novelist* (Clarendon Press, 1973), p. 180.
8. John Cowper Powys, *Dostoievsky* (first published 1946; Village Press, 1974), p. 19.
9. John Cowper Powys, *Porius* (Macdonald, London, 1951), p. 497.
10. John A. Brebner, *The Demon Within: A Study of John Cowper Powys's Novels* (Macdonald, London, 1973), p. 108.
11. Cavaliero, op. cit., p. 65.
12. Cavaliero, op. cit., p. 75.
13. J. C. Powys, 'The Owl, the Duck, and − Miss Rowe! Miss Rowe!' (Black Archer Press, Chicago, 1930).
14. Brebner, op. cit., p. 108.

CHAPTER 6: LAST LOOK BACK

1. John Cowper Powys (*Weymouth Sands*, Macdonald, London, 1963), p. 341. Hereafter cited as *WSds*.
2. John Cowper Powys, *Maiden Castle*, (Macdonald, London, 1966,) p. 466. Hereafter cited as *MC*.
3. Quoted by R. L. Blackmore, 'Writing the Autobiography', J. C. Powys, *Autobiography*, p. xviii.
4. V. S. Pritchett, *New Statesman*, 2 April 1965 (see Appendix).

CHAPTER 7: THE WELSH NOVELS

1. John Cowper Powys, 'Welsh Culture', *Obstinate Cymric* (1947, Village Press, London, 1973), p. 55.
2. John Cowper Powys, *Owen Glendower* (Bath, 1974), p. 8. Hereafter cited as *OG*.
3. Angus Wilson, 'John Cowper Powys as a Novelist', *The Powys Review* (Spring 1977), p. 14.
4. John Cowper Powys, *Porius* (Macdonald, London, 1951), p. 276. Hereafter cited as *P*.
5. John Cowper Powys, 'My philosophy', *Obstinate Cymric*, op. cit., p. 176.
6. J. C. Powys, 'Pair Dadeni', *Obstinate Cymric*, op. cit., p. 86.
7. Glen Cavaliero, *John Cowper Powys: Novelist* (Clarendon Press, 1973), p. 186.
8. John Cowper Powys, *In Defence of Sensuality* (Gollancz, 1930; reprinted Village Press, 1974), p. 132.
9. J. Keats, letter to R. Woodhouse, 27 October 1818, *Letters* (London, OUP, 1960), p. 226.

10. Cavaliero, op. cit., p. 128.
11. John Cowper Powys, 'My Philosophy', *Obstinate Cymric*, op. cit., p. 158.
12. Ibid., p. 165.
13. Bertrand Russell, *Mysticism and Logic* (1918, Penguin, London, 1953).
14. John Cowper Powys, 'My Philosophy', *Obstinate Cymric*, op. cit., p. 153.
15. Ibid., p. 155.

CHAPTER 8: SUMMING UP

1. John Cowper Powys, *The Inmates* (Village Press, London, 1974), p. vii.
2. John Cowper Powys, *Atlantis* (Macdonald, London, 1964), p. 183. Hereafter cited as *At.*
3. John Cowper Powys, *The Brazen Head* (Macdonald, London, 1969), p. 165.
4. John Cowper Powys, *All or Nothing* (Macdonald, London, 1960), p. 22.
5. Ibid., p. 219.
6. John Cowper Powys, *You and Me* (Village Press, London, 1975), p. 3.
7. John Cowper Powys, *Two and Two* (Village Press, London, 1974), p. 40.
8. Ibid., p. 76.
9. John Cowper Powys, *You and Me*, op. cit., p. 51.
10. John Cowper Powys, *Real Wraiths* (Village Press, London, 1974), pp. 7–8. Hereafter cited as *RW*.
11. Philip O'Connor, *Living in Croesor* (Hutchinson, London, 1962).
12. John Cowper Powys, *The Pleasures of Literature* (Village Press, London, 1975), p. 132.
13. *The Pleasures of Literature*, op. cit., p. 651.
14. Ibid., p. 650.
15. Jeremy Hooker, *John Cowper Powys* (University of Wales Press, Cardiff, 1973), p. 92.
16. Walter Pater, *Marius the Epicurean* (Dent, London, 1968), p. 32.
17. Ibid., p. 82.
18. Ibid., p. 145.
19. Walter Pater, 'Denys l'Auxerrois', *Imaginary Portraits* (Macmillan, London, 1925), p. 51.
20. Arthur Machen, *The Hill of Dreams* (Corgi, London, 1967), p. 31.
21. Ibid., p. 73.
22. Ibid., p. 92.
23. Ibid., p. 81.
24. Angus Wilson, 'John Cowper Powys as a Novelist', *Powys Review* (Spring 1977), p. 14.
25. Humphry House, *Coleridge* (1953, Rupert Hart-Davis, London, 1962), p.26.

APPENDIX: CRITICISM

1. The *New Statesman*, 2 April 1965.
2. Walter Allen, *Tradition and Dream* (first published Phoenix, 1964; republished Penguin, London, 1965), p. 71.
3. Lloyd Emerson Siberell, *A Bibliography of the First Editions of John Cowper Powys* (Cincinnati, 1934), Preface, p. 9.
4. Richard Heron Ward, *The Powys Brothers* (Bodley Head, London, 1935), p. 20.
5. John Cowper Powys, *Suspended Judgements* (first published G. Arnold

Shaw, New York, 1916; reprinted Village Press, London, 1975), p. 113.

6. Wilkinson, Louis (as Louis Marlow), *Swan's Milk* (Faber, London, 1934)
   Welsh Ambassadors (Chapman & Hall, London, 1936); *Seven Friends*
   (Richards Press, London, 1953).

7. R. C. Churchill, *The Powys Brothers*, Writers and Their Work, no. 150
   (Longmans, Green & Co., London, 1962).

8. Angus Wilson, 'Mythology in J. C. Powys's Novels', *A Review of English
   Literature*, IV., Number 1, January 1963, p. 9.

9. G. Wilson Knight, *The Saturnian Quest* (Methuen, London, 1964).

10. K. Hopkins, *The Powys Brothers* (Phoenix, London, 1967).

11. H. P. Collins, *John Cowper Powys: Old Earth Man* (Barrie and Rockliff,
    London, 1966).

12. D. Langridge, *John Cowper Powys: A Record of Achievement* (The
    Library Association, 1966).

13. G. Wilson Knight, *Neglected Powers: Essays on Nineteenth and
    Twentieth Century Literature* (Routledge and Kegan Paul, London,
    1971).

14. B. Humfrey (ed.), *Essays on John Cowper Powys* (University of Wales
    Press, Cardiff, 1972).

15. John A. Brebner, *The Demon Within: A Study of John Cowper Powys's
    Novels* (Macdonald, London 1973).

16. Glen Cavaliero, *John Cowper Powys: Novelist* (Clarendon Press, Oxford,
    1973).

17. Jeremy Hooker, *John Cowper Powys* (University of Wales Press, Cardiff,
    1973).

18. Morine Krissdottir, *John Cowper Powys and the Magical Quest* (Mac-
    donald, London, 1980).

19. Hooker, op. cit., p. 93.

Bibliography

A. Principal books by John Cowper Powys in chronological order with date and place of first publication. Some marginal pamphlets have been omitted.

Odes and Other Poems (W. Rider and Son, London, 1896)

Poems (W. Rider and Son, London, 1899)

Lucifer: A Poem (Macdonald, London, 1956) (Written in 1905)

Visions and Revisions (G. Arnold Shaw, New York, 1915)

Wood and Stone (G. Arnold Shaw, New York, 1915)

Confessions of Two Brothers (with Llewelyn Powys) (The Manas Press, Rochester, New York, 1916)

Wolf's-Bane: Rhymes (G. Arnold Shaw, New York, 1916)

One Hundred Best Books (G. Arnold Shaw, New York, 1916)

Rodmoor (G. Arnold Shaw, New York, 1916)

Suspended Judgements: Essays on Books and Sensations (G. Arnold Shaw, New York, 1916)

Mandragora: Poems (G. Arnold Shaw, New York, 1917)

After My Fashion (Pan Picador, London, 1980) (Written in 1919)

The Complex Vision (Dodd, Mead, New York, 1920)

Samphire: Poems (Thomas Seltzer, New York, 1922)

Ducdame (Doubleday, Page, New York, 1925)

The Religion of a Sceptic (Dodd, Mead, New York, 1925)

The Art of Forgetting the Unpleasant (Haldeman-Julius, Girard, Kansas, 1928)

Wolf Solent (Simon and Schuster, New York, 1929)

The Meaning of Culture (W. W. Norton, New York, 1929)

The Owl, The Duck, and – Miss Rowe! Miss Rowe! (William Targ, Chicago, 1930)

In Defence of Sensuality (Simon and Schuster, New York, 1930)

Dorothy M. Richardson (Joiner and Steele, London, 1931)

A Glastonbury Romance (Simon and Schuster, New York, 1932)

A Philosophy of Solitude (Simon and Schuster, New York, 1933)

Autobiography (Simon and Schuster, New York, 1934)

Weymouth Sands (Simon and Schuster, New York, 1934)

The Art of Happiness (Simon and Schuster, New York, 1935)

Maiden Castle (Simon and Schuster, New York, 1936)

Morwyn, or the Vengeance of God (Cassell, London, 1937)

The Pleasures of Literature (Cassell, London, 1938)

Owen Glendower (Simon and Schuster, New York, 1940)

Mortal Strife (Jonathan Cape, London, 1942)

The Art of Growing Old (Jonathan Cape, London, 1944)
Dostoievsky (John Lane, The Bodley Head, London, 1946)
Obstinate Cymric: Essays 1935–47 (Druid Press, Carmarthen, 1947)
Rabelais (John Lane, The Bodley Head, London, 1948)
Porius (Macdonald, London, 1951)
The Inmates (Macdonald, London, 1952)
In Spite of (Macdonald, London, 1953)
Atlantis (Macdonald, London, 1954)
The Brazen Head (Macdonald, London, 1956)
Up and Out (Macdonald, London, 1957)
Letters of John Cowper Powys to Louis Wilkinson, 1935–1956 (Macdonald,
    London, 1958)
Homer and the Aether (Macdonald, London, 1959)
All or Nothing (Macdonald, London, 1960)
Real Wraiths (Village Press, London, 1974)
Two and Two (Village Press, London, 1974)
You and Me (Village Press, London, 1975)

B. Principal books and articles about John Cowper Powys

Richard Heron Ward, *The Powys Brothers* (John Lane, The Bodley Head,
    London, 1935)
Louis Wilkinson (as Louis Marlow), *Welsh Ambassadors* (Chapman and Hall,
    London, 1936)
Louis Wilkinson (as Louis Marlow), *Seven Friends* (Richards Press, London,
    1953)
Angus Wilson, 'Mythology in J. C. Powys's Novels', *A Review of English Litera-
    ture*, IV, Number 1, January 1963 (John Cowper Powys number)
G. Wilson Knight, *The Saturnian Quest* (Methuen, London, 1964)
H. P. Collins, *John Cowper Powys: Old Earth Man* (Barrie and Rockliff,
    London, 1966)
Derek Langridge, *John Cowper Powys: A Record of Achievement* (The Library
    Association, London, 1966)
Kenneth Hopkins, *The Powys Brothers* (Phoenix House, London, 1967)
G. Wilson Knight, *Neglected Powers* (Routledge and Kegan Paul, London,
    1971)
Belinda Humfrey (ed.), *Essays on John Cowper Powys* (University of Wales
    Press, Cardiff, 1972)
John A. Brebner, *The Demon Within* (Macdonald, London, 1973)
Glen Cavaliero, *John Cowper Powys: Novelist* (Clarendon Press, Oxford, 1973)
Jeremy Hooker, *John Cowper Powys* (University of Wales Press, Cardiff, 1973)
Morine Krissdottir, *John Cowper Powys and the Magical Quest* (Macdonald,
    London, 1980)

Index

aeroplanes, 95

Aesthetes, 167–9

After My Fashion: published, 21; described, 21–5; religion in, 25–7; style, 26–7; assessed, 27–8; drowning in, 38

Albert of Cologne, 158

All or Nothing, 15, 159

Allen, Walter, 161, 175

Arch, Joseph, 7, 16

Art of Happiness, The, 132

Arthur, King, 104–5, 112, 133

astrology, 139

Atlantis, 156–8

Autobiography: and social class, 7; on early life, 7–11; on feelings, 20; and pornography, 51; and women, 83; and JCP's ambitions to be magician, 113; writing and publication, 119; described, 124–31; obsessions in, 154; and propagandist writing, 176

Bacon, Roger, 158

Blackmore, R.L., 179

Blaenau-Ffestiniog (Wales), 161

Bohemianism, 24–5

Bonaventura, St, 158

Boughton, Rutland, 90–2

Brazen Head, The, 118, 158

Brebner, John A., 118, 164, 178

Breckon, Richard, 178

Brighton, 9

Brontë, Emily, 92

Browning, Robert, 176

Burpham (Sussex), 21

Cader Idris, 137, 148–9

Cambridge University, 8

Cavaliero, Glen: on critical views of JCP, 2, 3, 104, 178–9; on *A Glastonbury Romance,* 115, 117; on *Porius,* 143; on JCP's religious rejection, 152; on JCP and Lawrence, 164

'cavoseniargizing', 140, 145, 149

Cerne Giant, 45–6, 159

Chesterton, G.K., 40

Coleridge, Samuel Taylor, 165–6, 172

Collins, H.P., 64, 94, 178

Compton-Burnett, Ivy, 6

Confessions of Two Brothers (with Llewelyn Powys), 14, 16, 107, 154

Connolly, Cyril, 43

Conscience, 126

Corwen (N. Wales), 132–3, 137

Cronos (god), 140, 143–4, 150

Dangerfield, George, 40–1

Davies, Frederick, 8

Dickens, Charles, 18–19, 28, 163, 176

Dinas Bran (N. Wales), 133–4

Dorchester, 132

Dorset, 53, 56, 65, 67, 70, 85

Dostoievsky, 107

Dostoievsky, Fyodor: influence on JCP, 9, 16, 18–20, 89, 151, 162; and cruelty, 19–20; Pritchett on, 174

drowning, 38, 94

dualism: JCP's attitude to, 14–15; in *Wood and Stone,* 17; in *After My Fashion,* 26; in *Ducdame,* 31–3, 36, 47, 49; in *Wolf Solent,* 47–9, 85–6, 88; and religious experience, 84, 153; in *A*